Eating Habits

Eating Habits
Food, physiology and learned behaviour

Edited by

Robert A Boakes

University of Sussex

David A Popplewell

University of Oxford

Michael J Burton

University of Sussex

JOHN WILEY & SONS

Chichester · New York · Brisbane · Toronto · Singapore

Library of Congress Cataloging-in-Publication Data:

Eating habits.

Includes index.
1. Food habits—Psychological aspects. 2. Eating disorders. 3. Children—Nutrition—Psycholocal aspects. 4. Psychology, Experimental. I. Boakes, Robert A. II. Popplewell, David A. III. Burton, Michael J.
TX357.E28 1987   616.3'98'0019   86-15776
ISBN 0 471 90744 8

British Library Cataloguing in Publication Data:

Eating habits.
1. Food habits
I. Boakes, Robert A. II. Popplewell, David A. III. Burton, Michael J.
152   GT2860

ISBN 0 471 90744 8

Typeset by Inforum Ltd, Portsmouth
Printed and bound in Great Britain

Contents

List of Contributors

Addresses of authors (July, 1986)

G. A. Bennett
Department of Clinical Psychology, Rochdale Health Authority, Birch Hill Hospital, Rochdale, OL12 9QB, England

L.L. Birch
Department of Human Development and Family Ecology, University of Illinois, 1105 West Nevada Street, Urbana, Illinois, 61081, USA

D.A. Booth
Department of Psychology, University of Birmingham, PO Box 363, Birmingham, B15 2TT, England

J.A. Deutsch
Department of Psychology, C-009, University of California, San Diego, La Jolla, California, 92093, USA

J. Le Magnen
College de France, 11 Place Marceline Berthelot, 75231 Paris, France

R.L. Palmer
Academic Department of Psychiatry, Leicester General Hospital, Gwendolen Road, Leicester, LE2 4PW, England

G.I. Szmukler
Department of Psychiatry, Clinical Sciences Block, Royal Melbourne Hospital, Melbourne, Victoria, 3050, Australia

P. Wright
Department of Psychology, Edinburgh University, 7 George Square, Edinburgh, EH8 9JZ, Scotland

Preface

To most of us it seems natural to accept some things as edible, but to reject, sometimes with violent disgust, other foods that may be equally nutritious. Such reactions are acquired at an early age. Not only do adult Frenchmen and adult Britons have quite distinct ideas on what is good to eat, but young children from these two countries also differ dramatically in their tastes and distastes. Over the past few decades the spread into Europe and North America of cuisines from different cultures has led to far more widespread appreciation than ever before that an individual's likes and dislikes reflect learned eating habits. Europeans and North Americans, may speak of 'acquiring a taste' for Cantonese dishes, Mexican chilis or Indian curries, but usually assume, wrongly, that such tastes are natural, not acquired, in people born as Cantonese, Mexican or Indian.

To most of us it may also seem natural that we eat for the first two decades of our lives enough food to keep our weight increasing steadily, for the next two decades enought to maintain that weight at a fairly constant value, and then tend towards rather too much for the rest of our lives so that, unless we are very poor, very careful, very energetic or very ill, we are likely to enjoy an obese old age. In this context, too, everyday belief accepts that an individual's weight is partly a matter of inherited physiology: 'No wonder she's as thin as a rake, look at her mother!' and partly reflect habits of consumption: 'It's surprising he hasn't even more of a belly, considering the amount of beer he gets through every evening'. Such lay beliefs may place more emphasis on genetics than is deserved, according to research on the transmission of eating habits from one generation to the next by social learning. As discussed by Birch in Chapter 5, observation of parents, siblings or companions can play a very important part in a young individual's acceptance or rejection of foods.

When psychologists have turned to the question of why people develop particular eating habits, they have usually looked at three very different sources of evidence. Disturbed eating patterns, loss of appetite, and abnormal concern with body weight are extremely common among people seeking help from clinical psychologists and psychiatrists. Most of the attention such patients receive is, of course, directed towards alleviating their problems. But, just as the study of visual illusions has been of incomparable value to our understanding of normal perception, so it is hoped that the study of abnormal eating habits — whether those of the bulimic discussed by Palmer in Chapter 1, of the anorexic discussed by Szmukler in Chapter 2 or of the obese discussed by Bennet in Chapter 3 — may shed light on the processes that maintain normal patterns of eating. It is for that reason that these topics are included in the present book. Thus Chapters 1 and 2 are only incidentally concerned with the treatment of bulimia and anorexia nervosa. Although Chapter 3 concentrates on the treatment of obesity, it is also concerned with the question of why most people do not need to seek professional help to control their weight.

The second, and most obvious, source of evidence on why people eat in the way they do is to study the development of food preferences and patterns of consumption in children. This is a strangely neglected area of research. For historical reasons the vast majority of developmental psychologists have chosen to concentrate on children's cognitive abilities or emotions. Even on a topic which is of central importance to any family with a young baby and which has generated a vast number of speculative claims and counter-claims, concerning the psychological implications of bottle- as opposed to breast-feeding, there have been very few direct studies, as Wright notes in Chapter 4. Similarly, there is little empirical research to offer solutions to the kind of everyday problem that many families meet of how to get their children to eat what is good for them, i.e. greens, not ice-cream. As Birch notes in Chapter 5, what research there is suggests that one very commonly adopted strategy: 'if you eat up your food, you can go and watch television' may be the worse possible one.

In many textbooks of psychology a chapter on eating is likely to devote far less space to abnormal patterns of human consumption and to the development of eating habits in children than to research involving the laboratory rat. Whatever the merits of animal models of human behaviour in other areas of psychology, there is clearly a great deal to be said in favour of studying the rat in order to understand general principles of feeding and drinking that might be relevant to man. Above all else, *Rattus*, like *Homo*, is an omnivore. It faces a comparable range of possible foods and is presented with what, in evolutionary terms, is the same kind of problem: choosing from among this range so as to maintain adequate intakes of the various chemicals required for bodily growth and health, while avoiding poison and disease. Furthermore, the solutions the rat has found to this problem are remarkably similar to those that the human race has evolved. For example, like man, the rat shows an innate delight in sweet tastes and innate aversions to sour and bitter tastes; like man, a rat will learn what to eat from its social group so that, for example, two neighbouring colonies of wild rats may perpetuate very different choices of food and ways of obtaining food, even though they live in environments that are identical in ecological terms; finally, like man, a rat will adjust its preferences and the sizes of its meals in the light of its experience of the consequences of various foods, that is, one rat's meat can become another rat's poison!

It is this final aspect of eating habits in rats which provides the focus for Chapters 6 and 7. The bulk of studies on feeding and drinking in rats have concentrated on the search for physiological mechanisms that might control such behaviour. In the main such studies have examined the role of particular parts of the brain or of specific neurochemicals and have developed general conceptual frameworks for such research, notably that of homeostasis, without a great deal of attention to the role of learning. No chapter in this book attempts to review the achievements of such research, since good introductions to the field can be found in most textbooks of physiological psychology or of the physiology of motivation. Instead, Chapters 6 and 7 treat that small part of this physiological tradition which has concentrated on the effects of past experience; Le Magnen is largely concerned with the way in which the palatability of a food may change as a rat learns about its nutritional consequences, while Deutsch reviews evidence supporting a new theory as to how rats learn to regulate the amount they eat in each meal.

The approach discussed in the final chapter has its origins in the same physiological tradition, but is concerned with evidence from experiments with human subjects. Booth claims that to understand such data one needs to take into account beliefs and other aspects of human cognition that may be inaccessible, unimportant or non-existent in the rat. He argues that a new 'cognitive experimental psychology of appetite' is needed which will coordinate research from the animal laboratory, experimental studies of human eating and surveys of food preferences and patterns of consumption, of the kind that today are more often examined by the market researcher or food producer than by psychologists.

No coherent field yet exists which could be called 'the cognitive experimental psychology of appetite'. Perhaps when such a development occurs, it will bring much greater understanding than we have now of the human tragedies that can occur when eating becomes abnormal in the ways described in the first three chapters. The editors would like to think that one contribution of the present volume might be to make this development more likely to happen.

This book stems from a conference held at the University of Sussex, Brighton, England, in April 1984. The event was organized in collaboration with the British Feeding and Drinking Group and the Experimental Analysis of Behaviour Group. Some of the chapters are based on papers presented at that conference, while others were subsequently solicited on subjects that did not appear on the conference programme. The editors were also the organizers of this conference and would like to take this opportunity to express their appreciation of the financial support provided by the Experimental Psychology Society and the Royal Society and of the facilities made available by the Laboratory of Experimental Psychology at the University of Sussex.

April, 1986   R.A. Boakes
                                                        D.A. Popplewell
                                                          M.J. Burton

CHAPTER 1

Bulimia: The Nature of the Syndrome, its Epidemiology and its Treatment

Robert L. Palmer
Academic Department of Psychiatry,
Leicester General Hospital, Leicester, UK

Gluttony is not new. People have always been given to excessive and unusual eating on occasions. The pattern of intermittent gorging which characterizes big carnivores is arguably as much part of our evolutionary heritage as the monotonous munching of the herbivore. Man is an omnivore and an opportunist. Certainly, within civilized societies the better off have often exploited and dramatized their position of privilege by ostentatious consumption. The poor have likewise indulged themselves when they have been able. Eating has undeniable social meaning and so may overeating. The Roman rich reputedly made themselves vomit between courses and stimulating the vagus for this end is an old trick. Nevertheless the bulimic syndrome characterized by episodes of excessive eating with a sense of loss of control and often followed by self-induced vomiting or purgation is seen as a 'new' condition: as a disorder of our times.

The word bulimia is used to describe a behaviour which may be considered in isolation from any supposed pathological significance. Secondly, it may be used to describe such behaviour as a symptom of some well-recognized disorder such as anorexia nervosa. Lastly it may be used to denote the central feature of a syndrome which has some claim to a separate existence within a classification of disorders. It is this last sense which is a recent development and discussion of this bulimic syndrome will be the chief subject of this chapter. However some discussion of bulimia as a behaviour and as a symptom is a

1

necessary preliminary. It may be argued that our understanding of bulimia as a syndrome results from convergence of ideas that are derived from the study of unequivocally abnormal states on the one hand and from observations of the variety of normal patterns of eating including our own experience on the other.

BULIMIA AS A BEHAVIOUR

The word bulimia means overeating and is said to derive from words meaning 'ox hunger'. It is specifically used to describe susbstantial overeating occurring in episodes and is often used interchangeably with the word 'binge'. This latter is familiar from writings on alcohol abuse where it likewise denotes an episode of unusual and excessive consumption. The word binge is part of the vocabulary of most people in a way that bulimia is not and it is therefore not infrequently used in surveys employing self-report methods to investigate eating habits. In this sense the experience of binge eating is commonplace. Certainly such surveys have tended to report high rates of subjects who admit to such behaviours. Usually one-fifth and sometimes over one-half of female subjects admit to binge eating at some time in their life (Cooper and Fairburn, 1983; Katzman, Wolchik and Braver, 1984; Halmi, Falk and Schwartz, 1981; Hawkins and Clement, 1980; Healy, Conroy and Walsh, 1985). Men also admit to having had binges, although rates tend to be lower and seem to decline with age in both sexes. However, such reports are difficult to interpret since the word binge is open to a wide variety of interpretations. It may often be used to denote the breaking of some inner subjective rule of eating rather than some objectively definable behaviour. Meadows, Palmer, Newball and Kenrick (1986) conducted a survey of eating attitudes in a population of women aged 18–22 years registered within general practices in Leicestershire. In this population 11.6% of subjects reported themselves as at least 'often' 'eating in binges lots of fattening foods', but less than 1% described themselves as 'eating and eating until I feel ill or go to sleep', a description which approximates to the DSM III criteria of a bulimic binge (see below). Likewise Conroy, Healy and Walsh (1985) in a large study of Irish college students found that 32% admitted to binge eating but only a quarter of these acknowledged loss of control within the binge. Such a characteristic would often be thought necessary if the eating was to be appropriately described as bulimic. It would seem therefore that self reports of binge eating are sensitive to the way in which questions are asked. Respondents may use the word to describe a wide variety of behaviours. Certainly it would be a mistake to equate such a report of binge eating with the kind of gross bulimic over-eating which is characteristic of many patients presenting at the clinic.

Self reports of bingeing may often denote merely a subjective judgement about having eaten in an inappropriate or self-indulgent fashion. In this regard it is perhaps not surprising that there seems to be a notable relationship between reports of bingeing and reports of dietary restraint usually for the purpose of slimming (Wardle, 1980; Clarke and Palmer, 1983). If subjects are judging what is proper for them to eat by some self-imposed standard of significant restraint, then 'letting go' and eating a meal of commonplace size may be judged to be a binge. However, there is no doubt that dietary restraint is the usual background for the unequivocably excessive intake of the true binge eater or bulimic. Furthermore there is some evidence which suggests that even in non-clinical situations the breakdown of restraint may lead to greater than average consumption. Thus Herman and Mack (1975) carried out an experiment in which subjects were classified according to whether or not they were habitual restrained eaters on the basis of a questionnaire measure. Both groups underwent an experimental 'taste test' in which the amount of ice cream they consumed (the covert dependent variable) was measured in relation to whether or not they had been given a dietary preload, namely a milk shake. Non-restrained subjects ate less ice cream after one milk shake and still less after two, whereas the habitually restrained subjects ate substantially more ice cream once they had consumed a preload of milk shake.

It is tempting to speculate that a physiological mechanism might underly this relative overconsumption in the face of previous deprivation and certainly such a mechanism could be thought of as making sense in evolutionary terms. However, if seems that cognitive factors are of considerable importance. It has been shown that it is the subjects' belief about the calorie content of the preload rather than its actual substance that determines subsequent eating behaviour (Polivy, 1976; Spencer and Fremouw, 1979). Furthermore, both anxiety and the belief that they have consumed alcohol but not alcohol as such, may also increase food consumption in restrained subjects (Herman and Polivy, 1975; Polivy and Herman, 1976; Wardle and Beinart, 1981). This tendency towards rebound overeating in the face of dietary restraint is described as counter-regulation in contrast to the regulation of a more normal eating pattern.

Herman and Polivy (1984) have recently proposed a boundary model for the regulation of eating in an attempt to reconcile observations which suggest a primary physiological control of eating with the other body of evidence which emphasizes the importance of psychological and social factors. They suggest that normal consumption is regulated within boundaries rather than to a set-point. Aversive and essentially physiological control occurs at the boundaries of considerable deficit (hunger) or excess (satiety). Between these boundaries there is a 'zone of biological indifference' in which psycho-social and cognitive pressures are of importance in determining consumption. Most individuals contained within a social pattern of eating rarely experience notably aversive hunger or satiety. However, the highly restrained dieter attempts to impose a cognitive barrier on the upper limit of consumption well short of satiety and perhaps even at a point which leads to the experience of some aversive hunger.

This so-called diet boundary is construed as entirely cognitive and represents the dieters self-imposed quota for consumption. If, however, within an individual eating episode or perhaps within a dieting day, this barrier is for some reason breached, Herman and Polivy suggest that what they call the 'what the hell' effect occurs in which the lapsed dieter eats in a less constrained fashion until the previously redundant physiological satiety barrier is reached. They further suggest that the dieter may eat even more than the non-dieter in such circumstances since she has come to be relatively unresponsive to what they describe as 'physiological subleties' and stops only when the upper satiety barrier becomes truely aversive. Presumably this upper barrier may indeed be shifted as a result of chronic dietary restraint or low weight or both. Furthermore Herman and Polivy tentatively suggest that the true binger 'for whatever psychodynamically complex reason she might have, does transgress this satiety boundary. She stops, not when eating becomes unpleasant, but when it becomes impossible (i.e. when she reaches her limit of physical capacity).'

In summary, bulimia in as much as it may be said to occur in non-morbid states may well be characteristic mainly of habitual restrained eaters who transgress their rules and give in and eat excessively. Certainly it is likely that this is the kind of 'normal' bulimic behaviour which is most related to the overeating of the sufferer from the bulimic syndrome. The occasional socially promoted and personally acceptable excessive indulgence which is part of most people's experience is probably of less relevance.

BULIMIA AS A SYMPTOM

Bulimia as a symptom is clearly recognized as a feature of some obese subjects, some sufferers from anorexia nervosa, and possibly as a feature of a few patients with organic brain disease.

The popular idea of overweight people as gluttons has little support from systematic observation. Indeed, although it is logically necessary that an obese person has in the long run taken in more food than was necessary to sustain their energy requirements, the study of eating behaviour in obese people has tended to find that their intake is commonplace or even less than average. There is great variety. Nevertheless eating binges with a sense of compulsion have been described in a minority of obese subjects (Loro and Orleans, 1981). However, many obese people engage in frequent attempts to slim by means of eating restraint and presumably such dieters would be over represented amongst obese people in contact with medical or other services. Thus it is probable that restrained eating provides the background for many if not all of the binge eating described in obese subjects. Interestingly, too, the enhanced sensitivity to external cues for eating which was observed in obese subjects and thought to be of importance in their vulnerability to weight gain, seems itself to be largely a function of eating restraint and is not prominent in obese subjects who are not attempting to slim (Hibscher and Herman, 1977).

If bulimic overeating is usually associated with dietary restraint and undereating, it is hardly surprising that it should occur in people who fulfill diagnostic criteria for anorexia nervosa. Anorectic subjects limit their intake radically and their restraint characteristically seems to be in the service of ideas about keeping their weight low and avoiding weight gain. Bulimic episodes have long been recognized in otherwise typical anorectic subjects and there have been many clinical descriptions. Indeed Gull (1873) in one of the earliest accounts of the disorder mentions brief periods of voracious appetite as occurring on occasions in abstinent patients. A number of recent papers have drawn attention to the group differences between purely restricting/abstinent anorectics and bingeing/vomiting anorectics. Thus Casper, Eckert, Halmi, Goldberg and Davis (1980) reported that just under half of their series of 105 anorectics 'periodically resorted to bulimia'. In addition to more commonly inducing vomiting the bulimic subjects were more extroverted, tended to be older, were more likely to admit to a strong appetite and show kleptomania. Furthermore, they had more affective symptoms and more somatic complaints. These findings are broadly supported by other series of patients (Garfinkel, Moldofsky and Garner, 1980; Beumont, George and Smart, 1976). Furthermore, Strober, Salkin, Burroughs and Morrell (1982) showed that the parents of bulimic and anorectic subjects tended to have particular personality characteristics. Fathers of bulimics were more impulsive and mothers were more depressed and both reported more disatisfaction with family relationships than the parents of restrictive anorectics. There was also more affective disorder in the families of bulimic anorectics.

In summary, then, at least a substantial minority of anorectic subjects show bulimia and the frequency of the symptom tends to rise with the duration of the illness. There seem to be consistent behavioural and psychological correlates of such behaviour and bulimia may complicate treatment and worsen prognosis. However, some anorectics gain weight and in that sense 'recover' but go on to develop the features of a bulimic syndrome at normal weight. Indeed the disorders occur along a continuum with intermediate forms. These issues will be discussed again below. In anorectic subjects, bulimic behaviour is characteristically followed by self-induced vomiting or purgation.

In addition to its appearance in obese patients and those with anorexia nervosa bulimic overeating has been reported as a symptom in organic brain disease. Thus, a few patients with hypothalamic lesions develop bulimia (Reeves and Plum, 1969; Celesia, Archer and Chung, 1981) and recently Krahn and Mitchell (1984) have reported a case of bulimia associated with increased intracranial pressure probably due to aquaductal stenosis which was improved by the insertion of a shunt. More generally Rau and Green (1975) have speculated that a neurological deficit may underly the behaviour of many subjects with egodystonic overeating which they call compulsive eating. (Unusually they would wish to confine the use of the word binge to egosyntonic overeating.) They have reported that some patients with the former show EEG abnormalities and respond to anticonvulsant therapy.

BULIMIA AS A SYNDROME

The idea that bulimia might be a feature of a not uncommon syndrome seperable from anorexia nervosa, obesity or other disorders, seems to have emerged during the 1970s. Different authors sought to describe a disorder occurring at normal weight in which episodic overeating with loss of control was associated with a variety of other features both psychological and behavioural. The definitions varied slightly as did the names which were coined for these 'new' disorders.

Bruch (1973) described a group of people in whom a normal body weight was maintained only with great care and restraint and in whom abnormal weight control methods occurred together with distressing binge eating. She called these subjects 'thin–fat people'. Later Boskind-Lodahl (1976) described what she called 'bulimarexia' as a syndrome featuring binge eating accompanied by vomiting, occurring mainly in female college students. Palmer (1979) suggested the term 'dietary chaos syndrome' to describe a state of disordered eating including bingeing together with psychological features including preoccupation with weight and eating control. The syndrome might arise either as a progression from classical anorexia nervosa or without prior major weight loss. Other names suggested for similar syndromes have included Kibarashi-gui (Nagami and Yabana, 1977), subclinical anorexia nervosa (Button and Whitehouse, 1981), and the abnormal/normal weight control syndrome (Crisp, 1981). However, two terms have emerged out of this array of nomenclature to find a measure of acceptance.

Perhaps the best established is simply the term 'bulimia' which is enshrined as a diagnosis within the Third Revision of the *Diagnostic and Statistical Manual of the American Psychiatric Association* (DSM III). The diagnostic criteria listed there are as follows:

(A) Recurrent episodes of binge eating (rapid consumption of a large amount of food in a discrete period of time, usually less than two hours).
(B) At least three of the following:

1. consumption of high-calorific, easily ingested food during a binge;
2. inconspicuous eating during a binge;
3. termination of such eating episodes by abdominal pain, sleep, social interruption or self-induced vomiting;
4. repeated attempts to lose weight by severely restrictive diets, self-induced vomiting, or use of cathartics or diuretics;
5. frequent weight fluctuations greater than 10 lb due to alternative binges and fasts.
(C) Awareness that the eating pattern is abnormal, and fear of not being able to stop eating voluntarily.
(D) Depressed mood and self-deprecating thoughts following eating binges.
(E) The bulimic episodes are not due to anorexia nervosa or any known physical disorder.

The term bulimia and these criteria can be criticized on a number of grounds. Firstly, the use of the word bulimia for the syndrome is perhaps unfortunate in view of its established use to refer to a symptom. Ambiguity can certainly arise in the discussion of anorectic subjects with bulimia and indeed in any person displaying the symptom of bulimia without the syndrome. Furthermore, the criteria make relatively little reference to psychopathology. Criterion E makes the distinction from anorexia nervosa an absolute one which may be fair nosological technique although it fails to recognize the fuzzy borderline between this syndrome and that of anorexia nervosa.

The second term to have achieved widespread acceptance is 'bulimia nervosa'. This term was introduced in a key paper by Russell (1979) in which he described a series of 30 patients with what he called 'an ominious variant of anorexia nervosa'. The criteria suggested for the diagnosis of bulimia nervosa are as follows.

1. Patients suffer from powerful and retractable urges to overeat.
2. They seek to avoid the 'fattening affects of food' by inducing vomiting or by using purgatives, or both.
3. They have a morbid fear of becoming fat.

Russell's patients were collected over a number of years within a practice with a high reputation for treating patients with anorexia nervosa. The need for a new term arose because of the failure of some of these severely ill subjects to fully conform to diagnostic criteria for anorexia nervosa. However, the majority of the subjects had had previous anorexia nervosa. These criteria may perhaps be criticized on the grounds of being too narrow. Thus, by insisting upon the use of abnormal weight control methods such as vomiting or purgative abuse they exclude those subjects who respond to binge eating by fasting rather than by these behaviours. Likewise the criterion of a 'morbid fear of becoming fat' may be characteristic and emphasizes the link with the similar fears of the anorectic but nevertheless does scant justice to the complicated fears and ideas which characterize such patients. Often bulimic subjects may be as fearful of the bulimic behaviour itself as of becoming fat, although such a fear is usual.

In general the DSM III criteria for bulimia, in spite of their rather complex nature, probably define a wider range of subjects than do Russell's apparently simpler criteria for bulimia nervosa. The former seemed to have arisen largely through an awareness of morbid binge eating occurring in both patient and non-patient populations, whereas the latter certainly arose through observations of patients presenting to an anorexia nervosa service. In that disordered eating can occur with any degree of severity and with a variety of associated features, any diagnositic criteria are likely to act merely as landmarks on a continuum. With these reservations the current criteria for bulimia and bulimia nervosa are acceptable although they should be open to revision in the light of further data. In the meantime they should be used to define populations for research, although atypical subjects who fail to fill the criteria in some respects should not be excluded, but rather described, so that the limitations of these criteria come to be better known. For the remainder of this review the term bulimia will normally be used to denote the DSM III syndrome, bulimia nervosa will be used to denote subjects who fulfill Russell's criteria and who have been described in these terms, and the term 'binge eating' will be used to describe the symptom.

Not withstanding the plethora of terms and the various sets of diagnostic criteria all this work does seem to represent a developing concensus that there are substantial numbers of subjects who report recurrent episodes of binge eating in which they feel out of control, whose general behaviour and attitudes resemble somewhat those found in primary anorexia nervosa, but who fail to fulfill diagnostic criteria for that disorder mainly because they have failed to lose sufficient weight.

CLINICAL DESCRIPTIONS

There have been many clinical descriptions of bulimia and more recently a few autobiographical accounts of the subject from people who have suffered from the bulimic syndrome (Roche, 1984). There is agreement that the disorder is seen most frequently in young women although cases have been reported in older women and in men. Abraham and Beumont (1982) described a series of 32 consecutive patients presenting at an eating disorders clinic complaining of episodes of overeating. Most were at a normal weight, although five were obese. They deliberately sought to look at the phenomenon of binge eating without diagnostic preconceptions but it seems likely that at the time of the study the majority of subjects would have fulfilled the DSM III criteria for bulimia. They made six observations which were found to be common to all subjects. Similar observations occur in other accounts of bulimia in the literature. Firstly, their subjects construed bulimia as quite distinct from social 'overeating'. This differentiation was made mainly on a sense of subjective loss of control which characterized the true binge. The patients ate within the binge amounts of food which were notably excessive when judged against nutritional needs or social expectations. Furthermore, all patients tended to resist the urge to binge eat and usually took pains to hide the behaviour from others. There was an association with dysphoric mood states but these were often relieved during the binge. Lastly bulimia was invariably associated with forms of behaviour directed at weight loss.

Other behaviours and attitudes associated with the bingeing were more variable. A majority of subjects tended to eat quickly and sometimes ravenously food which at other times they would have avoided as being 'bad'. Foods thus classified would often be palatable, high carbohydrate, 'junk foods'. Individual binges might seem to be triggered by stressful social events or by eating something in the context of craving for particular foods or general hunger. In this respect the almost universal background of dietary restraint is important. Bingeing is usually a lone activity, although occasional subjects who have admitted to their bingeing will then carry out the behaviour in front of others sometimes in a way that suggests an attempt at emotional manipulation. Binges tend to be ended by running out of food, 'running out of steam', physical discomfort, social interruption or sleep. Most subjects feel bad and self-critical after a binge and it is usual for subjects to promise themselves that they will never do it again, and to set out on a strict diet or fast. Subjects who vomit may find that these negative feelings are relieved by bringing up the food they have eaten and a few go to great lengths to make sure that they have got rid of the food that they have consumed. Thus a subject may eat marker foods early in the binge which can be easily recognized when they are brought up in vomit. A number of authors have described repeated drinking of water followed by vomiting in an attempt to wash out all the food. Vomiting is continued until the vomit is 'clean'. Disposal of substantial quantities of vomited material can present a problem and the mother of one patient is reported to have used the vomit to fertilise the garden! When laxative medicines are used these tend to be taken immediately after a binge and in dosages varying from two or three times the recommended amount to large and unmeasured excess. Certainly dosages of 20 or more times the usual dose are by no means uncommon. The subject's attitude to her bingeing behaviour is usually predominantly negative but nevertheless ambivalent. Thus almost all subjects show some attempts to resist bingeing, although the same subjects may also plan binges. Both types of behaviour may be extreme. Thus subjects might prepare elaborate foods and buy items especially for a binge. On the other hand, some subjects make quite desperate attempts to control bingeing behaviour such as injuring fingers so as to stop them being used to induce vomiting. One subject is reported to have attempted to carry out a jaw wiring operation on herself. More common resistance behaviour would include avoiding situations where food is available, trying to find a distracting activity, avoiding being alone, freezing food so that it would not be eaten or otherwise contaminating available food. Smoking or drinking alcohol during a binge is relatively unusual, although both activities may occur at other times.

The mood associated with binge eating episodes is varied. Johnson and Larson (1982) used an unusual method to study the mood states of bulimic subjects. They issued a number of patients with a radio paging device which was set off at random during the day as a signal to the subject to make self reports on mood and behaviour. They demonstrated that their bulimic subjects experienced significantly more mood fluctuations and dysphoric states than their control subjects and binges tended to emerge from times when these subjects were feeling particularly weak and constrained. Mood states during the actual binge were rather more variable with many subjects describing anxiety, sometimes with autonomic accompaniments, whilst others described relief from tension and a temporary sense of well-being. Abraham and Beumont (1982) describe depersonalization and derealization as having been reported by three-quarters of their patients. Johnson-Sabine, Wood and Wakeling (1984) confirm the generally low mood of bulimic patients and their subjects tended to report lower moods on binge days than on binge-free days.

Physical complications of established bulimia are well recognized and occur particularly in subjects who use vomiting or purgation as weight control

methods. Mitchel, Pyle, Eckert, Hatsukami and Lentz (1983) reporting on a
large series of bulimic subjects showed that almost half showed some electrolyte disturbance, with 27% showing a metabolic alkalosis, 24% hypo-
chloraemia, and 14% hypokalaemia. Blood sugar disturbances were not found
but a few subjects showed notably elevated serum amylase levels. Rarer
physical complications include renal failure (Russell, 1979), acute gastric
dilatation (Mitchell, Pyle and Miner 1982), parotid gland swelling (Levin,
Falko, Dixon, Gallup and Saunders, 1980) dental caries (Pyle, Mitchell and
Eckert, 1981), and epileptic fits (Russell, 1979). Menstrual disturbance in
female bulimics is variable and far less consistent than is the case in anorexia
nervosa at low weight.

EPIDEMIOLOGY

There is no doubt that bulimic syndromes have rapidly achieved great promi-
nence within the last decade. Coverage in the popular media of mass communication has doubtless made some contribution to this phenomenon. Such
coverage is probably inevitable in a disorder which mainly afflicts young
women and which for many seems mixed up with a search for physical
attractiveness, glamour, and an improved image. Although most sufferers are
ashamed of their problem and seek to hide it, there have been a number of
well-publicized exceptions who have perhaps contributed some of their own
glamour to the disorder. It is possible that the dissemination via the media, of
knowledge about the use of vomiting and laxatives as weight control methods
has been a crucial factor in the emergence of these syndromes as widespread
problems. Furthermore the media have been employed as means of recruiting
subjects for study. Fairburn and Cooper have reported large series of subjects
who have responded to appeals for information from sufferers delivered by a
women's magazine (Fairburn and Cooper, 1982) and by a television programme (Fairburn and Cooper, 1984). The former appeal produced 620 responses
of which 83% seemed to fulfill diagnostic criteria for bulimia nervosa whilst the
television appeal produced over 6000 enquiries. Only 1800 or so could be
studied and in the end 1346 satisfactory questionnaires were received from
female respondents. Of these 579 fulfilled diagnostic criteria for bulimia
nervosa. By contrast there were only 47 male respondents of whom eight
probably fulfilled diagnostic criteria for bulimia nervosa. Such studies cannot
be used to estimate the prevalence of bulimia or bulimia nervosa although they
do confirm that there exists in the community substantial numbers of women
subjects, but few men, who closely resemble patients presenting at the clinic. In
both series a majority felt that they needed professional help with their
problems although only a minority had ever seen a psychiatrist. Rather more
had discussed the problem with a general practitioner. (Thirty per cent in the
magazine series and 63% in the television series.)

    There have been a number of attempts to estimate the actual frequency of such eating problems in a number of populations. Indirect evidence may be obtained from surveys whose principal aim is to examine eating attitudes and behaviours rather than particular syndromes (Clarke and Palmer, 1983; Mann, Wakeling, Wood, Monck, Dobb and Szmukler, 1983; Meadows, Palmer, Newball and Kenrick, 1986). These studies have usually used the Eating Attitudes Test (Garner and Garfinkel, 1979) and do provide an important, albeit indirect, index of the probability of finding eating disorder within a population. Nevertheless, there have been a number of studies which have sought to directly estimate the frequency of defined eating disorder. Unfortunately these too have often relied upon self-report measures. Most have been conducted upon student populations and have sought to discover the prevalence of DSM III bulimia. A number of studies of North American students have produced notably high prevalence estimates. Thus, Halmi, Falk and Schwartz (1981) studied 'summer session registrants at a suburban liberal arts campus at the State University of New York'. These summer students included many housewives and others who would not be typical of student populations. Overall 13% of students gave questionnaire responses suggestive of bulimia comprising 19% of the females and 5% of the males. However only six of the 355 subjects reported vomiting once or more per week. These high figures must be interpreted with caution in view of the unknown selection bias involved in becoming a member of the sample and the rather loose self-reporting criteria used. Nevertheless, Pyle, Mitchell, Eckert, Halvorson, Neuman and Goff (1983), Pope, Hudson, Yurgelum-Todd and Hudson (1984), and Katzman, Wolchik and Braver (1984) have all carried out similar and arguably better designed studies and have produced overall estimates of the prevalence of bulimia amongst their female respondents of 7.8%, 12% and 3.9%, respectively. The first two studies included males also and produced estimates of zero and 1.4% respectively. On this side of the Atlantic Freeman, Henderson and Annandale (1984) studied a large sample of first year university students at Edinburgh and obtained a 99% response rate to their questionnaire. They estimated that 4.6% of females and 0.16% of male students would fulfill DSM III criteria for bulimia. Likewise Healy, Conroy and Walsh (1985) studied 1063 college students in Dublin and found a 2% rate in female students and a rate in males which was difficult to estimate but was certainly well under 1%.

   Non-student samples have been studied on both sides of the Atlantic. In this country Cooper and Fairburn (1983) studied 369 attenders at a family planning clinic. Twenty-six per cent claimed to have had the binge eating at some time in their life and 4% were currently bingeing at a rate of more than one per week. Just under 5% had recently used laxatives as a method of weight control and just under 3% had vomited. Cooper and Fairburn attempted to apply Russell's criteria for bulimia nervosa and estimated that 1.9% of this population could be appropriately described as suffering from bulimia nervosa. It is interesting to note that a proportion of those reporting frequent binges or the use of abnormal weight control methods nevertheless did not answer positively the question 'Do you consider yourself currently to have an eating problem'

(Cooper, Waterman and Fairburn, 1984).

Meadows, Palmer, Newball and Kenrick (1984) used a two-stage method to study a complete sample of young women aged 18–22 registered with General Practitioners in Leicestershire. The Eating Attitudes Test (Garner and Garfinkel, 1979) was used as a screening device and high scorers were interviewed where possible. There was a 70% response rate to the questionnaire, but unfortunately only a 56% response rate to the request to interview high scorers. Nevertheless, only one case of bulimia was diagnosed in 411 respondents, although partial syndromes not fulfilling all the criteria were not uncommon. In the United States Pope, Hudson and Yurgelum-Todd (1984) studied 300 females who were approached in a shopping mall in Boston. Their questionnaire was designed to elicit information relevant to making a diagnosis of bulimia. The age range of the sample was from 13–65 and 80% were under 40. The data were interpreted as a showing a 10.3% rate of a history of bulimia with 14 subjects (4.7%) currently having the problem. Nine subjects (3%) gave a life-time history of the use of abnormal weight control methods and four were currently behaving in this way.

In summary, there is general consensus that these disorders are much more common in females than males and that the highest rates are to be found in young women. This fits well with clinical experience, but it must be said that such clinical preconceptions have led most of the research to be done in young female populations. In this respect it is of interest that Fairburn and Cooper's (1984) 'television study' produced a population with a mean age of 28 years and of whom nearly half were married and only 10% were in full-time education. Although most of the work to date has been carried out with student populations or in young people, it may well be that substantial numbers of cases are to be found in other groups. Nevertheless, there is some evidence to suggest that abnormal eating attitudes and perhaps associated disorders may be more common in student populations than in others of similar age (Clarke and Palmer, 1983; Meadows, Palmer, Newball and Kenrick, 1986). Furthermore, populations in the United States seem to report higher rates of bulimia than similar populations on this side of the Atlantic. However, at present, estimates rest upon the rather shaky foundation of studies using self-report measures and further studies using clinical confirmation of caseness are required.

It is by no means clear whether bulimia is associated with a particular background of social class, because of the selected nature of the populations which have been studied. Certainly attitudes to eating and weight which form a background to the disorder seem to be relatively evenly distributed through the population in recent studies (Meadows, Palmer, Newball and Kenrick, 1986).

Most studies that have addressed the issue seem to find that there are at least as many subjects to be found who partially fulfil diagnostic criteria as those who do so fully. Likewise there is a strong impression that cases found by questionnaire techniques in the community are by no means as severely troubled by their state as those who present at the clinic and are in every sense less severe. Often they feel that it is not relevant for them to seek professional help. It is important therefore not to extrapolate with too much confidence from estimates obtained by questionnaire studies to guesses about what services might be required to help such people. Likewise this prevalence data from a relatively new disorder gives little clue as to incidence, course, or prognosis. All that can be said with confidence is that for a proportion of bulimic subjects the disorder is both severe and long lasting and associated with considerable morbidity and even mortality. However, for the majority of subjects fulfilling diagnostic criteria this is probably not the case.

TREATMENT

Over the last few years there has been a gradual growth of literature on attempts to treat individuals with bulimic syndromes who seek help. Not surprisingly the majority of these have been written by psychiatrists or clinical psychologists. Most contributions have been in the form of single case reports or small series and few treatments have been adequately evaluated. Difficulties in assessing treatment arise from differences in case selection with a wide variety of severity even in cases fulfilling a particular set of criteria, the largely unknown natural history of these disorders, and technical problems such as small numbers and inadequate follow up. Certainly no one treatment has emerged as the treatment of choice.

There have been a number of studies reporting the use of various psychotropic drugs in the treatment of bulimic syndromes. One of the earliest was that of Wermuth, Davis, Hollister and Stunkard (1977) who compared the effect of the anticonvulsant phenytoin with a placebo preparation in a 12-week double-blind cross-over trial in 19 subjects with binge eating. They reported some modest improvement in the phenytoin treated group which interestingly persisted even when the patients were transferred to placebo. Patients receiving the placebo first did not benefit until they received the active drug. These workers could find no relationship between response and presence or absence of EEG abnormality in their subjects. Their work was a follow up to an even earlier study by Green and Rau (1974) which showed more dramatically positive results in a selected group of subjects. More recently Kaplan, Garfinkel, Darby and Garner (1983) described one dramatic response to Carbamazepine in the context of a small cross-over trial. It seems possible that a small number of bulimic subjects do have an anticonvulsant responsive state but it is unlikely that these drugs are useful in the majority.

A variety of antidepressant drugs have been tried in bulimic syndromes, a practice usually informed by the idea that there is a relationship between these syndromes and affective disorders. Thus, Hsu (1984) reported on the use of lithium, sometimes in conjunction with behaviour therapy, in the treatment of fourteen bulimic subjects who seem to have been quite severely disordered. Twelve had a marked or moderate response although the mixture of therapies and lack of a double-blind technique make the claim of a specific response merely suggestive. Similarly Walsh, Stewart, Wright, Harrison, Roose and Glassman (1982) reported on a series of six cases of DSM III bulimia who seemed to respond to treatment with monoamine oxidase inhibitors. Pope, Hudson, Jonas and Yurgelum-Todd (1983) carried out a 6-week double-blind placebo controlled trial of Imipramine in a dosage of 200 mg a day with subjects who fulfilled DSM III criteria for bulimia, although the authors note that 'most met DSM III criteria for other disorders as well, particularly affective and anxiety disorders'. There was a significant, if modest, advantage in terms of a reduction in binge eating amongst the Imipramine group and the authors report that most subjects continued to receive antidepressant therapy after the trial with benefit. The biggest, and arguably the best designed, trial of this kind compared the antidepressant Mianserin with a placebo in total of 50 cases fulfilling criteria for bulimia nervosa (Sabine, Yonace, Farrington, Barratt and Wakeling, 1983). There was a relatively high drop out rate in both groups over the 8-week trial period, but no significant difference was detected between the active drug and placebo. The whole issue about the use of antidepressant drugs in the therapy of bulimia has recently been reviewed (Hudson, Pope and Jonas, 1984) and these authors are hopeful that the use of antidepressant drugs may be an important new avenue of treatment. Nevertheless, the results published so far give only inconsistent support to this view. With a few exceptions, they seem to be only moderately efficacious in the short term in some cases. There is a need for further work. How long treatment should be continued in responsive subjects and whether there is any specific indication for particular antidepressants remains unknown.

Russell and his colleagues at the Maudsley Hospital recently experimented with the use of Fenfluramine and have noted a decrease in bulimic symptoms in subjects fulfilling criteria for bulimia nervosa when this drug is compared with placebo (Robinson, Checkley and Russell, 1985). However this drug has yet to be evaluated as a clinical treatment for the disorder. Previously the same group had reported on the suppression of bulimic symptoms with methylamphetamine (Ong, Checkley and Russell, 1983). In this regard it should be noted that many bulimic subjects gave a history of obtaining and using amphetamine and amphetamine-like substances in an attempt to contain their appetite and control their weight. Whether such substances have any useful and acceptable place in the clinical management of such disorders is uncertain, but rather unlikely.

There have been reports of a wide variety of psychotherapeutic interventions which have been used to treat bulimic subjects. Some have been informed by psychodynamic ideas and some by behavioural principles, but interestingly many authors have reported complex treatment packages involving cognitive, behavioural, and other elements. As with drugs, there are major problems of evaluation and most reports describe only small series of patients or even single cases. These include reports of treatment by structural family therapy (Schwartz, 1983), cognitive-behavioural therapy (Linden, 1980; Long and Cordle, 1982; Rosen and Leitenberg, 1982) and response prevention in severe and chronic cases (Freeman, Henderson and Anglim, 1984). Reports of group treatments by their nature tend to include more subjects, but are still usually uncontrolled. Whyte and Boskind-Whyte (1981) describe a brief, but very intensive, group treatment informed by feminist ideas. Johnson, Connors and Stucky (1983), Stevens and Salisbury (1984), and Roy-Byrne, Lee-Benner and Yager (1984) report on groups which seemed to combine psychodynamic with behavioural and goal setting techniques. All of these groups seem to have coincided with improvements in a majority of cases, but in most of the studies there was a significant drop out rate and some unresponsive subjects; also none had a control group. Dixon and Kievolt-Glaser (1981) and Schneider and Agras (1985) have reported on group treatments which were more clearly behavioural in orientation. The former authors had a very high drop out, but in the end nine out of eleven of their subjects were improved and five were binge free. Similarly, Schneider and Agras (1985) ran two groups each for 16 weeks in which 13 severely bulimic women were treated with cognitive and behavioural methods. By the end of the group just over half had stopped bingeing completely, although two had relapsed somewhat by the end of the six-month follow-up period.

By contrast to these small and preliminary studies three centres have reported the use of varied psychotherapeutic techniques on rather larger numbers of patients who were studied more carefully and in depth. Thus, Fairburn from Oxford has published a series of papers describing an individual cognitive behavioural technique for the treatment of bulimia nervosa (Fairburn, 1981, 1982, 1983, 1984). Most of the patients whom he has treated have been severely disordered and most have been so for a number of years. The treatment is individual and intense and lasts from 4 to 6 months. Initially patients are seen two or three times a week and the emphasis in treatment is on advice, self-monitoring, prescription of an eating pattern and the use of stimulus control techniques. Often there would be some joint interviews with family or friends. This regime usually results in a substantial degree of control over abnormal eating behaviour within a few weeks and the patient is then seen at weekly intervals for further behavioural advice together with training in problem solving and cognitive restructuring. In the third stage of treatment the patient is seen at fortnightly intervals and prepared for discharge with discussion of how to cope with future episodes of poor control. Fairburn's careful documentation of his intensive individual therapy has made an important contribution to the field of cognitive behavioural therapy in these disorders. Most subjects do well, although the work is essentially uncontrolled.

Lacey at St George's Hospital, London has by contrast reported a major trial of complex group treatment (Lacey, 1983). The treatment lasted for one half day per week over ten consecutive weeks and in all 30 patients were treated in six groups of five patients each. Each treatment session consisted of a half-hour individual session with one therapist followed by a 90-minute group session with the other patients and with two therapists. Patients were required to make a contract to attend the groups, to maintain their present weight, to eat along the lines advised by the therapists, and to record their eating in a dietary diary which was to be kept with them at all times. The individual sessions initially used simple behavioural and counselling techniques before moving on to insight-directed psychotherapy. The group was insight-directed throughout. The patients involved fulfilled both the DSM III criteria for bulimia and Russell's criteria for bulimia nervosa. The length of history of eating disorder varied from three to eighteen years and on average the subjects binged and vomited about three times per day. The outcome with treatment was remarkably good for the majority of patients, with 80% stopping vomiting and bingeing completely by the end of the treatment. A further four patients managed to stop soon after the end of treatment. Twenty-eight of the 30 patients were followed up for up to two years and 20 reported no bulimic or vomiting episodes and the remainder only occasional symptoms. Lacey noted the emergence of some depression and anger within the group as time went by, but felt that this was an appropriate expression of feelings which had been previously suppressed. This work needs to be replicated, but would seem to represent a potent and relatively economical treatment intervention with a high success rate.

Pyle and his colleagues from the University of Minnesota recently reviewed the two former approaches to the treatment of bulimia and have outlined their own treatment programme (Pyle, Mitchell, Eckert, Hatsukami and Goff, 1984). Their treatment regime grew out of the deluge of eating disordered patients seeking help from their clinic. It comprises an intensive evening group approach which lasts some two months and is run by a multidisciplinary team. Patients meet several times per week in groups of eight to ten and each session lasts about three hours and at least initially would include eating together. The programme seems to be based mainly on educational and behavioural principles with a continuing emphasis on mutual support within the group. Thus recovering patients may become volunteers helping within the programme and programme participants are required to make two calls nightly to other group members to provide support. Subjects are contracted from the beginning to cease bingeing and attend the group regularly. Less focused and more traditional group psychotherapy may be offered after the end of the two monthly programme. The results of the programme have yet to be reported in detail, but an initial review of 104 consecutive patients suggested that nearly half reported no bulimic behaviour from the first night of the programme and only 4% had four or more episodes of bulimic behaviour during the programme. Sixteen per cent failed to complete the treatment. Follow-up data are as yet unavailable. These results are of great interest and it will be important to know the long-term outcome of these patients. However, the general approach of an intensive multidisciplinary evening programme for the treatment of bulimia may be one that will find an important place at those centres where very large numbers of subjects present for treatment. Furthermore, it is possible that such techniques could be successfully used by lay or self-help organizations.

All in all attempts at the treatment of bulimia have been characterized by their variety and by the frequent recourse to mixed treatment packages which emphasize both behaviour control and the modification of ideas and attitudes. Broadly speaking the cognitive behavioural approach, whether conducted individually or in groups, would seem to be the most promising. However, given the large numbers of subjects who may well require some help with their eating problems, there is a real need to consider economy as well as efficacy in arranging treatment for the generality of subjects, whilst perhaps developing more powerful and intensive treatment approaches for the most severely affected patients.

THE NATURE OF BULIMIA

Since the recognition of bulimia and bulimia nervosa as syndromes there has been a good deal of speculation as to how these disorders should be best construed. Their definition as syndromes clearly implies a recognition of similarities between subjects who show binge eating behaviour, but it is also clear that groups thus defined vary. Certainly binge eaters differ in the extent to which their behaviour disturbs and disrupts their lives. It is possible to fulfil either set of criteria and have a mild disorder or one that is devastating. In general, however, the DSM III criteria for bulimia would seem to define a wider group than the criteria for bulimia nervosa which demand the use of abnormal weight control methods. Neither set of criteria specifies at length any necessary psychopathology and the degree to which subjects are psychologically disturbed is a further source of variation. However, it is possible to speculate that anyone suffering from a bulimic syndrome is likely to show an unproductive entanglement of issues of weight and eating control with wider personal issues, especially problems of self-confidence, self-worth, and self-esteem. The subject feels that these personal issues are importantly bound up with and influenced by her success or failure in modifying her body weight and controlling her eating. In this respect bulimic individuals may be unusual only in the degree to which they hold such beliefs or act upon them, since matters of body size and shape are of considerable importance for self-evaluation for many young women in our society. Indeed it is likely that this cultural context is essential as part of an explanation of the emergence of both anorexia nervosa and bulimia as relatively common disorders.

Restrained eating, usually for the purpose of slimming, forms the background of both disorders and it seems likely that the prevalence of clinical problems bears a similar relationship to the prevalence of slimming behaviour as does the prevalence of alcohol problems to the general consumption of alcohol within a society. Garner and Garfinkel (1980) have demonstrated that where such pressures to be slim are strongest, clinical eating disorder occurs more frequently. Nevertheless, pervasive cultural influences have little to add to the understanding of why one individual develops the disorder rather than another. At present no clear answer can be given to this question, but it may be useful to examine, firstly, the nature of weight and eating control itself, and, secondly, what evidence there is about the personal characteristics of individuals who develop the bulimic syndromes.

It is both a commonplace experience and observation that restrained eating, such as sustained slimming, tends to lead the subject to become more aware of hunger, more preoccupied with food, more responsive to external cues to eating, more likely to eat impulsively and to show a tendency to overeat once eating has begun. To someone who feels that the 'successful' control of these impulses and through them the manipulation of body weight holds the key to well-being and self-confidence, these consequence pose a real dilemma with the characteristics of a positive feedback; the greater the self-control, the greater is the experienced risk of loss of control. Furthermore, the greater the importance of the matter for self-evaluation, the greater is the fear of losing control. Almost certainly the commonest, and arguably the healthiest, response to this dilemma of dieting is to question the true worth of slimming and to give it up at least for a while. Most diets end with the person resuming their former pattern of eating and weight. If, however, the response to this dilemma is ever increasing efforts at control, there may be a serial postponement of a resumption of eating, increasing weight loss and the onset of anorexia nervosa (Palmer, 1982). It may be argued that bulimia is an intermediate position between these two responses with a pattern of increasingly frantic alternation between efforts at restraint and its abandonment, often with a mixture of pleasure, relief, and guilt. Undoubtedly other psychological issues enter into the vicious circle, but such a model does provide some understanding of the relationship between bulimia, anorexia nervosa and the background of slimming and ideas about weight from which they characteristically arise.

Within such a model it is still necessary to consider why some subjects respond to the dilemmas of restrained eating by developing bulimia and others do not. It is perhaps relevant to return to the lessons which may be learned from the extreme case of bulimia appearing in the context of anorexia nervosa. Those anorectic subjects who do develop bulimic overeating show a tendency to be more extroverted, impulsive, and emotional than those who remain as restricters. It could be that, when these characteristics are combined with the overvaluing of weight and eating control which is an aspect of all eating disorders, the stage is set for a pattern of eating in which overcontrol alternates with overconsumption. Such studies as there are do tend to confirm that bulimic subjects at normal weight resemble their lower weight counterparts in this respect (Katzman and Wolchik, 1984). This is hardly surprising, since in most series of subjects with bulimia at normal weight there are a substantial number who have gained that position following a period of anorexia nervosa. The proportion who have been anorectic previously doubtless depends upon the source of referral and other selective criteria, but in many series a quarter or even a half have been previously anorectic (Gandour, 1984). Rost, Newhams and Florin (1982) examined the sex-role attitudes, behaviour, and locus of control in a series of bulimic women and concluded that there was a notable gap between the women's stated sexual attitudes and their actual behaviour and, furthermore, that they had a notably external and fatalistic locus of control. It is possible to speculate that the bulimic woman is urging herself to solve her personal problems in terms of moulding herself into some stereotyped role, but feels incompetent to do so, particularly perhaps when she encounters the dilemmas of dieting outlined above. At this point her impulsivity and emotional lability may make her more vulnerable to the alternating pattern of bulimia rather than the rigid overcontrol of the anorectic. In this respect it is worthy of note that there is evidence which suggests that bulimics may also show an excess of other behaviours such as chemical and alcohol dependence (Mitchell, Hatsukami, Eckert and Pyle, 1985). It could be suggested that the relatively unstable mood of the bulimic may be an aspect of some inborn or other vulnerability to affective disorder. Such a view is supported by the reported higher family history of affective disorder in bulimic subjects (Hudson, Pope, Jonas and Yurgelum-Todd, 1983). Some authors have taken this argument further by seeking other links between affective disorder and bulimia and cite treatment response, depressive symptomatology, and neuroendocrine findings (Hudson, Pope and Jonas, 1984). Certainly there is some evidence to suggest that a blunted thyroid stimulating hormone response to the injection of thyrotrophin releasing hormone of a kind that is found in some depressives is also present in some bulimics (Gwirtsman, Roy-Byrne, Jager and Gerner, 1983; Norris, O'Malley and Palmer, 1985) and that the same may be true of the dexamethasone suppression test (Gwirtsman, Roy-Byrne, Jager and Gerner, 1983). However, such relatively subtle and non-specific changes must be interpreted with caution in a nutritionally disturbed group.

In social terms bulimic women seem often to have a relatively preserved adjustment at least in the less personal aspects of their lives. Many patients reported in the literature lead academically achieving and materially successful lives, although there may be a major selection bias. Likewise they may be sexually active, although many have high levels of sexual anxiety and insecurity and substantial numbers give a past history of adverse sexual experiences (Oppenheimer, Howells, Palmer and Chaloner, 1985; Howells, Oppenheimer and Palmer, 1986).

Bulimia and bulimia nervosa are related syndromes of varying severity which have emerged into full recognition only over the past few years. It seems likely that they reflect the casualties of our society's preoccupation with slimness, but that this general influence is revealed and manifest as clinical disorder only in people who are vulnerable in some way. It is possible that their vulnerability may have psychological, social, and even biological components. There is a clear and close relationship of severe bulimia with anorexia nervosa, but the prognosis of bulimia at normal weight is as yet uncertain, although it is clearly varied. The disorder provides a challenge for the researcher to find its nature and outcome and for the clinician to provide appropriately varied response to its variety of severity.

REFERENCES

Abraham, S.F. and Beumont, P.J.V. (1982) How patients describe bulimia or binge eating. *Psychological Medicine*, **12**, 625–635.

Beumont, P.J.V., George, G.C.W. and Smart, D.E. (1976). 'Dieters' and 'vomiters and purgers' in anorexia nervosa. *Psychological Medicine*, **6**, 617–622.

Boskind-Lodahl, M. (1976). Cinderella's stepsisters : A feminist perspective on anorexia nervosa and bulimia. *'Signs.' Journal of Women, Culture and Society*, **2**, 342–356.

Bruch, H. (1973). Thin-fat people. *Journal of the American Medical Women's Association*, **28**, 187–248.

Button, E.J. and Whitehouse, A. (1981). Subclinical anorexia nervosa. *Psychological Medicine*, **11**, 509–516.

Casper, R.C., Eckert, E.D., Halmi, K.A., Goldberg, S.C. and Davis, J.M. (1980). Bulimia: its incidence and clinical importance in patients with anorexia nervosa. *Archives of General Psychiatry*, **37**, 1030–1035.

Celesia, G.G., Archer, C.R. and Chung, H.D. (1981). Hyperphagia and obesity; relationship to medial hypothalamic lesions. *Journal of the American Medical Association*, **246** (2) 768–777.

Clarke, M.G. and Palmer, R.L. (1983). Eating attitudes and neurotic symptoms in university students. *British Journal of Psychiatry*, **142**, 299–304.

Cooper, P.J. and Fairburn, C.G. (1983). Binge-eating and self induced vomiting in the community: a preliminary study. *British Journal of Psychiatry*, **142**, 139–144.

Cooper, P.J., Waterman, G. and Fairburn, C.G. (1984). Women with eating problems : a community survey. *British Journal of Clinical Psychology*, **23**, 45–52.

Crisp, A.H. (1981). Anorexia nervosa at normal body weight! The abnormal/normal weight control syndrome. *International Journal of Psychiatry in Medicine*, **11**, (3), 203–233.

Dixon, K.N. and Kievolt-Glacer, J. (1981). An integrated therapy approach to bulimia. Paper presented at the Annual Meeting of the American Psychiatric Association. New Orleans, 1981.

Fairburn, C.G. (1981). A cognitive behavioural approach to the management of bulimia. *Psychological Medicine*, **11**, 707–711.

Fairburn, C.G. (1982). Binge-eating and its management. *British Journal of Psychiatry*, **141**, 631–633.

Fairburn, C.G. (1983). Bulimia nervosa. *British Journal Hospital Medicine*, **29**, 537–542.

Fairburn C.G. (1984). Bulimia: Its epidemiology and management. In A.J. Stunkard and E. Stellar (Eds), *Eating and Its Disorders*, (Eds), Raven Press, New York.

Fairburn, C.G. and Cooper, P.J. (1982). Self induced vomiting and bulimia nervosa : an undetected problem. *British Medical Journal*, **284**, 1153–1155.

Fairburn, C.G. and Cooper, P.J. (1984). Binge-eating, self induced vomiting and laxative abuse: a community study. *Psychological Medicine*, **14**, 410–410.

Freeman, C.P.L., Henderson, M. and Annandale, A. (1984). Binge eating in Edinburgh university students. Paper presented at International Conference on Anorexia nervosa and Related Disorders, University College, Swansea, September 1984.

Freeman, C.P.L., Henderson, M. and Anglim, M. (1984). Response prevention as a treatment technique in severe treatment-resistant bulimia. Paper presented at International Conference on Anorexia Nervosa and Related Disorders, University College, Swansea, September 1984.

Gandour, M.J. (1984). Bulimia : clinical description, assessment, etiology and treatment. *International Journal of Eating Disorders*, **3** (3) 3–38.

Garfinkel, P.E., Moldofsky, H. and Garner, D.M. (1980). The heterogeneity of anorexia nervosa : bulimia as a distinct subgroup. *Archives of General Psychiatry*, **37**, 1036–1040.

Garner, D.M. and Garfinkel, P.E. (1979). The Eating Attitudes Test : an index of the symptoms of anorexia nervosa. *Psychological Medicine*, **9**, 273–279.

Garner, D.M. and Garfinkel, P.E. (1980). Socio cultural factors in the development of anorexia nervosa. *Psychological Medicine*, **10**, 647–656.

Green, R.S. and Rau, J.H. (1974). Treatment of compulsive eating disturbances with anticonvulsant medication. *American Journal of Psychiatry*, **131**, 428–432.

Gull, W.W. (1873). Anorexia Nervosa. *Trans Clinical society (London)*, **7**, 22–28.

Gwirtsman, H.E., Roy-Byrne, P., Jager, J. and Gerner, R.H. (1983). Neuroendocrine abnormalities in bulimia. *American Journal of Psychiatry*, **140**, 559–563.

Halmi K.A., Falk, J.R. and Schwartz, E. (1981). Binge eating and vomiting : a survey of a college population. *Psychological Medicine*, **11**, 697–706.

Hawkins, R.C. and Clement P.F. (1980). Development and construct validation of a self-report measure of binge eating tendencies. *Addictive Behaviours*, **5**, 219–226.

Healy, K., Conroy, R.M. and Walsh, N. (1985). The prevalence of binge-eating and bulimia in 1063 college students. *Journal of Psychiatric Research*, **19**, 161–166.

Herman, C.P. and Mack, D. (1975). Restrained and unrestrained eating. *Journal of Personality*, **43**, 647–660.

Herman, C.P. and Polivy, J. (1975). Anxiety, restraint and eating behaviour. *Journal of Personality*, **84**, 666–672.

Herman, C.P. and Polivy, J. (1984). A boundary model for the regulation of eating. In A.J. Stunkard and E. Stellar (Eds), *Eating and Its Disorders*, Raven Press, New York.

Hibscher, J.A. and Herman, C.P. (1977). Obesity, dieting and the expression of 'obese' characteristics. *Journal of Comparative and Physiological Psychology*, **2**, 374–380.

Howells, K., Oppenheimer, R. and Palmer, R.L. (1985). Sexual attitudes in eating disordered patients (in preparation).

Hsu, L.K.G., (1984). Treatment of bulimia with lithium. *American Journal of Psychiatry*, **141**, 1260–1262.

Hudson, J.L. Pope, H.G., Jones, J.M. and Yurgelum-Todd, D. (1983). Family history study of anorexia nervosa and bulimia. *British Journal of Psychiatry*, **142**, 133–138.

Hudson, J.I., Pope, H.G. and Jonas, J.M. (1984). Treatment of bulimia with anti-depressants, theoretical considerations and clinical findings. In A.J. Stunkard and E. Stellar (Eds), *Eating and Its Disorders*, Raven Press, New York.

Johnson, C., Connors, M. and Stucky, M. (1983). Short term group treatment of bulimia; a preliminary report. *International Journal of Eating Disorders*, **2**, 199–208.

Johnson, C. and Larson, R. (1982). Bulimia — an analysis of moods and behaviours. *Psychological Medicine*, **44**, (4), 341–351.

Johnson-Sabine, E.C., Wood, K.H. and Wakeling, A. (1984). Mood changes in bulimia nervosa. *British Journal of Psychiatry*, **145**, 512–516.

Kaplan, A.S., Garfinkel, P.E., Darby, P.L. and Garner, D.M. (1983). Carbamazepine in the treatment of bulimia. *American Journal Psychiatry*, **140**, (9), 199–208.

Katzman, M.A. and Wolchik, S.A. (1984). Bulimia and binge eating in college women; A comparison of personality and behavioural characteristics. *Journal of Consulting and Clinical Psychology*, **52**, 423–428.

Katzman, M.A., Wolchik, S.A. and Braver, S.L. (1984). The prevalence of frequent binge eating and bulimia in a non clinical college sample. *International Journal of Eating Disorders*, **3**, 53–62.

Krahn, D.D. and Mitchell, J.E. (1984). Case report of bulimia associated with increased intracranial pressure. *American Journal of Psychiatry*, **141**, 1099–1100.

Lacey, J.H. (1983). Bulimia nervosa, binge eating and psychogenic vomiting: a controlled treatment study and long-term outcome. *British Medical Journal*, **286**, 1609–1613.

Levin, P.A., Falko, J.M., Dixon K., Gallup, E.M. and Saunders W. (1980). Benign parotid enlargement in bulimia. *Annals of International Medicine*, **93**, 827–829.

Linden, W. (1980). Multicomponent behaviour therapy in a case of compulsive binge eating followed by vomiting. *Journal of Behaviour Therapy and Experimental Psychiatry*, **11**, 297–300.

Long, C.G. and Cordle, C.J. (1982). Psychological treatment of binge-eating and self induced vomiting. *British Journal of Medical Psychology*, **55**, 139–145.

Loro, A.D. and Orleans C.S. (1981). Binge eating in obesity; preliminary findings and guidelines for behavioural analysis and treatment. *Addictive Behaviours*, **6**, 155–166.

Mann, A.H., Wakeling A., Wood K., Monck E., Dobb R. and Szmukler G. (1983). Screening for abnormal eating attitudes and psychiatric morbidity in an unselected population of 15 year old schoolgirls. *Psychological Medicine*, **13**, 573–580.

Meadows, G.N., Palmer, R.L., Newball, E.U.M. and Kenrick, J.M.T. (1986). Eating attitudes and disorder in young women: a general practice based survey. *Psychological Medicine*, **16**, 351–357.

Mitchell, J.E., Pyle, R.L. and Miner, R.A. (1982). Gastric dilation as a complication of bulimia. *Psychosomatics*, **23**, 96–97.

Mitchell, J.E., Pyle R.L., Eckert, E.D., Hatsukami, D. and Lentz, R. (1983). Electrolyte and other physiological abnormalities in patients with bulimia. *Psychological Medicine*, **13**, 273–278.

Mitchell, J.E., Hatsukami, D., Eckert, E.D. and Pyle, R.L. (1985). Characteristics of 275 patients with bulimia. *American Journal of Psychiatry*, **142**, 482–485.

Nagami, Y. and Yabana, F. (1977). On Kibarashi-gui (binge eating). *Folia psychiatrica et neurologica Japonica*, **31**, 159–166.

Norris, P.D., O'Malley, B.P. and Palmer, R.L. (1985). The TRH Test in bulimia and anorexia nervosa: a controlled study. *Journal of Psychiatric Research*, **19**, 215–219.

Ong, Y.L., Checkley, S.A. and Russell, G.F.M. (1983). Suppression of bulimic symptoms with methylamphetamine. *British Journal of Psychiatry*, **143**, 288–289.

Oppenheimer, R., Howells, K., Palmer, R.L. and Chaloner, D.A. (1985). Adverse sexual experiences in childhood and clinical eating disorders; a preliminary description. *Journal of Psychiatric Research* (in press).

Palmer, R.L. (1979). The dietary chaos syndrome : A useful new term? *British Journal of Medical Psychology*, **52**, 187–190.

Palmer, R.L. (1982). Anorexia nervosa. In K. Granville Grossman (Ed.), *Recent Advances in Clinical Psychiatry*, vol. 4, Churchill Livingstone, Edinburgh.

Polivy, J., (1976). Perception of calories and regulation of intake in restrained and unrestrained subjects. *Addictive Behaviours*, **1**, 237–243.

Polivy, J. and Herman, C.P. (1976). The effects of alcohol on eating behaviour; influence of mood and perceived intoxication. *Journal of Abnormal Psychology*, **85**, 601–604.

Pope, H.G., Hudson J.I., Jonas, J.M. and Yurgelum-Todd, D. (1983). Bulimia treated with imipramine : a placebo-controlled, double blind study. *American Journal of Psychiatry*, **140**, 554–558.

Pope, H.G., Hudson, J.I. and Yrgelum-Todd, D. (1984). Anorexia and bulimia among 300 suburban women shoppers. *American Journal of Psychiatry*, **141**, 292–294.

Pope, H.G., Hudson, J.I. Yurgelum-Todd, D. and Hudson, M.S. (1984) Prevalence of anorexia nervosa and bulimia in three student populations. *International Journal of Eating Disorders*, **3**, 45–51.

Pyle, R.L., Mitchell, J.E. and Eckert, E.D. (1981). Bulimia : A report of 34 cases. *Journal of Clinical Psychiatry*, **42**, 60–64.

Pyle, R.L., Mitchell, J.E., Eckert, E.D., Halvorson, P.A., Neuman, P.A. and Goff, G.M. (1983). The incidence of bulimia in freshman college students. *International Journal of Eating Disorders*, **2**, 75–85.

Pyle, R.L., Mitchell, J.E., Eckert, E.D., Hatsukami, D.K. and Goff, G (1984). The interruption of bulimic behaviours. *Psychiatric Clinics of North America*, 7, 275–286.

Rau, J.H. and Green, R.S., (1975). Compulsive eating : A neurophysiological approach to certain eating disorders. *Comprehensive Psychiatry*, 16, 223–231.

Reeves, A.G. and Plum, F. (1969). Hyperphogia, rage and dementia accompanying a rentromedical hypothalmic neoplasm. *Archives Neurology (Chicago)*, 20, 616–624.

Robinson, P.H., Checkley, S.A. and Russell, G.F.M. (1985). Suppression of eating by fenfluramine in patients with bulimia nervosa. *British Journal of Psychiatry*, 146, 169–176.

Roche, L. (1984). *Glutton for Punishment*, Pan Books, London.

Rosen, J.C. and Leitenberg, H. (1982). Bulimia nervosa : treatment with exposure and response prevention. *Behaviour Therapy*, 13, 117–124.

Rost, W., Newhams, M. and Florin, I. (1982). Bulimia nervosa — sex-role attitude, sex-role behaviour and sex-role related loss of control in bulimarexic women. *Journal of Psychsomatic Research*, 26, 403–408.

Roy-Byrne, P., Lee-Benner, K. and Yager, J. (1984). Group therapy for bulimia; a year's experience. *International Journal of Eating Disorders*, 3, 97–116.

Russell, G.F.M. (1979). Bulimia nervosa : an ominous variant of anorexia nervosa. *Psychological Medicine*, 9, 429–448.

Sabine, E.J., Yonace, A., Farrington, A.J., Barratt, K.H. and Wakeling, A. (1983). Bulimia nervosa; a placebo controlled double blind therapeutic trial of mianserin. *British Journal of Clinical Pharmacology*, 15, 195S–202S.

Schneider, J.A. and Agras, W.S. (1985). A cognitive behavioural group treatment of bulimia. *British Journal of Psychiatry*, 146, 66–69.

Schwartz, R.L. (1983), Bulimia and family therapy : a controlled study. *International Journal of Eating Disorders*, 2, 75–82.

Spencer, J.A. and Fremouw, W.J. (1979). Binge eating as a function of restraint and weight classification. *Journal of Abnormal Psychology*, 88, 262–267.

Stevens, E.V. and Salisbury, J.D. (1984). Group therapy for bulimic adults. *American Journal of Orthopsychiatry*, 54, 156–161.

Strober, M., Salkin, B., Burroughs, J. and Morrell, W. (1982). Validity of the bulimia-restricter distinction of anorexia nervosa. *Journal of Nervous and Mental Diseases*, 170, 345–351.

Walsh, B.T., Stewart, J.W., Wright L., Harrison, W., Roose, S.P. and Glassman, A.H. (1982). Treatment of bulimia with monoamine oxidase inhibitors. *American Journal of Psychiatry*, 139, 1629–1630.

Wardle, J. (1980). Dietary restraint and binge eating. *Behavioural Analysis and Modification*, 4, 201–209.

Wardle, J. and Beinart, H. (1981) Binge eating : A theoretical review. *British Journal of Clinical Psychology*, 20, 97–109.

Wermuth, B.M., Davis, K.L., Hollister, L.E., and Stunkard, A.J. (1977). Phenytoin treatment of the binge-eating syndrome. *American Journal of Psychiatry*, 134, 1249–1253.

Whyte, W.S. and Boskind-Whyte, M. (1981). An experimental-behavioural approach to the treatment of bulimarexia. *Journal of Psychotherapy: Theory, Research and Practice*, 18, 501–507.

CHAPTER 2

Anorexia Nervosa: A Clinical View

G.I. Szmukler

Royal Melbourne Hospital, Parkville, Victoria, 3050, Australia

Anorexia nervosa has been the subject of considerable attention in the past two decades. There is some evidence that it has increased in incidence (Jones, Fox, Babigan and Hutton, 1980; Szmukler, McCance, McCrone and Hunter, 1986) but the fact that more cases are being seen now than before is probably in part due to better recognition. The disorder has been well delineated and a good case has been made for its identity as a relatively discrete illness (Russell, 1970). This is based on the consistency with which the elements of the syndrome are encountered and the fact that it tends to 'breed true' over time, that is, the sufferer, even when the disorder is chronic, presents throughout a similar clinical picture. Although a comprehensive epidemiological study has yet to be done, the evidence based on schoolgirl studies suggests a prevalence of about one in 150–400 girls aged 16–18 years in the United Kingdom (Crisp, 1976; Szmukler, 1983).

The aims of this chapter are to describe the disorder as it presents clinically and to examine critically the explanations offered to account for its development. Throughout this presentation, the emphasis will be on the types of understanding which are of value to clinicians. The phenomena of anorexia nervosa which are of greatest interest to the psychiatrist will be teased out for special consideration, in particular the puzzling nature of the psychopathology.

THE CLINICAL PRESENTATION

The disorder occurs in females, although about one in ten cases is a male. The commonest age of onset is the middle to late teens but cases occur in prepubertal youngsters as well as in older subjects even into their 40s and 50s.

25

The most common initial event is the commencement of a diet which is usually unremarkable in its early stages. Occasionally the process is set in train by other causes of weight loss such as a physical illness (e.g. glandular fever) or a psychiatric disorder such as depression. Sometimes weight loss occurs for a reason which is neither obvious to the patient or the physician. At some point the weight loss becomes obviously excessive, yet the patient continues to restrict her intake and to intensify her efforts to lose even more weight. The subject of her weight becomes her major preoccupation and the attempts of her family and friends to persuade her to eat more are rebutted.

At this stage the characteristic features of anorexia nervosa will be evident:

1.   Weight loss: this is purposive and the result of eliminating 'fattening' foods from the diet. Weight loss may also be accelerated by other means including excessive exercise, self-induced vomiting, and the abuse of laxitives.
2.   An endocrine disorder: this is amenorrhoea in the female or a profound loss of sexual interest and potency in the male.
3.   A characteristic psychopathology: this may be quite complex but it usually involves a morbid fear of 'fatness' or weight gain. This will be discussed in some detail later.

There are usually a number of other changes which are less specific. A variety of psychological disturbances, particularly depressive and obsessional symptoms, are often present. A major change in the patient's personality is usually evident. A loss of interest in social activities and boyfriends is nearly always noted, as is an immersion in studies or work. Patients usually express a keen interest in food and not infrequently displace their mothers from the kitchen. Other's plates are loaded with carefully prepared and enticing foods, but the patient herself will retire to her bedroom to eat her cottage cheese and salad, the calorie content of which has been assiduously calculated. The patient finally and reluctantly agrees to see the physician, usually having been coerced into this by her family and friends. She is likely to deny that there is any problem. The illness rarely lasts less than 2 years and the outcome, for patients ill enough to be hospitalized, ranges from complete recovery in about 40–60% to a persisting, chronic course in about 20%. There is an appreciable mortality of about 5% over a 4 to 8 year follow-up period (Morgan and Russell, 1975; Hsu, Crisp and Harding, 1979).

Between 30% and 50% of patients with anorexia nervosa move into a phase of gross overeating (bulimia) with attempts to compensate for this, usually by starvation, self-induced vomiting or purgation. The morbid fear of fatness persists. This condition has been termed 'bulimia nervosa' (Russell, 1979).

CAUSES OF ANOREXIA NERVOSA

Garfinkel and Garner (1982) have provided an excellent review of the 'forces' leading to anorexia nervosa. These are presented within a model derived from

Weiner (1977) with the following features. Illness is seen as the result of an interplay of a number of predisposing forces. These predisposing factors may develop in different people in different ways, with only a few of those predisposed actually developing the illness and in these cases the exact interaction of predisposing factors also varies. Anorexia nervosa is viewed as a kind of final common pathway to which groups of interacting forces lead. Garfinkel and Garner discuss the factors implicated in the genesis of anorexia nervosa under three categories: predisposing factors, precipitating or initiating events, and perpetuating factors. The factors discussed are drawn from a number of conceptual levels — sociocultural, psychological, and biological Table 1 lists most of the factors which are regarded as playing a role in causing anorexia nervosa.

This kind of overview embodies an important truth about the causes of anorexia nervosa, namely, that a full account of these must be exceedingly complex. Different factors and differing interactions may occur in different cases while factors which may be important in the predisposition may play no role in the perpetuation of the illness. One approach to the aetiology of anorexia nervosa may be to construct a type of actuarial or risk factor analysis,

Table 1.   Possible aetiological factors in anorexia nervosa

Predisposing		
Socio-cultural	Slimness as an ideal Race Social Class	
Familial	Family history of affective disorder, alcoholism Family history of anorexia nervosa High aspirations Family dynamics (e.g. 'psychosomatic family')	

Psychological	Specific deficits:
	   Perceptual: body image disturbance; interoceptive
	   Conceptual: cognitive style
	Sense of ineffectiveness, deficits in autonomy
	Fear of maturation
	Personality (e.g. 'perfectionism')	

Biological	Genetic Neuroendocrine vulnerability Other illnesses, e.g. Turner's syndrome, urogenital malformation, diabetes mellitus, perinatal complications Diathesis for affective disorder	
Precipitating factors	Non-specific; external precipitant often identified	
Perpetuating factors	Starvation effects Perceptual—cognitive disturbances Positive reinforcement, e.g. being 'in control' Avoidance of aversive stimuli Stabilization of family dynamics	

in which the whole range of factors could be incorporated, but for this to be fruitful it would be necessary to study a vast number of cases and this would probably need to be followed by an elaborate statistical model for the inter-actions involved.

While it is important to bear the totality in mind, it is equally important to select for closer scrutiny those areas which are likely to be of greatest significance for discerning specific mechanisms resulting in anorexia nervosa. Using the common pathway analogy, it seems reasonable to suppose that we shall discover more that is 'essential' to the disorder by studying the less trodden byways rather than the well-used highways. For example, the social and psychological forces that result in dieting in girls are of interest and undoubted importance, but arguably more pertinent to an understanding of the disorder are the mechanisms by which normal dieting becomes abnormal.

Without wishing to diminish in any way the value of a multifactorial, risk factor approach, whose presentation by the previously mentioned authors I cannot improve on, I would like, in this contribution, to examine the aetiology of anorexia nervosa from a different perspective. This perspective is a uniquely psychiatric one which, I believe, serves to direct the observer to mechanisms possibly specific to the disorder. From the point of view of the clinician some features stand in stronger need of 'explanation' than others. To discuss this further some preliminary comments are necessary about the methods of the psychiatrist in evaluating the psychopathology of his patients.

'UNDERSTANDING' AND 'EXPLANATION'

The clinician assesses the presenting psychopathology by examining it within the context of the patient's life history, his current situation and his social and cultural background. As well as using the psychopathology for arriving at a descriptive diagnosis, the clinician attempts to 'understand' its development. The word 'understand' is used here in a special sense and refers to our comprehension of a particular kind of connexion. Karl Jaspers, whose *General Psychopathology* (1913) has exerted a profound effect on the study of psycho-pathology, put it as follows:

> Psychic events emerge out of each other in a way which we 'understand'. Attacked people become angry and spring to the defence, cheated persons grow suspicious. . . . It strikes us as something self-evident which cannot be broken down any further. . . . Where we understand how certain thoughts arise from moods, wishes or fears, we are 'under-standing' the connexions in a true psychological sense, that is by empathy. We 'understand' the speaker'. (pp. 302–304)

This 'everyday, practical understanding' is distinguished from 'causal expla-nation':

Understanding does not lead to any causal explanation except in an
indirect fashion, when it happens to come up against the un-
understandable. (p.305)

For that which is not 'understandable' we seek causal 'explanations' and these
causal explanations are of the same nature as causal explanations in the natural
sciences. In general when the clinician discerns psychologically meaningful
connexions to account for aspects of the patient's state he does not feel that a
causal explanation is especially necessary.

Psychological 'understanding' and causal 'explanation' are not mutually
disqualifying. There is no reason why causal relations underlying phenomena
which are understandable should not be investigated. It is simply that for the
clinician, causal explanations for that which is not understandable are of
greater interest than for that which is psychologically readily and empathically
understood.

An important point needs to be made about psychologically meaningful
connexions. Unlike causal relationships they are not of a kind which permit
general laws to be derived. They emerge from the unique experiences of an
individual and although, as we shall see, many are common, their organization
varies greatly between individuals. They refer to the particular rather than the
general. As Jaspers put it: 'Anything really meaningful tends to have a concrete
form and generalization destroys it'. (p. 314). By the standards of the natural
sciences, meaningful connexions are not 'objective' since they are discerned
subjectively, that is, by empathy. Detection is limited by the general epistemo-
logical principle that 'like knows like', so that, for example, only what is
capable of emotion can be sensitive to emotion. Observers are likely to vary
considerably in such capacities.

Although the status of 'understandable' connexions as knowledge is special
and not 'scientific' in the conventional sense, this is not to say that it is
unimportant. On the contrary, in the practice of psychiatry it is essential to the
formulation of a case and in planning treatment. For many patients who
present for help with difficulties, these may be totally 'understandable' and
the psychiatrist may have no need for recourse to causal explanations. The
interested reader is referred to an excellent discussion of the issues raised in this
section by Bolton (1984).

My intention in raising the distinction between 'understanding' and 'explanation' is not to claim superiority for the latter at the expense of the former,
but to look at the role of each in accounting for the development of anorexia
nervosa. Causal 'explanations' have been proposed where 'understanding' has
proved difficult and such 'explanations' are, or are implied to be, objective,
based on general 'laws', specific to the disorder and amenable to experimental
methods.

THE UNDERSTANDABILITY OF ANOREXIA NERVOSA

When viewed from the perspective elaborated here much of the experience of patients with anorexia nervosa can be understood. Sources of unhappiness and conflict can be readily discerned and include many that are common in adolesence. These include problems of establishing autonomy, of separating from the family, of coming to terms with sexual feelings, of accepting one's peculiarities, of making satisfactory peer relationships, and of achieving confidence in studies or work. Often special circumstances may compound these problems, for example, unattractive physical characteristics or growing up in a family in which independence is perceived as threatening. Some of these difficulties may be attributed by the adolescent to a particular source, for example, body shape, and this may become an area of special sensitivity. Unlike many other 'disabilities' body shape has the promising quality of being potentially controllable. The adolescent girl may decide that some weight loss would improve her figure and she may be influenced in this by the message from our culture that slimness is an important key to success. A perfectionistic girl may embark on the enterprise of weight loss with method and determination and should she succeed she will find some obvious rewards. Her appearance may improve and invite compliments from others. She may find the weight loss especially gratifying if she values the feeling of being in control. If her problems remain unaltered, she may intensify her efforts to diet in the hope that this will help more. With the investment of so much energy in losing weight this may become a special preoccupation. However, the more she starves, the more she will be troubled by hunger and the more she will fear losing control. Once the diet is broken, her special achievement will be lost and so she may seek to establish a margin of safety so that, even if she should 'break out', it will not represent a total disaster. Her starvation may thus become further intensified and as a consequence of this so will her preoccupation with weight and food. Other means may be introduced to keep her weight in check: exercise, purgatives, and vomiting. Since an ever-increasing amount of energy is being expended on weight control she finds it difficult to maintain her other interests. Her social life begins to suffer, in part because eating with others is to be avoided. This can be embarrasing and the situation might prove irresistably tempting. Alternative sources of satisfaction become fewer so that her special achievement assumes even greater importance. She has little energy to cope with the tasks of adolescent development and she falls progressively behind her peers. In the face of failures in these areas her weight control assumes even greater importance.

Described above are a handful of the psychologically meaningful connexions that we see in patients. Also evident from the description is the way in which the clinical approach enables us to comprehend complex interactions and vicious cycles in a way that is difficult to specify in a formal manner. Events having cultural, psychological, and physiological aspects can be assimilated in the life history and meaningfully juxtaposed or related to each other through understandable experience.

In this way much of the anorexic's behaviour is comprehensible. However, most clinicians would agree that a limit to this kind of understanding is reached and that some phenomena remain which are mystifying and justify special attention. It is this morbid core of experience and behaviour which calls for causal explanation. This core appears to comprise the patient's continued self-starvation and her attitude to it. The patient while apparently starving herself to death denies that she wants to die and in fact continues to make plans for the future on the assumption that she will carry on living. If it is pointed out to her that her behaviour seriously threatens her life, this will generally be denied or it might lead to emotional distress but usually without any alteration in her behaviour. The patient's dieting gives the appearance of being purposeful. She wants to be thin and she acts in accordance with this goal. However, why she wants to be emaciated is a puzzle. If asked directly the patient's replies are likely to be unimpressive. She may say that she enjoys the feeling of 'being in control' or if pushed further she may admit: 'I don't know why, I just want to'. On initial contact with the patient she may maintain that her self-starvation is not experienced as being imposed on her and that it is consonant with her will. However, the attitude of patients with anorexia nervosa to their self-starvation is not fixed and, commonly, when a trusting relationship has been established, the patient will begin to admit that rather than her controlling her eating, she feels controlled by it. She may reach a point where she will express a wish to gain weight, but concede that she cannot.

The patient's attitude to her body is a complex, but also puzzling, experience. She commonly expresses an abhorrence of being 'fat' but what this means for her is far from clear. The concept of 'fatness' for the patient differs from the conventional one. She may say that fatness for her is represented by a normal weight or more usually a weight far below a normal weight. Related to this is a denial of emaciation. Even at a weight which is barely compatible with life the patient may say that this is right for her or that she needs to lose a few pounds still. Other patients will admit they are thin but will give a weight which they are prepared to achieve which is absurdly low. Some patients although greatly emaciated will say that when they look in the mirror they see themselves as normal. Others still will say that they are disgusted with their thinness but if the scales register a weight increase they 'panic'. Conversely, a loss of weight brings relief. Again the attitude of a particular patient is not fixed and she may at one time deny that she is thin but at another concede that she is. Often related to the body concept are bizarre beliefs about the effects of food. Some patients will say, for instance, that even if they eat a relatively small amount of food they fear they will wake up the next day and be 'huge'.

The patient's attitude to her weight is even more puzzling when some other factors are taken into account. Challenging her perception that she is fat is the reading on her weighing scales. Patients are usually able to judge their weight in stones and pounds extremely accurately (Griffiths, 1967). How does the patient reconcile her perception with the objective measure? Some patients will say that for them, weight is meaningless. It is their shape which is important. Others say they trust their 'eyes more than the scales'. Others still will confess that the contradiction is troublesome and on occasions they may have suspected that the scales have been tampered with.

Russell, Campbell and Slade (1975) devised an experiment in which patients whose weight had been restored to normal were then allowed to eat freely. However, unbeknown to the patients, the weighing scales were systematically adjusted to read 0.2 kg less than the actual weight, incrementally each day for 2 weeks, and then by 0.2 kg more each day incrementally back to an accurate reading over the next 2 weeks. At the mid-point of the study, therefore, the scales were registering almost 3 kg less than the actual weight. The hypothesis was that anorexics would adjust their food intake according to what the 'scales said', whereas controls would not. The results showed that the real weight of the anorexics increased and then decreased over the one month experimental period, while that of the control group remained constant. Whatever the wider interpretation of the results, it is clear that the patients (at least when their weight had been restored) were able to control their weight very accurately. How is it then that so many continue to lose weight relentlessly following their discharge from hospital?

Usually following recovery from the illness, most patients are themselves mystified by it. If shown a photograph of themselves when emaciated, they are puzzled that they could have believed themselves to be fat. Many comment that the whole experience seems to them to have been like a 'bad dream', 'unreal' or 'mad'.

EXPLANATIONS FOR ANOREXIA NERVOSA

A number of explanations have been offered for the non-understandable phenomena of anorexia nervosa described above. These have been formulated in psychological or physical terms.

Psychological Explanations

Weight phobia   Anorexia nervosa has been regarded as essentially a 'phobia' of normal weight and its consequences (Crisp, 1980). The condition involves a regression, both biological and psychological, to a prepubertal state. This regression stalemates adolescent development and provides relief from the challenges of growth which, for a variety of reasons, the patient is unable to meet. Menstruation ceases, feminine curves are smoothed out and sexual feelings diminish. The girl is relieved of facing the challenges of psychological and physical maturation. Starvation has served to reverse the changes occurring at puberty and the patient's behaviour is directed to avoiding a weight at which pubertal changes will be re-established. This weight will vary from patient to patient but will usually be in the range of 45 to 50 kg. It is this behaviour which is termed 'phobic' and it is a weight commensurate with a rekindling of pubertal processes which is the feared object.

One may dispute the applicability of the term 'phobia' in this context — phobic patients appreciate the irrationality of their fears and see the appropriateness of treatment — but this is not germane to the explanation. The problem of this explanation concerns the attribution of causal significance to some of the disorder's consequences. In its support is offered its consistency with many of the clinical features and the observation that some patients in the course of treatment will put on some weight but will then 'get stuck' at a level just below that necessary for menstruation to resume. This explanation is less readily applicable to those patients whose illness commences long after puberty, particularly when they have married and had children. It is also not apparent from the terms of this explanation why the patient should continue to starve herself and lose weight. Forty kilogrammes should allow plenty of safety so why should she still be distressed at 35 kg? Clinical observation of some patients does lend some support to a wish on their part to avoid the changes of puberty, but this is in the nature of clinical understanding, in the sense previously defined, and does not attain the status of a causal explanation.

Specific Deficits

Bruch (1973) has proposed that a number of specific disturbances underlie the disorder. These are: (1) a body image disturbance; (2) interoceptive disturbances, i.e. difficulties in identifying accurately important affective and visceral (hunger and satiety) sensations; (3) an overwhelming sense of personal ineffectiveness. These disturbances are said to arise from previous unfavourable interactional patterns between infant and mother which will not be discussed here. Bruch characterized anorexia nervosa as a 'relentless pursuit of thinness' and in this respect her formulation differs fundamentally from the weight phobia notion.

A valuable attribute of Bruch's hypothesis is that it is in principle testable and a considerable body of research has been devoted to this task, particularly in the investigation of the body image disturbance. A number of methods have been devised which are based on an assessment of the patient's ability to estimate her size accurately. Disturbed body image has been defined as an overestimation by the patient of her body parts or body size. The techniques to measure this include a 'moveable caliper technique (Slade and Russell, 1973a), an 'image marking method' (Askevold, 1975), a 'distorting photograph technique' (Garner, Garfinkel, Stancer and Moldofsky, 1976) and a 'video distortion technique' (Meerman, 1983). Common to all of these is the requirement for the patient to indicate, mark or adjust the apparatus so that it corresponds to the dimensions of a particular body part (movable caliper technique) or of her whole body (distorting photograph or video techniques). A body perception index is then calculated which is based on the ratio of estimated width to real width.

The original study by Slade and Russell (1973a) gave rise to straightforward results. Compared with normal controls, patients with anorexia nervosa significantly overestimated their body widths at specific regions (face, chest, waist, and hips). Furthermore, it was found that overestimation decreased with weight gain in hospital and that it was positively related to a poor prognosis after discharge. The fact that overestimation was relatively greater at a lower weight suggested a mechanism which could account for progressive weight loss, i.e. by the establishment of a vicious cycle. Unfortunately, subsequent investigations have not produced consistent findings. Using the caliper technique a number of studies have found that while anorexics overestimate their size so do controls (Button, Franscella and Slade, 1977; Garner, Garfinkel, Stancer and Moldofsky, 1976). The conditions under which the experiments are performed can be crucial in determining the results. These include the degree of illumination in the room (Button, Fransella and Slade, 1977); the patient's belief about her prior carbohydrate consumption (Crisp and Kalucy, 1974); allowing the patient to view herself in a mirror (Pierloot and Houben, 1978). In one study when the experimenters invited their patients to drop their guard, some substantially reduced the degree of overestimation (Crisp and Kalucy, 1974). Other studies have shown that age is associated with overestimation, this being more likely for younger girls (Halmi, Goldberg and Cunningham, 1977). Other studies still have found that obese subjects (Slade and Russell, 1973b) and pregnant women (Slade, 1977) also overestimate their size.

Studies using the 'distorting photograph technique' have also tended to show that about 50% of both anorexics and controls overestimate, although the anorexics tend to overestimate more grossly (Garner, Garfinkel, Stancer and Moldofsky, 1976). One study using a 'video distortion technique' found that the anorexics showed a greater variability in body size estimation although they did not differ in mean values from normal controls (Touyz, Beaumont, Collins, McCabe and Jupp 1984). Another study using a video distortion technique found that all of the groups examined underestimated (Meerman, 1983). Obviously the method used, in addition to the details of how it is used, affects the results.

It appears that for progress to be made many variables need to be controlled and that the conclusions drawn will necessarily be very conditional. The task is even more complicated still. Most investigators seem to have ignored the fact that the object in their studies is a human subject who is not necessarily blind to the hypothesis being tested. Under these circumstances, the validity of the estimations must be suspect. The patient's relationship with the investigator, for example, whether she wishes to please or not, could have a major influence on the results.

Even if anorexics were to be shown to overestimate more than controls, there still remains the possibility that this could be a result rather than a cause of the illness. Overestimation may be a feature of weight loss whatever the cause and not be at all specific to anorexia nervosa. The case for a specific deficit in anorexia nervosa would be considerably strengthened if it could be shown that it persists, for a time at least, following weight restoration. Garfinkel, Moldofsky and Garner (1979) retested 16 patients one year after an initial assessment. Neither anorexic subjects nor controls showed significant change in body size estimates over the year, the correlation between estimates from one year to the next for the patients being 0.70. Although the patients had gained a significant amount of weight they still averaged only 83% of standard weight for height, age and sex. Five of the patients on follow-up weighed 100 to 110% of standard weight and their estimates were still very similar from one year to the next and averaged about 5% overestimation. These findings are in contrast to those of Slade and Russell (1973a) where weight gain resulted in less overestimation. The evidence that overestimation is a relatively durable feature is thus fairly meagre at present.

Bruch also postulated that there is a disturbance in the perception and interpretation of interoceptive stimuli such as hunger, satiety, fatigue, cold and sexual feelings. Clinically, many patients do seem to have difficulties in identifying or at least naming internal feeling states but these are difficult to investigate empirically. Garner, Garfinkel, Stancer and Moldofsky (1976) reported that some patients with anorexia nervosa showed an abnormal response on a 'satiety aversion to sucrose test'. Unlike normal controls, anorexic subjects did not experience any difference in the rated pleasantness of sucrose tastes before versus after the ingestion of a glucose load. This lack of satiety aversion tended to occur in those patients who also overestimated their body size. Retesting of some of these patients one year later showed a persistence of the abnormalities (Garfinkel, Moldofsky and Garner, 1979). However, similar difficulties arise in interpreting these findings as were encountered with the body image studies.

A 'pervasive sense of ineffectiveness' in anorexia nervosa finds some clinical support but is more difficult to study. Such a state is less likely to be specific to anorexia nervosa and when assessed in a clinical population it may be to a significant degree related to the demeaning fact of being a patient.

A variety of conceptual disturbances in anorexia nervosa have also been described (Bruch, 1973; Garner and Bemis, 1982). The latter have described these in formal terms, e.g. 'selective abstraction', 'dichotomous or all-or-none reasoning', 'superstitious thinking'. These have been described as 'proximal' causes of the behaviour which underlie the patient's belief that it is absolutely essential that she be thin. So far, however, no evidence is available to substantiate even a limited causal influence for these cognitions.

Functional analysis   Recently Slade (1982) has presented what he terms a 'functional analysis' of anorexia nervosa. This is again an explanation in psychological terms and presents an analysis of the process leading to anorexia nervosa in ABC terms — 'antecedents' which determine the initial occurrence of the 'behaviour' and 'consequences' which determine its maintenance and change over time.

Predisposing factors are summed to provide a 'setting' necessary for the development of the disorder. The setting context comprises:

1. 'A general dissatisfaction with life and self'. This arises from adolescent conflicts of the dependence/independence type, interpersonal problems, and from 'stress and failure experiences'.
2. 'Perfectionistic' tendencies.

The combined setting conditions above interact to produce 'a need for complete control over some aspect of the life situation and/or total success in one area'. Of the limited number of candidates for 'total control', control over bodily functions is an obvious one. Given this setting, relatively innocuous psychosocial stimuli trigger initial dieting in those with a non-specific setting condition, common in Western society, of weight sensitivity. Once dieting behaviour has commenced, at least two types of consequence are posited which strongly reinforce the behaviour and lead to a 'downward spiralling effect, the end of which is full-blown anorexia nervosa'. The first is the positive reinforcement of 'successful behaviour in the context of perceived failure in all other areas of functioning'. This is dependent on the initial setting conditions. The second is negative reinforcement by the avoidance of two kinds of aversive stimuli: (a) weight gain, which acquires an overvalued importance, since weight loss has occurred in someone who perceives herself as having failed in everything else; (b) worrying thoughts, since the anorexic has such a single-minded preoccupation with food and weight that she can think of little else. Those problems which led to the initial setting conditions, e.g. failure experiences, are thus avoided and starvation is reinforced.

A key point in Slade's analysis is that the reinforcers derive their potency from the antecedent context. The major setting condition of 'general dissatisfaction with life and self' is an essential prerequisite for successful dieting to act as a positive reinforcer. The analysis also assigns a specificity to dieting because of its unique suitability to satisfy the need for complete control of some aspect of the life situation. Slade argues that the 'secondary gain' established from the effects of starvation on others, for instance, obtaining control over parents, is a less potent reinforcer, since this sort of reinforcement is less certain and often ambiguous.

This analysis combines complexity and parsimony because of the dependence of parts of the 'system' on each other. It also has considerable specificity. Slade claims that the model is testable since it should be possible to devise suitable measuring instruments for each of its elements and to establish the 'effective time relationships between hypothesized causal factors and symptomatology'. He also believes that, if treatment directed at the targets suggested by the model were to result in improvement, this would also support its veracity.

This analysis verges towards a systems view without fully abandoning linear causes. When a 'spiralling downwards' into anorexia nervosa is discussed, this suggests some kind of positive feedback or deviation amplifying process and thus circular causal relationships of the type: A causes B which causes A which causes, B, and so on. An example would be starvation resulting in the avoidance of problems leading to the initial setting conditions, which thus become worse and which therefore result in more starvation, and so on. Although deviation amplification seems to be an emergent property of Slade's analysis he stops short of recognizing this.

Some aspects of this functional analysis do seem to be testable. In theory the setting conditions could be evaluated, but this would depend on testing subjects before they developed the disorder. An assessment of the reinforcers is more difficult, particularly for the negative reinforcers. Even if the avoidance of worries can be measured in some way, it is hard to envisage how this can be manipulated independently of the condition which it is said to be reinforcing. The preoccupation with weight and food appears to be a necessary attribute or consequence of the starvation in anorexia nervosa and it thus appears impossible to separate the reinforcer from the condition which is said to be reinforced, i.e. it may be like saying that starving reinforces starving behaviour.

Common to all of these explanations is, firstly, the difficulty whether they are not in fact descriptions in the guise of explanations and, secondly, in the evaluation of causes which are also consequences of the disorder. They all appear strongest in suggesting perpetuating factors which come into play once the illness is established and this may be because they have been derived from the observation of clinic patients. Reconstructions of what went before are extremely inferential and, when circular, causal mechanisms are in operation, the past becomes more indeterminate still.

Physical Explanations

Another type of explanation for anorexia nervosa is one in which biological causes are given ultimate primacy and where the psychological features are seen as arising from these, having meaning only in so far as they are attempts by the patient to rationalize, accommodate or account for what are fundamentally meaningless experiences. The analogy is with the psychological symptoms of, say, general paralysis of the insane (late neurosyphilis). These are to some degree intelligible when considered in the light of the patient's past experiences and preoccupations, but the 'necessary' cause of the illness is the neuropathology due to the spirochaete. The psychological disturbances resulting from organic brain changes are limited in their forms, relatively non-specific, and determined by 'prepotent' structures. They reflect various levels of psychological organization. Brain damage appears to 'release' psychological processes (e.g. paranoid thinking) which are normally kept in check by higher level integration.

A recent study has suggested that there is a significant genetic component in anorexia nervosa (Holland, Hall, Murray, Russell and Crisp, 1984). Of 30 female twin pairs, 55% of the monozygotic and 7% of the dizygotic pairs were concordant for anorexia nervosa. Although a higher concordance rate in monozygotic twins could be ascribed to special psychological difficulties and a tendency to indentification in such a twin pair, the possibility of a constitutional predisposition seems more likely.

Numerous biological disturbances are seen in patients with anorexia nervosa. Most of those studied have been neuroendocrine systems and other functions, such as temperature regulation, which are dependent on an intact hypothalamus. The hypothalamus has been selected for investigation because the regulation of eating and of sexual functions are dependent on its normal activity. A major problem of studies aimed at detecting disturbances here is that they might be the consequences of the starvation. Most of the hormonal abnormalities show a tendency to revert to normal with weight restoration, e.g. changes in growth hormone, thyroid function, corticosteroids (Brown, 1983).

The system which has excited the greatest interest as a reflector of abnormal function in the hypothalamus is the hypothalamic–pituitary–ovarian axis. Disturbances here cannot be entirely accounted for by changes in weight, although below a critical weight, which varies from patient to patient, menstruation is impossible. Patients with anorexia nervosa have extremely low luteinizing hormone (LH), follicle stimulating hormone (FSH), and oestrogen levels. It is well documented that amenorrhoea may precede weight loss and it is also a common finding that it may persist for months or even years following weight restoration (Russell, 1977a). Recovery of hormonal function with weight gain occurs in an orderly manner which is similar to the sequence occurring in normal puberty. The final step is a positive feedback response at the hypothalamus to oestrogen which produces the surge of luteinizing (LH) necessary for menstruation to occur. Wakeling, de Souza and Beardwood (1977) showed an absence of this response in 9 of 12 patients who had recovered to a healthy weight. The authors suggested that a remission of the psychopathology, as well as weight restoration, might be necessary for normal function to be re-established. Other consequences of anorexia nervosa apart from the weight loss have been suggested to play a role in the disturbance of menstruation. These include hyperactivity and an abnormal pattern of dietary intake (Weiner, 1983). Amenorrhoea in association with psychological disturbances is also well recognized. Thus at this stage, a 'primary' hypothalamic disturbance remains possible, but the supporting evidence is equivocal.

A number of theories have been advanced which propose that neurotransmitter disturbances may account for the disorder. These are generally based on their putative roles in the regulation of eating in animals and the effects of their alteration by pharmacological agents in animals and man. The best formulated of these is the hypothesis of Barry and Klawans (1976) of a disturbance in the regulation of dopaminergic systems. However, the evidence for such disturbances in anorexia nervosa is at present slim. Studies of small numbers of weight-restored patients have suggested that there may be an impaired response of growth hormone to L-dopa as well as an impaired response of prolactin to chlorpromazine, a dopamine antagonist (Halmi and Sherman, 1977; Halmi, Owen, Lasley and Stokes, 1983). However, the limited techniques so far available present to assess neurotransmitter function render such findings difficult to interpret, as does the absence of an established theroretical basis for neurotransmitter control of eating in humans.

Another kind of proposal is that anorexia nervosa is a variant of affective disorder, taking on a particular form in adolescence where it is coloured by the weight preoccupation which is so common in this age group. Clinically, depressive symptoms are common in anorexia nervosa but are not usually sufficient to make a diagnosis of a depressive illness (Halmi, Dekirmenjian, Davis, Casper and Goldberg, 1978) Some studies have shown, however, that a high proportion of relatives of anorexic patients have a history of primary affective disorder and that this proportion is similar to that of the relatives of patients with an effective disorder (Winokur, March and Mendels, 1980). An abnormal dexamethasone suppression test, present in about 50% of patients with a diagnosis of major depressive illness, has also been found in some patients with anorexia nervosa but this may be a consequence of the emaciation (Gerner and Gwerstman, 1981). Against anorexia nervosa being a variant of affective disorder is the consistency of the clinical syndrome even with long-term follow-up (Morgan and Russell, 1975; Hsu, Crisp and Harding, 1979). There is also little evidence at present that anorexia nervosa responds to antidepressant medication. A reasonable conclusion at this stage is that a diathesis for affective disorder acts as a predisposing factor for the develop-ment of anorexia nervosa.*

Mrosovsky (1983) has discussed possible animal models of anorexia nervosa and concluded that most animal anorexias involve a lowering of the 'set point' for weight, which is then normally defended. This does not appear to be the case in anorexia nervosa where patients appear to be struggling to maintain a weight below their set weight. However, a curious animal anorexia has been described recently by Epling, Pierce and Stefan (1983). Rats and mice placed on a restricted feeding schedule (a single 90-minute period per day) will ordinarily maintain a healthy, though slightly lower than normal, weight. When a running wheel is also provided, locked during the feeding period but accessible for the remainder of the time, the rodents' activity levels rise exponentially and their consumption of food drops dramatically after a few days. The animals on this schedule will starve to death in the presence of food sufficient in quantity to maintain life. The authors suggest that food restriction when combined with activity may play a role in human anorexia nervosa, especially since hyperactivity is a common feature in such patients. There is of course an enormous difference in the feeding pattern between rodents and humans, but the relationship between self-starvation and activity may be worthy of investigation particularly to discover whether heightened activity, which may be a product of starvation, may in addition intensify the self-starvation.

Recently we have suggested that the clinical picture of anorexia nervosa resembles in most essential respects that of dependence syndromes (Szmukler and Tantam, 1984). A comparison was made between anorexia nervosa and

---

* Footnote: Since this chapter was first prepared, there has been much discussion concerning the relationship between anorexia nervosa and affective disorder; see an excellent review of this area by Strober and Katz (in press).

the alcohol dependence syndrome as delineated by Edwards and Gross (1977). In both conditions the patient engages in a behaviour (drinking/dieting) which is normally carried out in moderation and in which the subject induces deliberately an abnormal physiological state. This state is experienced as pleasant or calming. Even when the behaviour begins to have obvious destructive consequences, the patient denies that it is out of control and offers of help are rejected. The patient's life becomes increasingly organized around the need for a drink in the one instance or the need to starve in the other. Tolerance develops, this being suggested in the case of anorexia nervosa by the patient's need to increasingly restrict her intake or to lose a few pounds still. Unpleasant experiences ensue when the state of dependence is interrupted, when alcohol is not available in the one instance, or when the state of starvation is broken by an increased intake of food in the other. In both instances the patient feels an intense dysphoria with physiological accompaniments (Luck and Wakeling, 1980) and consequently seeks to avoid such occurrences in the future. In time the patient will usually come to admit that her behaviour has a subjective compulsive quality which is difficult to resist. Both conditions also show a rapid reinstatement of dependence where after a period of 'abstinence' from drinking or starving, dependence ensues again when the 'addictive' behaviour is attempted in moderation.

It is suggested that as with exposure to alcohol, exposure to starvation, most commonly due to dieting, leads to the development of starvation dependence in subjects who are in some way vulnerable and that the more widespread the exposure, the greater the number of subjects who become dependent. This is supported by the finding that ballet students have a much higher incidence of anorexia nervosa than normals (Garner and Garfinkel, 1980).

At this stage this hypothesis is speculative and its support derives almost solely from clinical observations. However, a number of its features can be tested, most importantly those related to the physiological mechanisms which might underlie the development of tolerance and withdrawal effects. It is highly specific for anorexia nervosa and posits a necessary cause for its development. We regard the search for such specific causes as valuable, although it may prove to be in vain.

CONCLUSIONS AND IMPLICATIONS FOR TREATMENT

Despite our increasing familiarity with the disorder, the pathogenesis of anorexia nervosa remains elusive.

For the clinician an examination of the individual case will usually lead to a reasonable understanding of many of the factors involved, particularly those relating to conflicts in the patient's life and her understandable attempts to deal with them. The influence of social factors such as pressures to be thin, as well as family factors which might be acting to constrain normal development, will also be evident. The final clinical picture presents a complex mix of what may be

regarded as non-understandable disturbances due to the illness and the patient's understandable reactions to these, the latter being coloured by her
personality and her life situation. A number of causal explanations with a high
degree of specificity for the former type of disturbance have been reviewed, but
as yet none can be accepted. No necessary cause or causes have been identified
nor has an indispensible or 'prepotent' link in the genesis of the disorder. The
only factor which might be a common predisposition in all cases is an initial loss
of weight but care is needed here since weight loss is itself a feature of the
syndrome.

The failure to discover any specific causal mechanism in anorexia nervosa
has contributed to lack of any specific treatments, apart perhaps from a
particular psychotherapeutic approach, first developed by Bruch, which takes
special account of the posited specific psychological deficits discussed earlier.
Here, importance is attached to helping the patient identify inner feeling states
and cues and achieve a sense of mastery over her fate. Cognitive-behavioural
strategies have recently been developed which have built further on some of
these principles (Garner and Bemis, 1982), but insufficient time has elapsed for
these to be evaluated. Drug treatments, so far tested, have not been shown to
be effective (Szmukler, 1981).

Among specialists in the field, there is a broad consensus in the approach to
treatment (Garfinkel and Garner, 1982). At present, treatment can be considered to have two aspects. The first involves the restoration of weight to a
healthy level. Most authorities agree that this is a priority, both to save life and
as a prerequisite for other treatment approaches to be successful. Vicious
cycles such as those due to starvation effects, which may serve to perpetuate the
disorder, are also reversed. For severe cases of the type which are seen in our
clinic, weight restoration is achieved either by admitting the patient to hospital
for skilled nursing care (Russell, 1977b) or, particularly for younger patients
living at home, by engaging the family in treatment and helping the parents to
establish parental control to feed their youngster (Dare, 1983). Formal behavioural treatment programmes do not appear necessary for weight gain to be
achieved (Eckert, Goldberg, Halmi, Casper and Davis, 1979) although restrictions and privileges in one form or another are usually involved. In general,
little attention is paid to the particularities of the diet, the aim being to ensure
that it is reasonably well balanced with sufficient carbohydrate to ensure weight
gain at a rate of 1 to 2 kg per week.

Often reversal of the starvation results in the patient feeling better in her
mood and more optimistic about the future. Occasionally, it results in an
apparent cure with little further treatment being required. Usually, however,
weight restoration is followed by what could be considered the second phase of
treatment aimed at helping the patient to maintain a healthy weight. This may
need to be prolonged for a year or more and usually takes the form of a
psychotherapeutic relationship, either individual or family, in which the
patient's life problems which are considered to predispose her to the illness are
tackled. These generally involve the types of adolescent conflicts previously

described. Causal 'explanations' recede in importance and the treatment is largely informed by psychologically understandable connexions along the lines previously discussed.

REFERENCES

Askevold, F. (1975). Measuring body image. *Psychotherapy and Psychosomatics*, **26**, 71–77.

Barry, V.C. and Klawans, H.L. (1976). On the role of dopamine in the pathophysiology of anorexia nervosa. *Journal of Neural Transmission*, **38**, 107–122.

Bolton, D. (1984). Philosophy of psychiatry. In P. McGuffin, M. Shanks and R. Hodgson (Eds), *Scientific Principles of Psychopathology*, Academic Press, London.

Brown, G.M. (1983). Endocrine alterations in anorexia nervosa. In P.L. Darby, P.E. Garfinkel, D.M. Garner, and D.V. Coscina (Eds), *Anorexia Nervosa: Recent Developments in Research*, Alan R Liss, New York, pp. 231–247.

Bruch, J. (1973). *Eating Disorders*, Basic Books, New York.

Button, E.J., Fransella, F. and Slade P.D. (1977). A reappraisal of body perception disturbance in anorexia nervosa. *Psychological Medicine*, **7**, 235–243.

Crisp, A.H. (1980). *Anorexia Nervosa: Let Me Be*, Academic Press, London.

Crisp, A.H. and Kalucy, R.S. (1974). Aspects of the perceptual disorder in anorexia nervosa. *British Journal of Medical Psychology*, **47**, 349–361.

Crisp, A.H. Palmer, R.A. and Kalucy, R.S. (1976). How common is anorexia nervosa? A prevalence study. *British Journal of Psychiatry*, **128**, 549–554.

Dare, C. (1983). Family therapy for families containing an anorectic youngster. In: G.J. Bargman (Ed.), *Understanding Anorexia Nervosa and Bulimia*, Ross, Columbus, Ohio, pp. 28–36.

Eckert E.D., Goldberg, S.C., Halmi, K.A., Casper, R.C. and Davis, J.M. (1979). Behaviour therapy in anorexia nervosa. *British Journal of Psychiatry*, **134**, 55–59.

Edwards, G. and Gross, M.M. (1976). Alcohol dependence: provisional description of a clinical syndrome. *British Medical Journal*, **i**, 1058–1061.

Epling, W.F., Pierce, W.D. and Stefan, L. (1983). A theory of activity-based anorexia. *International Journal of Eating Disorders*, **3**, 27–46.

Garfinkel, P.E. and Garner, D.M. (1982). *Anorexia Nervosa: A Multidimensional Perspective*, Brunner Mazel, New York.

Garfinkel, P.E., Moldofsky, H. and Garner, D.M. (1979). The stability of perceptual disturbances in anorexia nervosa. *Psychological Medicine*, **9**, 703–708.

Garner, D.M. and Bemis, K. (1982). A cognitive behavioural approach to anorexia nervosa. *Cognitive Therapy and Research*, **6**, 1–27.

Garner, D.M. and Garfinkel, P.E. (1980). Sociocultural factors in the development of anorexia nervosa. *Psychological Medicine*, **10**, 647–656.

Garner, D.M., Garfinkel, P, Stancer, H.C. and Moldofsky, H. (1976). Body image disturbances in anorexia nervosa and obesity. *Psychosomatic Medicine*, **38**, 327–336.

Gerner, R.H. and Gwirtsman, H.E., (1981). Abnormalities of dexamethasone suppression test and urinary MHPG in anorexia nervosa. *American Journal of Psychiatry*, **138**, 650–653.

Griffiths R.D.P., (1967). An investigation of hypotheses derived from the clinical observation of anorexia nervosa. M. Phil., University of London.

Halmi, K.A., Goldberg, S.C. and Cunningham, S., (1977). Perceptual distortion of body image in adolescent girls: distortion of body image in adolescence. *Psychological Medicine*, **7**, 253–257.

Halmi, K.A. and Sherman, B.M., (1977). Dopaminergic and serotoninergic regulation of growth hormone secretion in anorexia nervosa. *Psychopharmacological Bulletin*, **13**, 63–65.

Halmi, K.A., Dekirmenjian, H., Davis, J.M., Casper, R. and Goldberg, S., (1978). Catecholamine metabolism in anorexia nervosa. *Archives of General Psychiatry*, **35**, 458–460.

Halmi, K.A., Owen, W.P., Lasley, E. and Stokes, P., (1983). Dopaminergic regulation in anorexia nervosa. *International Journal of Eating Disorders*, **2**, (4), 129–134.

Holland, A.J., Hall, A., Murray, R., Russell, G.F.M. and Crisp, A.H., (1984). Anorexia nervosa: a study of 34 twin pairs and one set of triplets. *British Journal of Psychiatry* (in press).

Hsu, L.K.G., Crisp, A.H. and Harding, B., (1979). Outcome of anorexia nervosa. *Lancet*, **1**, 61–5.

Jaspers, K., (1913). *General Psychopathology* (transl. J. Hoenig and M.W. Hamilton, 1963), Manchester University Press, Manchester.

Jones, D.J., Fox, M.M., Babigan, H.M. and Hutton, M.A., (1980). Epidemiology of anorexia nervosa in Monroe County, New York 1960–1976. *Psychosomatic Medicine*, **42**, 551–558.

Katz, J.L., Boyar R., Roffwarg, H., Hellman, L. and Weiner, H., (1978). Weight and circadian luteinizing hormone secretory pattern in anorexia nervosa. *Psychosomatic Medicine*, **40**, 549–567.

Luck, P. and Wakeling, A., (1980). Altered thresholds for thermoregulatory sweating and vasodilatation in anorexia nervosa. *British Medical Journal*, **281** (ii), 906–908.

Meerman, R., (1983). Experimental investigation of disturbances in body image estimation in anorexia nervosa patients and ballet and gymnastic pupils. *International Journal of Eating Disorders*, **2**(4), 91–100.

Morgan, H.G. and Russell, G.F.M., (1975). Value of family background and clinical features as predictors of long-term outcome in anorexia nervosa: four year follow up study of 41 patients. *Psychological Medicine*, **5**, 355–371.

Mrosovsky, N. (1983). Animal models of anorexia nervosa. In G.J. Bargman (Ed.), *Understanding Anorexia Nervosa and Bulimia*, Report of 4th Conference on Medical Research, Ross, Columbus, Ohio, pp. 67–73.

Pierloot, R.A. and Houben, M.E., (1978). Estimation of body dimensions in anorexia nervosa. *Psychological Medicine*, **8**, 317–324.

Russell, G.F.M. (1970). Anorexia nervosa: its identity as an illness and its treatment. In: J. Harding Price (Ed.), *Modern Trends in Psychological Medicine*, vol. 2, Butterworths, London, pp. 131–164.

Russell, G.F.M. (1977a). The present status of anorexia nervosa. *Psychological Medicine*, **7**, 363–367.

Russell, G.F.M. (1977b). General management of anorexia nervosa and difficulty in assessing the efficacy of treatment. In R.A. Vigersky (Ed.), *Anorexia Nervosa*, Raven Press, New York, pp. 277–289.

Russell, G.F.M. (1979). Bulimia nervosa: an ominous variant of anorexia nervosa. *Psychological Medicine*, **9**, 429–448.

Russell, G.F.M., Campbell, P.G., and Slade, P.D. (1975). Experimental studies on the nature of the psychological disorder in anorexia nervosa. *Psychoneuroendocrinology*, **1**, 45–56.

Slade, P.D., (1977). Awareness of body perception during pregnancy. An analogue study. *Psychological Medicine*, **7**, 245–252.

Slade, P.D., (1982). Towards a functional analysis of anorexia nervosa and bulimia nervosa. *British Journal of Clinical Psychology*, **21**, 167–179.

Slade, P.D., Russell, G.F.M., (1973a) Awareness of body dimension in anorexia nervosa. Cross-sectional and longitudinal studies. *Psychological Medicine*, **3**, 188–199.

Slade, P.D., Russell, G.F.M. (1973b). Experimental investigations of bodily perception in anorexia nervosa and obesity. In J. Reusch and A.H. Schmale (Eds), *Psychotherapy and Psychosomatics*, Karger, Basel, pp. 359–363.

Strober, M. and Katz, J. (in press). Depression in the eating disorders: A review and analysis of descriptive, family and biological findings in anorexia nervosa and bulimia nervosa. In D.M. Garner and P.E. Garfinkel (Eds.), *Diagnostic Issues in Anorexia Nervosa and Bulimia Nervosa*. Bruner/Mazel, New York.

Szmukler, G.I. (1981). Drug treatment in anorectic states. In J.T. Silverstone (Ed.), Academic Press, London, pp. 159–181.

Szmukler, G.I. (1983). Weight and food preoccupation in a population of English schoolgirls. In G.J. Bargman (Ed.), *Understanding Anorexia Nervosa and Bulimia*, Report of 4th Ross Conference on Medical Research, Ross, Columbus, Ohio, pp. 21–27.

Szmukler, G.I. and Tantam, D. (1984). Anorexia nervosa: starvation dependence. *British Journal of Medical Psychology*, **57**, 303–310.

Szmukler, G.I., McCance, C., McCrone, L. and Hunter, D. (1986). Anorexia nervosa: a psychiatric case register study from Aberdeen. *Psychological Medicine*, **16**, 49–58.

Touyz, S.W., Beaumont, P.J.V., Collins, J.K., McCabe, M. and Jupp, J. (1984). Body shape perception and its disturbance in anorexia nervosa. *British Journal of Psychiatry*, **144**, 167–171.

Wakeling, A., DeSouza, V. and Beardwood, C.J. (1977). Effects of administered oestrogen on luteinizing hormone release in subjects with anorexia nervosa in acute and recovery stages. In R.A. Vigersky *Anorexia Nervosa*, Raven Press, New York, pp. 199–210.

Weiner, H. (1977). *Psychobiology and Human Disease*, Elsevier, North Holland, New York.

Weiner, H. (1983). The hypothalamic-pituitary-ovarian axis in anorexia and bulimia nervosa. *International Journal of Eating Disorders*, **2**, (4), 109–116.

Winokur, A., March. V., Mendels, J., (1980). Primary affective disorder in relatives of patients with anorexia nervosa. *American Journal of Psychiatry*, **137**, 695–698.

CHAPTER 3

Behaviour Therapy in the Treatment of Obesity

Gerald A. Bennett
Department of Clinical Psychology,
East Dorset Health Authority,
Branksome Clinic, Layton Road,
Poole, Dorset BH12 2BJ, UK

THE PROBLEM OF OBESITY

The Hazards of Obesity

Obesity is a condition in which the amount of fat in the body is excessively large. This is reflected in body weight which is, except in unusual circumstances (such as athletes with strikingly developed musculature), a good indicator of obesity and has been used as such in most studies.

Obesity has important consequences for health and well-being, including reduced life expectancy and increased likelihood of developing a range of diseases. Recent reports on the health consequences of obesity, produced on both sides of the Atlantic, have agreed on the specific dangers of obesity (Bray, 1979; DHSS/MRC, 1976; Royal College of Physicians, 1983).

Greater obesity is associated with lower life expectancy, and this effect is especially marked in the 10% of the population that is more than 25% above the average population weight (or, equivalently, more than 35% above 'ideal' weight) (Berger, Berchtold, Gries and Zimmerman, 1981). The effect on mortality is more marked for men than for women, and for the young than for the old. Greater obesity is associated with greater risks of cardiovascular disease, and sudden death. It is associated with the occurrence of several risk factors for coronary heart disease, such as hypertension and raised serum cholesterol levels. The extent to which it poses a risk factor independent of these associated factors is still a matter of controversy.

45

Greater obesity is correlated with glucose intolerance and increased risks of developing diabetes mellitus, especially in persons with a personal or family history. It is associated with greater risks under surgery or with anaesthetic. The probability of developing gall bladder disease rises with increasing obesity, as do the risks of complication in pregnancy. There is an association between increasing weight and increased risk of cancer, especially (in men) of cancer of the colon, rectum, and prostrate, and (in women) of cancer of the breast, uterus, and cervix (Lew and Garfinkel, 1979). A further common result of obesity is the aggravation of degenerative and joint diseases such as arthritis.

Adverse social and psychological consequences of obesity have also been documented, but their study has proved less conclusive. Accounts of prejudice against obese persons must be balanced by other findings, such as studies of the general population, which show that obese persons suffer, if anything, less from anxiety and depression (e.g. Crisp and McGuinness, 1976), and may even have a higher income (McLean and Moon, 1980).

The Benefits of Losing Weight

Many of the hazards of obesity can be reversed by weight loss and it is this reversibility that makes weight reduction such an important endeavour. Dropping to a more normal weight increases life expectancy to more normal levels (Dublin, 1953). Blood pressure can be reduced by much smaller weight losses; clinically significant improvements, allowing sufferers to discontinue anti-hypertensive medication, can result from weight reductions of the order of 10 kg (Reisin, Abel, Modan, Silverberg, Eliahou and Modan, 1978). A survey of non-drug treatments of hypertension concluded that weight reduction was the most effective (Andrews, MacMahon, Austin and Byrne, 1982). Weight reduction often results in beneficial changes in cholesterol levels and other aspects of blood chemistry and can cause improvements in glucose tolerance and the likelihood of developing diabetes mellitus (Horton, 1981). Although it cannot repair the damage caused by degenerative and joint diseases weight reduction can lighten the burden and reduce pain.

There is insufficient evidence to make definitive statements about improvements in gallbladder disease, surgical risk, anaesthetic risk, or psychological functioning.

The beneficial effects of weight reduction on mortality and morbidity make it a worthwhile endeavour. The medical benefits from weight reduction vary from person to person, according to their personal and family history of disease, as well as their age or sex.

The Causes of Obesity

Many factors can play a role in the development and maintenance of obesity, necessitating a multifactorial perspective.

Genetic Obesity often follows family lines and evidence from twin studies and other family studies, although not completely consistent, implicates a heritable component (Foch and McClearn, 1980).

Social Social and cultural factors are also important. In industrialized societies obesity is more prevalent in lower social classes, while the reverse pattern has been observed elsewhere, such as in India (Siddamma, 1979). Social mobility has been observed to be accompanied by changes in the prevalence of obesity, so that, in America, upward mobility has been associated with decreasing obesity, whilst downward mobility is associated with increasing obesity (Stunkard, 1980).

Psychological Several psychological factors have been proposed as possible causes of obesity. Psychodynamic clinicians (e.g. Bruch, 1973) have suggested that obesity is the result of deep-seated emotional problems and represents the person's mode of coping with them. The implication of this suggestion, that weight reduction would deprive them of this means of coping and thus precipitate emotional distress, has been clearly disconfirmed (e.g. Brewer, White and Baddeley, 1974). Weight reduction has most frequently been found to cause emotional improvements. It has also been suggested that obese persons are more likely than others to eat when under stress, and that this tendency could act as a cause of obesity. Linked to this is the speculation that stress-induced eating could develop out of early feeding patterns (Bruch, 1973). One way in which this could occur would be for the mother to respond with food to both distress and hunger, thus depriving the child of the opportunity of learning to discriminate between these states. Subsequently distress, like hunger, would elicit eating. The developmental speculation remains untested and there is no clear evidence that obese persons are more likely than others to eat under stress (Robbins and Fray, 1980; Ruderman, 1983; Slochower, 1983). In general there is no strong reason to believe that obese persons are more neurotic (McReynolds, 1983; Bennett, 1986c), more externally responsive (Rodin, 1981), or unusual in their pattern of eating (Gilbert, 1983). In order to be considered as causes of obesity, psychological factors have to be integrated with others. Emotions have little direct effects on energy expenditure (Blaza and Garrow, 1980) and therefore they must achieve their effects indirectly, through food intake or physical activity. If, as will be seen below, there is no clear evidence that the obese do consume more food, or do expend less energy through physical activity, then psychological factors cannot be seen as important causes of obesity.

Energy balance Obesity develops through an excess of energy intake over energy expenditure; once established it may be maintained by energy balance. The possibility that obesity results from some defect in energy balance has occasioned much research (reviewed by Garrow, 1978, 1981) which has consistently failed to find any clear differences in energy intake through food consumption between non-obese and obese persons.

The major part of energy expenditure is accounted for by metabolic processes, metabolic rate remaining fairly constant within an individual, and being principally determined by age, lean body mass, and body weight (so that it tends to be higher in younger and heavier persons). This most important part of energy expenditure is subject to large individual differences, which may well predispose some persons to obesity. In recent years it has been suggested that part of this individual variability may reflect differences in the extent to which individuals 'waste' energy as heat (through thermogenesis). A possible role for brown adipose tissue in controlling this has also been hypothesized (Miller, 1975; James and Trayhurn, 1981). Although it is clear that there are large variations in energy needs (with low needs causing vulnerability to obesity), the reasons for this, and the underlying mechanisms, remain a matter of controversy. Bodily activity accounts for another, relatively small, proportion of energy expenditure, and comparisons of activity levels between obese and non-obese persons (reviewed by Brownell and Stukard, 1980) are complicated by the higher energy costs of activity for the obese.

The study of energy balance has so far failed to elucidate any clear differences between obese and non-obese persons in energy intake, energy expenditure, or the control of energy flow.

A Set Point for Bodyweight?

Although no metabolic mechanism has been established, there is evidence of some stability of bodyweight over time. Experimental studies of underfeeding in humans show a fall in bodyweight, accompanied by a slowing of metabolic processes and a fall in metabolic rate, limiting the rate of weight reduction. When food intake returns to pre-experimental levels, metabolic rate increases and weight sluggishly returns to the pre-experimental range (Keys, Brozek, Henschel, Mickelson and Taylor, 1950). Similarly, experimental studies of overfeeding have found weight to increase up to a certain range, and to slowly return in the direction of the previous lower rate after food intake reduces to previous, lower, levels (Sims and Horton, 1968). Both of these phenomena, together with the observation of stability of bodyweight over long periods of time, have suggested the notion of a 'set' weight, which is defended from perturbations, analogous to the maintenance of a fixed body temperature (Keesey, 1980). The effects of overfeeding may be limited by 'wasting' energy through thermogenesis, while the effects of underfeeding may be limited by consequent reductions in metabolic weight. The implication of genetic factors is also seen as consistent with the view of bodyweight being 'set'. Nevertheless there are other factors operating, such as a degree of conscious regulation of bodyweight, and it may not be necessary to postulate a 'set point' for obesity in man (Garrow, 1978). If there is a 'set point' which is defended, rather than a conservative system which minimizes changes in weight, the mechanism involved remains to be demonstrated.

Conclusions

Genetic and social factors are clearly implicated in the causation of obesity. Studies of energy balance have identified mechanisms contributing to the stability of bodyweight, but have not yet identified any defect of energy balance in the obese. The 'cause' has not yet been identified and it is unlikely that any individual factor will be identified as a single cause of all cases of obesity. There are many ways of becoming and staying obese and many disparate factors influence bodyweight. A multifactorial perspective is required.

THE TREATMENT OF OBESITY

The Basis of the Treatment

Reducing obesity involves reducing the amount of adipose tissue in the body, and this can be achieved by establishing a negative energy balance in which energy expenditure exceeds energy intake. Such an imbalance results in the utilization of energy stored in the body, principally as fat. Beyond the surgical removal of adipose tissue all methods require the establishment of a negative energy balance. The size of loss depends on two things: (a) the size of the energy imbalance and (b) the energy value of the weight loss.

If a person is in energy balance and then reduces their energy intake, the size of this reduction will be the major determinant of the energy imbalance. A second determinant is the effect of this reduction of food intake in reducing metabolic rate. This fall in metabolic rate with reduced food intake may well be biologically adaptive during periods of food scarcity, and has the effect of reducing the size of energy imbalance caused by dieting.

The energy value of weight loss varies according to what is being lost. In the early stages of a diet energy is taken from the less energy dense glycogen store (producing losses of several kg), but once this limited store is depleted energy is taken from the more energy-dense adipose tissue, with a lower rate of weight loss.

Thus if a person reduces energy intake by a constant amount (say 1000 kcal daily) the rate of weight loss will diminish as a result both of increases in the energy value of what is lost and also of decreases in the size of the energy imbalance. A rapid loss of up to several kilogrammes in the first week would be expected to fall to a rate less than 1 kg each week (gradually slowing over time with the reducing metabolic rate). Deliberately increasing physical activity may increase energy expenditure by a significant amount, thus contributing to energy imbalance and weight loss. Although it has been suggested that increased physical activity may have stimulating effects on metabolic rate (Mayer, 1968), there is no definitive evidence for this (Thompson, Jarvie, Lahey and Cureton, 1982).

The principle of bringing about a negative energy balance in order to produce reduction in obesity is well established. The means of bringing this about are more difficult to arrange.

Methods of Weight Reduction

Some of the methods of weight reduction which have been so widely used as to permit evaluation are considered below. Quantitative literature reviews by Wing and Jeffery (1979a), Stuart, Mitchell and Jensen (1981), and others permit conclusions to be drawn about the size of weight loss achieved using them. In doing so it is important to distinguish between short-term and long-term effects, because of the general tendency for slimmers to regain lost weight. Apart from exercise and bypass surgery, these methods attempt to help obese persons achieve a negative energy balance by aiding them to restrict their food intake by manipulating their appetite, behaviour patterns, or the opportunity to eat.

Fasting   Supervised fasting is one of the simplest methods of weight reduction, reducing food intake completely. This is carried out in a medical setting because of the significant risk of complications, and even of sudden death. The mean length of treatment in the 15 studies reviewed by Stuart, Mitchell and Jensen (1981) was 17 weeks, with mean weight loss of 35 kg. Few studies report follow-up, and where they do the results are poor. Supervised fasting is a very expensive technique with poor long-term results.

Dieting   Where obese people are given dietary advice as the main source of help, combined with regular weighing and counselling, they tend to lose weight while attending. Stuart, Mitchell and Jensen, (1981) reported a mean post-treatment loss of 11.6 kg over an average 24 weeks of treatment. The long-term results are rarely reported. A recent development has been very-low-calorie-diets (VLCDs) (of below 600 kcal per day), composed either of normal food, or of special preparations. These achieve losses similar in size to those produced by starvation but, being safer, can be employed with outpatients (Mancini and Howard, 1981). Studies of the long-term effects of VLCDs (reviewed by Wadden, Stunkard and Brownell, 1983) have found fairly rapid replacement of lost weight. A typical result was that of Genuth, Vertes and Hazelton (1978) who reported that, after 22 months follow-up, 56% of patients had regained more than half of their weight loss.

Anorectic Drugs   Anorectic drugs are widely used to help suppress food intake and represent a financial burden on the NHS of the order of £4,000,000 per year. They achieve modest weight losses while the person takes them, but these are largely regained when the drug is withdrawn. Stuart, Mitchell and Jensen (1981) found a mean loss over 75 studies of anorectic drugs of 5.4 kg over a mean treatment duration of 11.6 weeks.

Jaw-wiring   Wiring the jaws together to prevent the ingestion of solid, but not liquid, foods aids the restriction of food intake in a very direct manner. Weight reduction tends to occur while the jaws are wired, and if they are wired for long enough large amounts of weight, of the order of 35 kg, may be lost. Much of this is regained once they are unwired (Harding, 1980). Some patients find the conspicuousness and the claustrophobic qualities of jaw wiring to be rather unpleasant (Bjorvell, Hadell, Jonsson, Molin and Rossner, 1984).

Commercial weight reduction groups Commercial weight reduction groups such as Weight Watchers and Slimming Magazine Clubs are readily available at a cost to most obese people and provide dietary advice and social support. The average length of membership is about 26 weeks and the mean weight loss about 9 kg (Ashwell, 1978). Little is know about the long-term results. The cost per kg lost exceeds £2.00.

Physical exercise Achieving a negative energy balance by increasing energy expenditure through exercise alone has been shown to cause weight loss (Gwinup, 1975). Exercise alone has not often been reported as a treatment method. The mean weight loss achieved over a mean duration of 19 weeks in the seven studies reviewed by Stuart, Mitchell and Jensen was 7.3 kg. No long-term follow-ups were available.

Bypass surgery Bypass surgery reduces the absorptive capacity of the gut, so as to reduce the amount of food digested or absorbed. This is achieved by surgically bypassing a middle section of the intestines: an upper section is reconnected to a lower section, thereby 'leapfrogging' the intervening section. The underlying principle of this jejunoileal bypass operation is that after it the patient could eat as much as before, but lose weight. Bypass surgery attempts to reduce energy intake, but not food intake: it is reserved for the extremely obese person and produces substantial and lasting losses, of the order of 50 kg (Stuart, Mitchell and Jensen, 1981). Side-effects such as frequent diarrhoea are common and there is a mortality rate of about 3%. Gastric bypass surgery achieves similar beneficial results with fewer side-effects, and a similar mortality rate. Despite the assumptions underlying the development of these operations, it is clear that an important effect is to reduce food intake (Bray, 1980).

Conclusions about the Treatment of Obesity

None of these techniques is entirely adequate in producing large, well-maintained weight losses without unpleasant or harmful side-effects. The difficulty in achieving this goal reflects the difficulties of the task of weight reduction, these being establishing and maintaining a negative energy balance for long enough to produce clinically significant weight losses and then to sustain energy balance in order to maintain the new lower weight. The greater part of energy requirements is accounted for by the relatively unchanging metabolic needs and there is relatively little scope for increasing energy expenditure by increasing levels of physical activity. The savings to be achieved by reducing energy intake are potentially greater, and most treatment techniques have been concerned with this. Consciously reducing food intake is central to many of the techniques described. Unfortunately, none of these has been shown to produce large, durable weight losses by safe means that could be made widely available.

The large weight losses produced by supervised fasting show that significant weight reduction is biologically possible: metabolic resistance to dieting does not make weight loss impossible. Closely supervised inpatients in hospital units can lose weight because of the strong constraints on their behaviour and the lack of opportunities for acquiring food. The major problem is for slimmers living in their natural environment to produce and maintain such changes in behaviour.

Behaviour Change in the Treatment of Obesity

The task of obesity reduction requires changes in food intake and, possibly, also in bodily activity. Reducing food intake may require changes in the purchase, selection, preparation, and consumption of food, and may have social and religious ramifications. Changing deeply ingrained habits is difficult to achieve, and behavioural resistance may be as potent as biological resistance. The basis of weight reduction — establishing a negative energy balance — has been described, together with the likely resultant weight loss. Implementing the task of weight control requires changes in related patterns of behaviour, and this behavioural change is at the heart of most methods of weight reduction.

BEHAVIOUR THERAPY FOR OBESITY

The Role of Behaviour Therapy

Many obese persons who are unable to carry out the task of weight reduction and who seek help in doing this require help in changing their behaviour, and mainly in changing their eating habits. Indirect means of producing these changes, such as psychoanalysis, have been employed to help them do this (Rand and Stunkard, 1983), but the most frequently used and most successful approach has been the direct approach of behaviour therapy. This is the attempt to produce beneficial changes in behaviour through the application of principles and procedures derived from the experimental study of behaviour. It is a widely used approach which has been found valuable in so many areas (Rimm and Masters, 1979). As an endeavour explicitly and primarily concerned with the production of changes in patterns in behaviour, it has been applied to the production of changes in the behaviours supporting the task of weight reduction. In attempting to produce behavioural changes that promote a negative energy balance and, thus, weight loss, the targets of change have tended to be selecting and ingesting food, and also engaging in physical activities that have a significant energy cost.

Several different treatment strategies have been developed and become the core of the behavioural approach. Some have attempted to engage the treatment targets directly (e.g. by altering food preferences), while others have approached them indirectly (e.g. by modifying the social support for dieting). The main principles guiding the development of these approaches have been those of operant and classical conditioning. There has been very little influence from the psychological study of appetite and food intake and a great deal of influence from the applications of the behavioural approach to other areas of indulgent behaviour such as stopping smoking or controlling drinking (Miller, 1980). Three main approaches — aversion therapy, external control, and self-control — emerged as distinct and seperate therapeutic approaches. The last of these has become most influential and in recent years has formed the basis of developments of the behavioural approach. Each technique will be described and then evaluated from two points of view: the justification of its rationale and its clinical effects.

Aversion Therapy

The first techniques to be employed in the treatment of obesity were aversive techniques, attempting to produce lasting changes in food preferences and food selection. The means of doing this was by pairing the eating (or imagined eating) of a specific food with an aversive experience (such as smelling a foul odour or receiving an electric shock). Repeated pairings were assumed to result in decreasing palatability of the food through a process of Pavlovian conditioning; this shift in preference for the food was assumed to facilitate control over eating and, thus, weight reduction.

The rationale of aversion therapy A clear conceptual basis for aversive procedures has been provided by the phenomenon of taste aversions (Garb and Stunkard, 1974; Milgram, Krames and Alloway, 1977; Logue, Ophir and Strauss, 1981). Developing such aversions by tasting food close in time to experiencing some form of gastrointestinal upset appears to be a highly prepared form of learning (Seligman, 1970). Aversions can develop after one conditioning trial, and even with several hours delay between tasting the food and experiencing the upset. Taste aversions develop most easily to novel foods and less preferred foods and often persist for many years. These and other characteristics show strong similarities to taste aversions documented in many species. The preparedness of this form of learning may result from its protective biological function in a world where many naturally occurring toxic events cause sickness (Rozin, 1976). If aversion therapy is seen as a method of producing taste aversions, then it might most usefully employ as aversive stimuli agents that cause gastrointestinal upset. One limitation of the model is the relative difficulty in establishing aversions to familiar preferred foods, which are the very foods to which dieters may wish to develop aversions.

The clinical effects of aversion therapy   Experimental evaluations of aversive techniques in weight reduction programmes have found them to be consistently ineffective in producing weight loss, and often no more effective than a waiting list control. These poor results have arisen whether the unpleasant stimulus has been a foul smell (Cole and Bond, 1983), electric shocks (Stollak, 1967), or an unpleasant image (Diament and Wilson, 1975).

External Control

In external control techniques the motivating consequences of behaviour are used to influence it. Slimmers enter into a set of arrangments which ensure that success in their task is followed by positive consequences and failure is followed by unpleasant consequences: motivating consequences become contingent on task-related behaviours. An explicit agreement or contract is set up between the slimmer and some other person (usually the therapist), specifying:

1.   targets to be attained at specific occasions;
2.   the circumstances in which the slimmers progress towards the target is to be monitored;
3.   consequences which will follow the attainment or non-attainment of the target.

In the first published application of this procedure to weight reduction (Mann, 1972) subjects agreed to deposit valuables or money with the therapist and to attend for weigh-ins at frequent intervals. Weight loss goals were agreed as targets to be attained at weigh-ins. Subjects agreed that if they attended weigh-ins and achieved their weight-loss targets then a specified portion of their deposit would be returned to them. If they failed to attend, or if they attended but failed to reach their target, that portion would be forfeited and sent to a charity.

This method of contingency contracting (deposit contracting) has been most widely used. Since the assumption has been that the procedure will be more effective, the stronger the incentives employed, fairly large monetary deposits have been used (e.g. of $225 by Wing, Epstein, Marcus, and Shapira, 1981). In some programmes (e.g. Quale, 1975) forfeited money or valuables were sent to an organization repugnant to the individual.

With the requirement for objective unambiguous targets, weight loss, rather than the behaviours leading to it, has often been used. Other reported targets include attendance at treatment sessions, reported calorie intake (Jeffery, Thompson and Wing, 1978), or maintained weight loss (Mann, 1976). A conceptually similar procedure, used to promote the maintenance of weight loss by Garrow and Gardiner (1981), employed the avoidance of unpleasant physical sensations as an incentive. Patients who had lost weight were fitted with snugly fitting nylon cords around their waist, sealed in position. Increases in weight would result in unpleasant sensations, effectively punishing the behaviours leading up to them.

The rationale of external control treatments   The rationale for these external control techniques comes from Ferster, Nurnberger and Levitt's (1962) operant analysis of the difficulties of weight control. They observed that restrained eating is less likely to persist than unrestrained eating because the naturally occurring reinforcement of the former is considerably delayed, while that of the latter is immediate. The contingencies embodied in the contract are an attempt to reverse this natural imbalance. It is assumed that behaviours leading to weight loss will be strengthened by the reinforcement.

The technique has been used in the control of other appetitive behaviours such as smoking (e.g. Paxton, 1981), drinking (Miller, 1972) or drug usage (e.g. Stitzer, Bigelow and McCaul, 1983). That the contingent application of motivating consequences can promote weight loss is seen in real life examples, such as the action of the New Orleans Police Force in requiring overweight police officers to lose 5lb (2.3 kg) each month (Scrignar, 1980). Failure to reach this target would result in a sliding scale of penalties ranging from a written reprimand to suspension without pay. While these contingencies were in force the officers lost weight; when they were withdrawn weight loss ceased.

Clinical evaluation of external control   Experimental evaluations of this technique have found that having weight loss as the target produced larger losses than having an attendance contract (Jeffery et al., 1978). The use of a further weight contract after the end of treatment has been found to result in continued loss (Wing, Epstein, Marcus and Shapiro, 1981). Clinically significant losses, of the order of 10 kg, were produced in these and other applications of this technique (e.g. Mann, 1972). Contingency contracting has been found to be a simple treatment procedure, capable of exerting powerful influence on patients' behaviour while a contract is in force. This influence vanishes once the contract ceases, so that weight is frequently regained. Studies in which significant amounts of weight were lost through contingency contracting, found that about half of this was regained during the year after treatment ceased (Jeffery, Gerber, Rosenthal and Lindquist, 1983; Jeffery, Bjornson-Benson, Rosenthal, Kurth and Dunn, 1984).

Although, once the contract is in force, participants are relatively passive objects of the behavioural influence, voluntarily entering into the contract can be seen as an active form of self-control. Intentionally seeking out and entering into circumstances which will influence one's behaviour is a technique of self-control extending back at least as far as Ulysses having his sailors bind him to the mast lest he should respond to the song of the Sirens.

Self-control Treatments

'Self-control' techniques attempt to help dieters achieve increased control over their eating so as to enable them to successfully reduce their food intake. This approach attempts to help them regulate their own behaviour by controlling the influences on it (so that it might be more accurately described as a 'self-regulation' approach, since this is only one of the several meanings connoted by the term 'self-control'). This approach was first described in a seminal paper by Ferster, Nurnberger and Levitt (1962) and was subsequently refined and implemented in more sophisticated ways by Stuart (1967, 1971) and, later, by others. Implicit in many applications is an educational assumption: that therapy is concerned with teaching dieters how to modify their behaviour so as to be able to control their eating. This educational assumption implies that treatment need only be brief and sees participants as active students rather than as passive patients. Stuart achieved results which were, by contemporary standards, exceptionally good. After 12 weeks of treatment subjects had lost an average of 6 kg; at one year follow-up this had increased to 14.5 kg (Stuart, 1967; 1975). In the wake of Stuart's reports, this approach has been widely adopted and most subsequent developments have built on, rather than supplanted, it. The self-control approach has been very widely disseminated and employed, partly because of the attractiveness of the notion of self-regulation of behaviour to both the consumers and providers of health services. Its popularity is illustrated by the fact that almost 80% of published studies of behaviour therapy have been of the self-control approach (Bennett, 1986d).

The core components of the self-control approach described by Ferster, Nurnberger and Levitt (1962) and Stuart (1967) are: (a) changing mealtime eating behaviour, (b) rearranging eating cues, (c) self-monitoring, and (d) programming incompatible behaviours. These distinct but overlapping components have constituted the core of subsequent applications to which have been added other techniques. Clinical programmes have varied in their degree of individualization of treatment advice, i.e. the extent to which recommendations have been based on an analysis of the dieters' eating habits. Stuart and others published treatment manuals which provide detailed accounts of the procedures used, and of how to implement them. These facilitate replications of studies and several manuals (Stuart and Davis, 1972; Mahoney and Mahoney, 1976; Ferguson, 1976) have formed the basis of many published accounts. The four main strands of the self-control approach will be described separately and their rationales considered separately. However, since they have mainly been used together in an integrated approach, their clinical effects will be considered together.

Changing mealtime eating behaviour   Dieters are recommended to change their eating behaviour by gradually implementing the following guidelines:

1.   Interrupt eating for predetermined intervals; during these intervals put

down eating utensils. Begin where you can manage (e.g. short intervals late in the course of the meal) and then gradually increase the length and timing of pauses, so that they occur several times in the course of meals, lasting several minutes at a time.

2.   When you eat, do nothing else. Cease engaging in other tasks while eating and concentrate on the taste of the food. Make eating a 'pure experience'.

3.   Slow the process of ingestion. Put small amounts of food in your mouth at a time, and replace your utensils until after you have swallowed your food. Chew food for longer. Concentrate on the flavour, savour it, and enjoy it as a sensuous experience.

4.   Eat all meals in one place, preferably well away from routine activities.

5.   Always leave some food on your plate.

These guidelines are usually given as advice for dieters to follow on their own, gradually incorporating them into their habitual eating behaviour. Some treatment programmes have incorporated *in vivo* practice, eating meals in sessions (e.g. Schumaker, Wagner, Grodnitzky and Lockwood, 1976) and this public activity has formed an important component of residential and semi-residential programmes (e.g. Musante, 1976).

The rationale of changing mealtime eating behaviour   These suggestions were first produced by Ferster, Nurnberger and Levitt (1962) because of three aspects of their analysis of the problems of dieters: chaining, stimulus control and eating style.

First was their judgement of the importance in eating of chains of behaviour, sequences in which each behaviour makes possible a subsequent behaviour and also reinforces the previous behaviour. The chain as a whole is reinforced by the consummatory response. With the passage of time, behaviour chains tend to become automatic and hard to control. Ferster and colleagues recommend interrupting behaviour chains to increase control over eating because this 'causes eating performance to become a series of discrete acts which are more easily interrupted than a continuous performance' (p.91). In particular they recommend interrupting towards the end of the chain, near the final reinforcer. This is the rationale for interposing delays and segmenting and lengthening the components of eating.

A second feature of their analysis was the observation that eating may come under the influence of the circumstances in which it tends to occur. 'The characteristic circumstances when an individual eats will subsequently control his disposition to eat' (Ferster *et al.*, 1962, p. 92). Under 'disposition to eat' is included not only the behavioural disposition, or habit, but also elicited physio-logical responses, including salivation. Interventions flowing from this analysis include narrowing the range of circumstances in which eating occurs, and separating eating from other associated activities (recommendations 2, 4, 5). The intention was to promote the extinction of eating dispositions associated with various cues by unreinforced exposure, and to develop more adaptive stimulus control.

A third feature of their analysis lay in their observations that obese persons eat more rapidly than others. They suggested that by reducing eating rate, not only would the behaviour become more controllable, but the person 'may eventually achieve a normal state of satiety with less food intake' (p.98). Implicit in this was the notion of normalization: if only the obese ate like the non-obese they would be able to control their eating.

Evaluation of the rationale of changing mealtime eating behaviour Although there is a hint of normalization in these recommendations, their coherence does not depend on assumptions about the differences between the obese and non-obese, but rather on assumptions about the specific effects of the procedures. Unfortunately, there is little evidence on which to base an evaluation.

One reason for the development of slowed eating was the assumption that it would allow natural satiety to develop so that the dieter would no longer override this mechanism by rapid consumption. Thus, consuming food slowly should inhibit subsequent appetite and eating. There is surprisingly little evidence on which to evaluate this assumption. One study found that slowing eating had effects on the salivary response (Wooley, Wooley and Turner, 1975), but studies of food consumption obtained mixed results (Wing and Jeffery, 1979b; Mahoney, 1975). Such inconsistent results do not allow clear conclusions to be drawn about the effects of slowed eating.

Current conceptions of satiety (e.g. Van Itallie and Vanderweele, 1981; Booth, 1980) emphasize the complexity of processes involved and do not support the simple notion of a fixed time course for the rise of satiety, as assumed by Ferster and colleagues. Indeed some models of feeding, embodied in computer simulations, suggest that slowing eating may delay the onset of satiety and increase fat stored in the body (Booth and Mather, 1978).

A related issue, less central to the rationale of these procedures, is that of differences between the obese and non-obese in eating style. Following Ferster and colleagues' (1962) anecdotal observations that the obese eat more rapidly, and in more various circumstances, the notion of an 'obese eating style' was developed. This style was characterized as rapid food intake, achieved through the consumption of large bites at short intervals, consuming all the food present. In order to test this hypothesis many studies have been carried out, both in the natural environment and also in the laboratory. The results (reviewed by Stunkard and Kaplan, 1977, and Spitzer and Rodin, 1981), although not all mutually consistent, do not show any clear separation of the obese and non-obese in eating behaviour.

One important conclusion to be drawn from these studies is that eating style varies considerably according to the circumstances in which it occurs. Although the search for clear non-obese differences in eating behaviour has failed to find them, it has provided evidence for the plasticity of this behaviour and, thus, for the rationale of self-control procedures focusing on the circumstances in which eating habitually occurs.

Rearranging eating cues This concentrates on changes to be made in the dieter's natural environment and is concerned with rearranging environmental cues for eating and other food-related behaviours. Several groups of procedures have been recommended and employed, including the following:

1. Eat at planned regular times.
2. At home eat only in a particular spot, always using the same utensils and china.
3. Reduce contact with food cues as far as possible (e.g. remove food from all places in the house other than the kitchen, clear away leftovers immediately, store food in opaque containers, etc.).
4. Buy food soon after eating a meal.
5. Prepare meals shortly after consuming meals.
6. Make 'diet foods' more attractive.

The rationale for rearranging eating cues The basis for these was the analysis that eating (and other food-related activities such as shopping) can come under the influence of such cues as time of day, location, sight and smell of food, activities, etc. As a result of association with these cues, subsequent contact with them can elicit eating. Thus it was seen to be important to:

(a) Narrow the range of circumstances in which eating occurs, thus establishing a strong association between eating and desirable stimuli and weakening that between eating and others, allowing them to extinguish (guidelines 1, 2 and 4 under the section above);
(b) Reduce the number of cues associated with eating (thus guidelines 3, 4 and 5);
(c) Strengthen cues associated with desirable behaviours (thus guidelines 4, 5 and 6).

Evaluation of the rationale of rearranging eating cues Very little work has been done on these assumptions and techniques and no firm statements can be made about their short-term effects.

The notion that the onset and form of eating are importantly determined by immediate external cues has been the object of much investigation. One important stimulus for this investigation was Schachter's hypothesis (1971) that there are important differences between the factors influencing appetite in the obese and non-obese. Schachter suggested that the appetite and eating of non-obese persons are strongly affected by internal stimuli (such as stomach contractions), but are relatively unaffected by external stimuli, and that the reverse pattern holds for obese persons. This bold hypothesis provoked a stream of attempted replications and extensions (reviewed by Rodin, 1981), much of which failed to confirm it. This literature leads to the conclusions that the dimension of responsiveness to external cues is an important determinant of eating behaviour, but that obese and non-obese persons are not clearly differentiated on it. For both obese and non-obese persons external food cues (such as the sight or smell of food) are a potent influence on starting eating, food choice, eating behaviour, and the amount eaten. Large individual differences in susceptibility to these exist (Sahakian, Lean, Robbins and James, 1981) and it is possible that acquired stimulus control of eating may be a stronger influence in more externally responsive dieters, and that these may benefit more from this procedure. Although the search for obese/non-obese differences in this area has failed to find them, it has provided support for the rationale of rearranging eating cues as a means of controlling eating.

Self-monitoring   Self-monitoring is widely used in behaviour change programmes. In self-control weight reduction programmes it is used by having the dieter record each instance of eating, what was eaten, and the circumstances in which this occurred (e.g. prior mood, prior events, location, time of day, the presence of others, etc.). The amount of information to be recorded can vary from simple food quantity through a large number of characteristics. The means of acutally recording the details can vary tremendously, and dieters and clinicians have shown greater flexibility in using a range of methods, from filling in complex forms, to tapping into a pocket calculator, to moving beads around a bracelet.

The rationale of self-monitoring   Ferster, Nurnberger and Levitt (1962) recommended self-monitoring as a means of gathering information about eating habits, and also of helping slimmers to gain a fuller and more concrete awareness of these habits. It was assumed that this technique provides accurate information about eating patterns and also increases awareness of these habitual behaviours. Helping dieters to become more aware of automatic habitual behaviours was assumed to allow them to exercise more control over them.

Evaluation of the rationale of self-monitoring   The accuracy of such information is brought into question by findings of inaccuracy in judgements of food intake in studies carried out both in the laboratory (e.g. Brownell, Heckerman, Westlake, Hayes and Monti, 1978) and *in vivo* (e.g. Green, 1978). It has been suggested (notably by Kanfer and Karoly, 1972) that self-monitoring has reactive effects on behaviour because it results in self-evaluation. They suggest that comparison of performance against some target results in motivating consequences which may affect future behaviour.

Programming incompatible behaviours   Programming incompatible behaviours involves the dieter in the following ways:

1.   listing high probability behaviour patterns which are incompatible with eating and which can easily be carried out;
2.   identifying the times and places in which uncontrolled eating tends to occur;

3. engaging in the high probability behaviours at or just before the identified 'danger' occasions.

The purpose is to interfere with the circumstances in which uncontrolled eating tends to occur. Parts 1 and 2 are usually carried out in sessions, making plans for the slimmer to carry out between sessions.

The rationale of programming incompatible behaviours In proposing this procedure Ferster and colleagues saw it as strengthening a 'healthy repertoire' of behaviour which would reduce the possibility of eating. Thus, new responses would be learned to stimuli which had previously served as occasions for eating, and the previous associations would be allowed to extinguish.

Increasing levels of physical activity Although the major emphasis of this treatment approach is changing eating habits, some programmes also emphasize the extension of behavioural techniques to increasing levels of activity. Contingency contracting has been employed to increase the amount of aerobic exercise (Epstein, Wing, Thompson and Griffin, 1980; Wysocki, Hall, Iwata and Riordan, 1979). The use of rearranging cues, self-monitoring, target setting, and self-reinforcement has also been reported in the same context (Martin and Dubbert, 1982).

Clinical evaluation of self-control treatments The size of weight loss produced in self-control programmes depends on (and is limited by) such factors as the length of treatment and the means used to achieve a negative energy balance. The most frequently used means of achieving a negative balance in self-control treatments is calorie restriction, a 'conventional diet' providing a daily intake of the order of 1000 kcal. If adherence to this were perfect, then weekly weight losses of the order of 0.5 kg would be expected.

The losses reported in programmes utilizing conventional diets have varied with their duration, typically 5 kg for 10 weeks, 7 kg for 15 weeks, 10 kg for 20 weeks, and 14 kg for 26 weeks. Greater losses have been reported for programmes which (a) are set up to provide an optimal clinical service, rather than to test experimental hypotheses, (b) involve experienced therapists (rather than graduate students who form the most frequently reported therapists), and (c) involve more contact hours or more weeks of treatment (e.g. in residential settings) (Bennett, 1986d). Self-control treatments can produce clinically significant reductions in obesity. The potential benefits of losing significant amounts of weight (surveyed at the beginning of this chapter) can be attained through behavioural programmes. Although few behavioural studies have systematically studied the physical effects of weight reduction, those which have done so have reported beneficial changes in blood pressure and cardiovascular fitness (e.g. Dubbert and Wilson, 1984); sometimes changes in blood pressure have been sufficient to allow hypertensives to discountinue their antihypertensive medication (Craighead, Stunkard and O'Brien, 1981).

Controlled comparisons have found such programmes to produce post-treatment losses that are greater than those produced by dietary advice alone, or the combination of dietary advice with social pressure, but which are smaller than those produced by anorectic drugs or surgical procedures (Wilson and Brownell, 1980; Stuart, Mitchell and Jensen, 1981; Bennett, 1986d).

The losses from self-control treatments tend to be well maintained over follow-up periods of at least one year: they neither increase nor decrease. The size of weight loss at follow-up is primarily determined by weight loss at the end of treatment (and thus by treatment length, etc.). The maintenance of losses produced by self-control treatments is superior to that of those produced by anorectic drugs or by dietary advice, and probably superior to those produced by fasting or jaw-wiring (Stuart, Mitchell and Jensen, 1981; Bennett, 1986d).

Although the contribution to total weight loss of each of the individual components of the self-control approach has not been experimentally investigated, there is evidence that weight loss maintenance can be enhanced if programmes include a strong exercise component (e.g. Dahlkoetter, Callahan and Linton, 1979) or training in rearranging eating cues (e.g. Carroll and Yates, 1981).

These behavioural treatments have been found to consistently generate changes in behaviour and also to produce weight reduction. However, the amounts of change in these two areas have not been found to be closely related, either in the short term or in the long term (Brownell and Stunkard, 1978). Greater compliance with key recommendations is not associated with greater weight loss; poor compliance does not predict failure in losing weight. Methodological features may have affected this (Lansky, 1981), but nevertheless negative findings have been reported so often as to raise grave doubts about the central role hypothesized for changes in these areas of behaviour. Changing eating habits was assumed to mediate dietary adherence and, thus, weight loss. Consistent failure to observe a close relationship between them brings the assumption into question, and highlights the need for a closer analysis of eating behaviour and the effects on this of treatment techniques. Such a fine-grained analysis might lead to more appropriate and effective individualization of treatment; the value of such an approach in shedding light on the system controlling food consumption has been shown by studies of anorectic drugs (Blundell, 1984).

There is wide variation between individuals in weight loss achieved through self-control programmes, but this variation has not been accounted for by any pretreatment characteristics. Despite many studies of behavioural, psychometric, demographic, physiological, and other characteristics, none has been identified that can reliably predict outcome or aid in selection for treatment.

Studies of self-control treatments which have included measures of emotional state or level of self-esteem have generally found reductions in anxiety or depression and increases in self-esteem (Wing, Epstein, Marcus and Kupfer, 1984). This general effect of emotional improvement stands in marked contrast to isolated reports of emotional deterioration reported in non-behavioural treatments (Stunkard and Rush, 1974).

EXTENSIONS TO SELF-CONTROL TREATMENTS OF OBESITY

The distinct benefits of behavioural treatments are limited in the ways described above. Attempts to improve the effectiveness of this approach have taken three main directions: (a) enlisting wider social influence; (b) combining it with other methods of weight reduction; (c) augmenting the self-control component.

Enlisting Wider Social Influence

The initial educational assumption of self-control programmes has not been confirmed. Participants lose weight during the programme, but do not continue to lose weight once contact with the programme comes to an end. Participation does not produce the ability (as had originally been assumed) to control weight henceforth; it helps slimmers to produce limited, stable reductions. This stability is of value, and represents a worthwhile achievement; however, it does not represent adequate attainment of self-control of eating. The more intensive the contact provided by the treatment programme, the greater the loss promoted. More experienced therapists achieve better results (Hall, Bass and Monroe, 1978; Jeffery et al., 1978; Paulsen and Beneke, 1978). Experimental studies of the patient–therapist relationship have shown this to affect outcome (Janis, 1982). Groups produce better results than individual therapy (e.g. Jones, Owen and Bennett, 1986; Kingsley and Wilson, 1977). Although this form of treatment attempts to teach people how to manage their behaviour so as to lose weight on their own, participation in it does have an immediate, probably social, influence. External control treatments show the value of producing arrangements which strongly influence the weight-loss behaviour of persons living in their natural environment. External control and social influence can act to reinforce, sustain, and extend self-control and it may prove productive to extend self-control techniques to include an external component. One way of doing this is to enlist continuing influences in the person's natural environment in order to produce an environment that sustains weight-loss behaviour. Attempts to do this have centred on the dieter's family and working environment.

Members of a person's immediate family, especially their spouse, constitute one of the strongest potential influences on them and are often present when eating occurs, at home or outside it. They can initiate or influence the slimmer's exposure to food cues and affect exercise habits. Their actions can control access to or constitute important types of reinforcement or punishment. A complex treatment package which attempts to involve the slimmer's spouse directly in the task of weight reduction has been developed (Brownell, Heckerman, Westlake, Hayes and Monti, 1978). In this spouses attend treatment sessions together with their partners, and are taught jointly, as a couple, how to apply a range of behavioural techniques to facilitate eating control and weight loss by the dieter. Teaching sessions, advice, and behaviour rehearsal are employed in teaching the couple how to change relevant patterns of behaviour. Brownell and colleagues found that slimmers receiving couples training showed larger weight losses in treatment and afterwards than those receiving self-control training alone. Weight loss continued after the treatment programme came to an end, an occurrence that is not often reported in self-control treatments. Subsequent studies of training couples in this way have tended to confirm the value of this approach. Producing changes in relevant family patterns of behaviour, which may persist after treatment ends, promises to be a valuable means of providing an environment sustaining weight-loss behaviour.

Another environment with potential influence on weight control is the work setting. At the very least, weight reduction programmes can be provided in work settings, making them very accessible; this has been done in many organizations (Foreyt, Scott and Gotto, 1980). Worksites have other potential influences on weight-loss behaviour, such as the social influence between co-workers, opportunities for exercise, and the fact that meals are frequently provided and consumed at work. The potential for unilateral external control by employers has already been exemplified by the action of the New Orleans Police Department. Some attempts have been made to harness the potential influence of the workplace to the task of weight control (Colvin, Zopf and Myers, 1983). One of the problems encountered — high attrition rates (Stunkard and Brownell, 1980) — has been significantly reduced by the application of contingency contracts based on attendance (Follick, Fowler and Brown, 1984). The potential of the workplace as an environment sustaining weight control has yet to be fully exploited.

The promising early results of widening the area of social influence involved in behavioural programmes suggests that going beyond self-control to include environmental support may result in increased long-term effectiveness.

Combining Self-control with other Methods of Weight Reduction

The upper limit for weight reduction in any behavioural programme is set by the means it uses to achieve a negative energy balance. Most programmes involve a conventional diet, and attempt to help participants adhere to it. Because post-treatment weight loss is rare, the ultimate weight loss achieved through behavioural treatment will be affected by the means it uses to achieve weight loss. Therefore, in order to achieve maximal clinically significant losses it may prove valuable to combine self-control procedures (which produce well-maintained losses) with other approaches giving larger losses (which are poorly maintained). Such a combination might link the advantages of both approaches, producing a large and well-maintained loss in weight. To date most attempts to combine self-control procedures with other methods have involved anorectic drugs.

Craighead, Stunkhard and O'Brien (1981) compared the effects of fenfluramine (an anorectic drug), self-control treatment, and a combination of the two. At the end of treatment weight losses in both drug conditions exceeded that of the self-control condition. The losses in the two drug conditions were gradually regained after treatment ended, while the loss in the behavioural treatment remained at the same level. At the year follow-up the loss of the behavioural treatment significantly exceeded those of the others. Combining the self-control treatment with fenfluramine produced greater short-term losses, but smaller long-term losses, than the self-control treatment alone. Similar, although less clear-cut, results have been found in similar studies of combining self-control with fenfluramine (Brownell and Stunkard, 1981; Craighead, 1984).

The effects of combining behaviour therapy with a Very Low Calorie Diet (VLCD), investigated in a pilot study by Wadden, Stunkard, Brownell and Day (1984), appear to be more promising. At the end of treatment the average loss was 20.5 kg: only 10% of this had been regained by the 12 months follow-up. These large, well-maintained losses point towards the potential value of the integration of behavioural treatments with other means of producing rapid weight loss.

Augmenting the Self-control Component

Self-control treatments do not enable slimmers to go on and control their weight effectively. One reason for this may lie in the inadequacy of the self-control component, which is essentially that described by Ferster, Nurnberger and Levitt (1962), and based on a contemporary analysis of the behavioural component of self-control. The weakness of this approach has been shown by the failure to find a clear relationship between changing eating habits and success in weight loss. Developing a more adequate means of helping dieters to regulate their own behaviour may require a concept of self-control wider than that of self-regulation. This quest has led to three main developments, in the areas of (a) cognitive control, (b) coping with relapse, and (c) controlling meal size.

Cognitive control Several types of evidence point to the importance of cognitive factors such as beliefs, expectations, evaluations, self-instructions, and images. Studies of the natural history of dieting find that successful, but not unsuccessful, dieters report the use of self-restraining self-instructions (Leon, Roth and Hewitt, 1977). Occasions when self-restraint fail ('volitional breakdowns') have been found to be preceded by dysfunctional patterns of thought such as dichotomous thinking or self-serving rationalizations (Sjoberg and Persson, 1979). Changes in cognitive factors (such as preoccupation with eating) during behavioural programmes have been found to be related to success, in a way in which behavioural changes have not (Jeffery, Vender and Wing, 1978). In the experimental study of food intake the (largely cognitive) notion of restrained eating (Herman and Polivy, 1980) — consciously inhibiting food intake — has been found influential. Beliefs can strongly influence food intake whether they concern eating speed (Mahoney, 1975), the content of tablets (Pudel, 1975; Experiment 3), or the energy value of meals (Wooley, 1972). Visual images of food can provoke similar physical responses to those provoked by exposure to food (Wooley and Wooley, 1981). In the light of such evidence, attempts have been made to utilize cognitive control as a means of self-control in the treatment of obesity.

Several treatment programmes have attempted to apply cognitive therapy procedures, techniques of cognitive change developed for other clinical problems, including impulse-control disorders (Meichenbaum, 1977). Different types of techniques have been used in different circumstances, according to whether uncontrolled eating was associated either with the absence of cognitive activity (e.g. impulsive eating when faced with food cues) or with the occurrence of maladaptive or dysfunctional patterns of thoughts. An example of the latter might be dichotomous thinking of the type, 'Since I've gone over my diet it doesn't matter what I eat'. In the first case (absence of cognitive activity) the technique of self-instructional training could be used, in the attempt to train the person to develop appropriate inhibitory self-statements and then, through practice to the point of overlearning, to learn to apply them in problematic situations. In the second case (the involvement of dysfunctional thoughts) a different approach, developed by Beck (1976), might be more appropriate. This involves teaching the person to become aware of such unhelpful thoughts and to examine their validity, by logical analysis or by testing them out through 'experiments'. If they continue to occur, the thoughts could be dealt with 'answering' them with appropriate responses (this being learnt by self-instructional training).

Positive results were obtained for these sorts of cognitive treatments by Dunkel and Glaros (1978) and Block (1980), but the studies only followed up subjects for relatively short periods. Similar treatments, employed in studies with 12-month follow-ups by Collins, Rothblum and Wilson, 1986) and Bennett (1986a; 1986b; 1986e) found no real benefit from cognitive treatments. A further cognitive treatment approach involves training dieters in general problem-solving skills, so that they can approach difficulties which they encounter as examples of problems to be solved, rather than as unique obstacles. Two treatment trials have found some benefit from training in problem-solving skills (Black and Scherba, 1983; Straw and Terre, 1983). Although the evidence for the role of cognitive processes in self-control and weight control is strong, the study of procedures for modifying these processes has hardly begun.

Relapse prevention   Maintaining a new lower weight is the hardest part of the task of weight loss, reflecting as it does the operation of physiological, behavioural, social, and other forms of resistance. The maintenance of treatment-induced gains is a problem in the treatment of all indulgent behaviours (such as cigarette smoking, alcoholism, drug abuse) and this communality has led to the study of the relapse process in each and the development of a general model of relapse (Marlatt and Gordon, 1980). This model emphasizes the importance of two factors and implies that relevant training will enable dieters to resist relapse. The first factor is the nature of high-risk situations, in which restraint is placed under severe pressure; the most important of these in weight control appear to be characterized by the occurrence of negative emotions (such as dysphoria), or by the occurrence of positive emotions in a social interaction (Cummings, Gordon and Marlatt, 1980; Rosenthal and Marx, 1981). Training patients to identify and cope with these is seen to be of value. The second factor is the dieter's perception of what has happened once a 'slip' occurs (e.g. as either an isolated event or as evidence of inability to cope). Marlatt and Gordon see this perception as a crucial determinant of whether or not relapse will then occur and argue that patients should be prepared in advance for slips and taught how to cope with them. Training in these two areas would be expected to help dieters resist relapse.

Relapse prevention treatments have been developed only recently and insufficient evidence is yet available to permit a clinical evaluation. A recent evaluation of the effects of adding relapse prevention training to a self-control training programme found improvements in weight loss at one year, but only when there was some contact with the programme in the follow-up period (Perri, Shapiro, Ludwig, Twentyman and McAdoo, 1984).

Eating control   The central focus of behavioural techniques for changing eating behaviour has been on starting eating and influences on this. Stopping eating, and its determinants, have received much less attention, despite the crucial role of meal size in determining energy intake. The two strategems used to affect satiety (slowing eating, leaving food on the plate) were first described by Ferster, Nurnberger and Levitt in 1962 and reflect assumptions about satiety current at the time. The lack of emphasis in treatment on controlling meal size has occurred despite the increasing emphasis on satiety and its determinants by basic research into appetite. The limitations of the assumptions of Ferster, Nurnberger and Levitt are shown by findings the satiety may be nutrient-specific (Rolls, Rolls and Rowe, 1983) or may be induced more strongly by certain foods, such as protein. Findings that satiety can be influenced by learning processes such as conditioning (Booth, 1983) opens a range of possibilities of behavioural control.

An innovative attempt to apply Booth's findings and utilize conditioned satiety in the treatment of obesity (Bradley, Poser and Jonson, 1980) was found to have little clinical effect. A possible means of helping dieters to modify meal size lies in directly training them to discriminate early sensations of satiety and then to use these as a cue for stopping eating. Discrimination training was successfully used to teach an obese person to become more aware of sensations of gastric motility associated wih hunger (Griggs and Stunkard, 1964). If an easily measurable physiological index of early satiety were established, then satiety discrimination training would be a possibility, perhaps along parallel lines to some methods used to train alcoholics in controlled drinking. In these methods problem drinkers were initially trained to accurately discriminate between a range of blood alcohol concentrations. This was followed by practice, in a bar setting, of drinking up to, but not beyond, a specified concentration. Such treatment programmes have reported very good clinical results (Sobell and Sobell, 1973) and suggest ways in which satiety training might be integrated with practice in 'controlled eating'.

Until the present, all clinical advances in the behavioural treatment of obesity have come either from extending the coverage of treatments or from applying techniques found to be useful in the treatment of other addictive behaviours. No clinical advance has yet come from the experimental study of food intake, but this discipline appears to be very relevant to clinical work in the treatment of obesity. Helping obese patients to develop control over eating may be a task where fruitful integration can develop.

REFERENCES

Andrews, G., McMahon, S., Austin, A. and Byrne, D. (1982). Hypertension: comparison of drug and non-drug treatments. *British Medical Journal*, **284**, 1523–1526.

Ashwell, M.A. (1978). Commercial weight-loss groups. In G.A. Bray (Ed.), *Recent Advances in Obesity Research*, vol. 2, Newman Publishing, London.

Beck, A.T. (1976). *Cognitive Therapy and the Emotional Disorders*, Guildford Press, New York.

Bennett, G.A. (1986a). An evaluation of self-instructional training in the treatment of obesity. *Addictive Behaviors*, **11**, 125–134.

Bennett, G.A. (1986b). Cognitive rehearsal in the treatment of obesity: a comparison against cue avoidance and social pressure.

Bennett, G.A. (1986c). Is there a pathognomic profile in obesity? *Medicographia*, **8**, 22.

Bennett, G.A. (1986d). Behavior therapy for obesity: A quantitative review of the effects of selected treatment characteristics on outcome. *Behavior Therapy*, in press.

Bennett, G.A. (1986e). Expectations in the treatment of obesity. *British Journal of Clinical Psychosis*, in press.

Berger, M., Berchtold, P., Gries, F. and Zimmerman, H. (1981). Indications for the treatment of obesity. In P. Bjorntorp, M. Cairella and A. Howard (Eds), *Recent Advances in Obesity Research*, vol. 3, John Libbey, London.

Bjorvell, H., Hadell, K., Jonsson, B., Molin, C. and Rossner, S. (1984). Long-term effects of jaw fixation in severe obesity. *International Journal of Obesity*, **8**, 79–86.

Black, D.R. and Scherba, D.S. (1983). Deposit money: a component in a self-directed minimal intervention program for weight control. *Behaviour Therapy*, **14**, 333–340.

Blaza, S.E. and Garrow, J.S. (1980). The effect of anxiety on metabolic rate. *Proceedings of the Nutrition Society*, **39**, 13A.

Block, J. (1980). Effects of RET on overweight adults. *Psychotherapy; Theory, Research and Practice*, **17**, 277–280.

Blundell, J.E. (1984). Systems and interactions: An approach to the pharmacology of eating and hunger. In A.J. Stunkard and E. Stellar (Eds.), *Eating and its Disorders*, Raven Press, New York.

Booth, D.A. (1980). Acquired behaviour controlling energy intake and output. In A.J. Stunkard (Ed.), *Obesity*, Saunders, Philadelphia.

Booth, D.A. (1983). How nutritional effects of foods can influence people's dietary choices. In L.M. Barker (Ed.), *The Psychobiology of Human Food Selection*, Ellis Horwood, Chichester.

Booth, D.A., and Mather, P. (1978). Prototype model of human feeding, growth, and obesity. In D.A. Booth (Ed.), *Hunger Models: Computable Theory of Feeding Control*, Academic Press, London.

Bradley, I., Poser, E. and Johnson, F. (1980). Outcome expectation ratings as predictors of success in weight reduction. *Journal of Clinical Psychology*, **36**, 500–502.

Bray, G.A. (1979). *Obesity in America*. National Institute of Health Publication No. 79–358, US Department of Health, Education, and Welfare, Washington.

Bray, G.A. (1980). Jejunoileal bypass, jaw-wiring and vagotomy for massive obesity. In A.J. Stunkard (Ed.), *Obesity*, Saunders, Philadelphia.

Brewer, C., White, H. and Baddeley, M. (1974). Beneficial effects of jejunoileostomy on compulsive eating and associated psychiatric symptoms. *British Medical Journal*, iv, 314–316.

Brownell, K.D. and Stunkard, A.J. (1978). Behavior therapy and behavior change: Uncertainties in programs for weight control. *Behaviour Research and Therapy*, **16**, 301–302.

Brownell, K.D. and Stunkard, A.J. (1980). Physical activity in the development and control of obesity. In A.J. Stunkard (Ed.), *Obesity*, Saunders, Philadelphia.

Brownell, K.D. and Stunkard, A.J. (1981). Couples training, pharmacotherapy, and behavior therapy in the treatment of obesity. *Archives of General Psychiatry*, **38**, 1224–1229.

Brownell, K., Heckerman, C.L., Westlake R.J., Hayes, S.C. and Monti, P.M. (1978). The effects of couples training and partner cooperativeness in the behavioural treatment of obesity. *Behaviour Research and Therapy*, **16**, 323–333.

Bruch, H. (1973). *Eating Disorders: Obesity, Anorexia Nervosa and the Person Within*, Basic Books, New York.

Carrol, L.J. and Yates, B.T. (1981). Further evidence for the role of stimulus control training in facilitating weight reduction after behavioral therapy. *Behavior Therapy*, **12**, 287–291.

Cole, A.D. and Bond, N.W. (1983). Olfactory aversion conditioning and overeating: a review and some data. *Perception and Motor Skills*, **57**, 667–678.

Collins, R.L., Rothblum, E.D. and Wilson, G.T. (1986). The comparative efficacy of cognitive and behavioral approaches to the treatment of obesity. *Cognitive Therapy and Research*, **10**, 299–318.

Colvin, R.H., Zopf, K.J. and Myers, J.H. (1983). Weight control among coworkers: effects of monetary contingencies and social milieu. *Behavior Modification*, 7, 64–75.

Craighead, L.W. (1984). Sequencing of behavior therapy and pharmacotherapy for obesity. *Journal of Consulting and Clinical Psychology*, **52**, 190–199.

Craighead, L.W., Stunkard A.J. and O'Brien, R.M. (1981). Behavior therapy and pharmacotherapy for obesity. *Archives of General Psychiatry*, **38**, 763–768.

Crisp, A.H. and McGuiness, B. (1976). Jolly fat: Relation between obesity and psychoneurosis in the general population. *British Medical Journal*, **1**, 7–9.

Cummings, C., Gordon, J. and Marlatt, G. (1980). Relapse: prevention and prediction. In W. Miller (Ed.), *Addictive Behaviors*, Pergamon Press, Oxford.

Dahlkoetter, J., Callahan, E.J. and Linton, J. (1979). Obesity and the unbalanced energy equation exercise vs. eating habit change. *Journal of Consulting and Clinical Psychology*, **47**, 898–905.

DHSS/MRC (1976) *Report on Research on Obesity*, Compiler W.P.T. James, HMSO, London.

Diament, C. and Wilson, G.T. (1975). An experimental investigation of the effects of covert sensitisation in an analogue eating situation. *Behavior Therapy*, **6**, 499–509.

Dubbert, P.M. and Wilson, G.T. (1984). Goal-setting and spouse involvement in the treatment of obesity. *Behaviour Research and Therapy*, **22**, 227–242.

Dublin, L.I. (1953). Relation of obesity to longevity. *New England Journal of Medicine*, **248**, 971–974.

Dunkel, L. and Glaros, G. (1978). Comparison of self-instructional and stimulus control treatments for obesity. *Cognitive Research and Therapy*, **1**, 75–78.

Epstein, L., Wing, R., Thompson, J. and Griffin, W. (1980). Attendance and fitness in aerobic exercise; the effects of contracts and lottery procedures. *Behavior Modification*, **4**, 465–479.

Ferguson, J. (1976). *Learning to Eat*, Bull Publishing Company, Palo Alto, California.

Ferster, C., Nurnberger, J. and Levitt, E. (1962). The control of eating. *Journal of Mathetics*, **1**, 87–109.

Foch, T.T. and McClearn, G.E. (1980). Genetics, bodyweight, and obesity. In A.J. Stunkard (Ed.), *Obesity*, Saunders, Philadelphia.

Follick, M.J., Fowler, J.L. and Brown, R.A. (1984). Attrition in worksite weight-loss interventions: the effects of an incentive procedure. *Journal of Consulting and Clinical Psychology*, **52**, 139–140.

Foreyt, J.P., Scott, L.W. and Gotto, A.M. (1980). Weight control and nutrition education programs in occupational settings. *Public Health Reports*, **95**, 127–136.

Garb, J. and Stunkard, A.J. (1974). Taste aversions in man. *American Journal of Psychiatry*, **131**, 1204–1207.

Garrow, J.S. (1978). *Energy Balance and Obesity in Man*, 2nd edn, Elsevier, Amsterdam.

Garrow, J.S. (1981) *Treat Obesity Seriously*. Churchill Livingstone, Edinburgh.

Garrow, J.S. and Gardiner, G. (1981). Maintenance of weight loss in obese patients after jaw-wiring. *British Medical Journal*, **282**, 858–860.

Genuth, S.M., Vertes, V. and Hazelton, J. (1978). Supplemented fasting in the treatment of obesity. In G.A. Bray (Ed.), *Recent Advances in Obesity Research*, vol. 2, Newman, London.

Gilbert, S. (1983) Pathology of eating. *Pharmacological Therapy*, **20**, 133–149.

Green, L. (1978) Temporal and stimulus factors in self-monitoring by obese persons. *Behavior Therapy*, **9**, 328–341.

Griggs, R.C. and Stunkard, A.J. (1964). The interpretation of gastric motility. 2 Sensitivity and bias in the perception of gastric motility. *Archives of General Psychiatry*, **11**, 82–89.

Gwinup, G. (1975) Effect of exercise alone on the weight of obese women. *Archives of Internal Medicine*, **135**, 676–680.

Hall, S.M., Bass, A. and Monroe, J. (1978). Continued contact and monitoring as follow up strategies: a long-term study of obesity treatment. *Addictive Behaviors*, **3**, 139–147.

Harding, P.E. (1980). Jaw-wiring for obesity. *Lancet*, **i**, 534–535.

Herman, C.P. and Polivy, J. (1980). Restrained eating. In A.J. Stunkard (Ed), *Obesity*, Saunders, Philadelphia.

Horton, E. (1981). Effects of altered caloric intake and composition of the diet on insulin resistance in obesity. In P. Bjorntorp, M. Cairella and A. Howard (Eds.), *Recent Advances in Obesity Research*, vol. 3, John Libbey, London.

James, W.P.T. and Trayhurn, P. (1981). Thermogenesis and obesity. *British Medical Bulletin*, **37**, 43–48.

Janis, I.L. (1982) *Short-term Counselling: Guidelines Based on Recent Research*, Yale University Press, New Haven.

Jeffery, R.W., Bjornson-Benson, W.M., Rosenthal, B.S., Kurth, C.L. and Dunn, M.M. (1984). Effectiveness of monetary contracts with two repayment schedules on weight reduction in men and women from self-referred and population samples. *Behavior Therapy*, **15**, 273–279.

Jeffery, R.W., Gerber, W.M., Rosenthal, B.S. and Lindquist, R.A. (1983). Monetary contracts in weight control: Effectiveness of group and individual contracts of varying size. *Journal of Consulting and Clinical Psychology*, **51**, 242–248.

Jeffery, R.W., Thompson, P. and Wing, R. (1978). Effect on weight reduction of strong monetary contracts for calorie restriction or weight loss. *Behaviour Research and Therapy*, **16**, 363–379.

Jeffery, R.W., Vender, M. and Wing, R. (1978). Weight loss and behavior change one year after behavioral treatment for obesity. *Journal of Consulting and Clinical Psychology*, **46**, 368–369.

Jones, S.E., Owens, H.M. and Bennett, G.A. (1986). Does behaviour therapy work for dietitions: An experimental evaluation of the effects of three procedures in a weight reduction clinic. *Human Nutrition*, **40A**, 272–281.

Kanfer, F.H. and Karoly, P. (1972). Self-control: a behaviourist excursion into the lion's den. *Behavior Therapy*, **3**, 398–416.

Keen, H. (1975). The incomplete story of obesity and diabetes. In A. Howard (Ed.), *Recent Advances in Obesity Research*, vol. 1, Newman Publishing, London.

Keesey, R.E. (1980). A set-point analysis of the regulation of bodyweight. In A.J. Stunkard (Ed.), *Obesity*, Saunders, Philadelphia.

Keys, A., Brozek, J., Henschel, A., Mickelson, O. and Taylor, H.L. (1950). *The Biology of Human Starvation*, University of Minnesota Press, Minneapolis.

Kingsley, R.G. and Wilson, G.T. (1977). Behavior therapy for obesity: a comparative investigation of long-term efficacy. *Journal of Consulting and Clinical Psychology*, **45**, 288–298.

Lansky, D. (1981). A methodological analysis of research on adherence and weight loss. *Behavior Therapy*, **12**, 144–149.

Leon, G.R., Roth, L. and Hewitt, M.I. (1977). Eating patterns, satiety, and self-control behaviour of obese pesons during weight reduction. *Obesity and Bariatric Medicine*, **6**, 172–181.

Lew, E.A. and Garfinkel, L. (1979). Variations in mortality by weight among 750,000 men and women. *Journal of Chronic Diseases*, **32**, 563.

Logue, A., Ophir, I. and Strauss, K. (1981). The acquisition of taste aversions in humans. *Behaviour Research and Therapy*, **19**, 319–333.

McClean R.A. and Moon, M. (1980). Health, obesity and earnings. *American Journal of Public Health*, **70**, 1006.

McReynolds, W.T. (1983). Toward a psychology of obesity: Review of research on the role of personality and level of adjustment. *International Journal of Eating Disorders*, **2**, 37–57.

Mahoney, M.J. (1975). The obese eating style: bites, beliefs and behaviour modification. *Addictive Behaviors*, **1**, 47–53.

Mahoney, M.J. and Mahoney, B.K. (1976). *Permanent Weight Control*, Norton and Company, New York.

Mancini, M., and Howard, A.N. (1981). Evaluation of very-low-calorie diets. Proceedings of a satellite symposium to the third International Congress on Obesity (Ischia, October 1980). *International Journal of Obesity*, **5**, 193–352.

Mann, R.A. (1972). The behaviour-therapeutic use of contingency contracting to control an adult behaviour problem; weight control. *Journal of Applied Behavioral Analysis*, **5**, 99–109.

Mann, R.A. (1976). The use of contingency contracting to facilitate durability of behaviour change; weight loss maintenance. *Addictive Behaviors*, **1**, 245–249.

Marlatt, G.A. and Gordon, J.R. (1980). Determinants of relapse: Implications for the maintenance of behaviour change. In P.O. Davidson and S.M. Davidson (Eds), *Behavioral Medicine: changing Health Lifestyles*, Brunner/Mazel, New York.

Martin, J.E. and Dubbert, P.M. (1982). Exercise applications and promotion in behavioral medicine: current status and future directions. *Journal of Consulting and Clinical Psychology*, **50**, 1004–1017.

Mayer, J. (1968). *Overweight: Causes, Cost and Control*, Prentice-Hall, Englewood Cliffs, New Jersey.

Meichenbaum, D. (1977). *Cognitive-behavior Modifications*, Plenum Press, New York.

Milgram, N.W., Krames, L. and Alloway, T.M. (Eds) (1977). *Food Aversion Learning*, Plenum Press, New York.

Miller, D.S. (1975). Thermogenesis in everyday life. In E. Jequier (Ed.), *Second International Congress on Energy Balance*, Geneva.

Miller, P.M. (1972). The use of behavioural contracting in the treatment of alcoholism. *Behavior Therapy*, **3**, 595–596.

Miller, W. (Ed.) (1980). *Addictive Behaviors*, Pergamon Press, Oxford.

Musante, G.J. (1976). The dietary rehabilitation clinic: evaluative report of a behavioral and dietary treatment of obesity. *Behavior Therapy*, **7**, 198–204.

Paulsen, B.K. and Beneke, W. (1978). Leader characteristics as a determinant of treatment effectiveness in a weight control program. *International Journal of Obesity*, **2**, 387–388.

Paxton, R. (1981). Deposit contracts with smokers: varying frequency and amount of repayments. *Behaviour Research and Therapy*, **19**, 117–123.

Perri, M.G., Shapiro, R.M., Ludwig, W.W., Twentyman, C.T. and McAdoo, W.G. (1984). Maintenance strategies for the treatment of obesity: An evaluation of relapse prevention training and posttreatment contact by mail and telephone. *Journal of Consulting and Clinical Psychology*, **52**, 404–413.

Pudel, V. (1975). Psychological obervations on experimental feeding in the obese. In A. Howard (Ed.), *Recent Advances in Obesity Research*. vol. 1, Newman Publishing, London.

Quale, F.R. (1975). A behaviour contracting approach to weight control. *Scandinavian Journal of Behavior Therapy*, **4**, 117–124.

Rand, C.S.W. and Stunkard, A.J. (1983). Obesity and psychoanalysis: Treatment and four-year follow-up. *American Journal of Psychiatry*, **140**, 1140–1144.

Reisin, E., Abel, R., Modan, M., Silverburg, D.S., Eliahou, H.E., and Modan, B. (1978). Effect of weight loss without salt restriction on the reduction of blood pressure in overweight hypertensive patients. *New England Journal of Medicine*, **298**, 1.

Rimm, D.C. and Masters, J.C. (1979). *Behavior Therapy. Techniques and Empirical Findings*, 2nd edn, Academic Press, New York.

Robbins, T.W. and Fray, P.J. (1980). Stress-induced eating: fact, fiction, or misunderstanding? *Appetite*, **1**, 103–133.

Rodin, J. (1981). Current status of the internal-external hypothesis for obesity. What went wrong? *American Psychologist*, **36**, 361–372.

Rolls, B.J., Rolls, E.T. and Rowe, E.A. (1983). The influence of variety on human food selection and intake. In L.M. Barker (Ed.), *The Psychobiology of Human Food Selection*, Ellis Horwood, Chichester.

Rosenthal, B.S. and Marx, R.D. (1981). Determinants of initial relapse episodes among dieters. *Obesity and Bariatric Medicine*, **10**, 94–97.

Royal College of Physicians of London (1983). Obesity. *Journal of the Royal College of Physicians of London*, **17**, 1–65.

Rozin, P. (1976). The selection of food by rats, humans, and other animals. In J. Rosenblatt, R.A. Hinde, C. Beer and E. Shaw (Eds), *Advances in the Study of Behavior*, vol. 1, Plenum, New York.

Ruderman, A.J. (1983). Obesity, anxiety, and food consumption. *Addictive Behaviors*, **8**, 235–242.

Sahakian, B., Lean, M., Robbins, T. and James, W.P.T. (1981). Salivation and insulin secretion in response to food in non-obese men and women. *Appetite*, **2**, 209–216.

Schachter, S. (1971). Some extraordinary facts about obese humans and rats. *American Psychologist*, **26**, 129–144.

Schumaker, J.F., Wagner, M.K., Grodnitsky, B. and Lockwood, G. (1976). Eating behaviors and the effectiveness of behavioral training and psychotherapy approaches to weight reduction. *Obesity and Bariatric Medicine*, **5**, 136–139.

Scrignar, C.B. (1980). Mandatory weight control program for 550 police officers choosing either behavior modification or 'willpower'. *Obesity and Bariatric Medicine*, **9**, 88–92.

Seligman, M. (1970). On the generality of the laws of learning. *Psychological Review*, **77**, 406–418.

Siddamma, T., (1979). Obesity and socioeconomic status among children. *Child Psychiatry Quarterly*, **12**, 83–88.

Sims, E. and Horton, E. (1968). Endocrine metabolic adaptation to obesity and starvation. *American Journal of Clinical Nutrition*, **21**, 1455–1470.

Sjoberg, L. and Persson, L. (1979). A study of attempts by obese patients to regulate eating. *Addictive Behaviors*, **4**, 349–359.

Slochower, J.A., (1983). *Excessive eating: The role of emotions and environment*, Human Sciences Press, New York.

Sobell, M.E. and Sobell, L.C. (1973). Individualised behavior therapy for alcoholism. *Behavior Therapy*, **4**, 49–72.

Spitzer, L. and Rodin, J. (1981). Human eating behavior: a critical review of studies in normal weight and overweight individuals. *Appetite*, **2**, 293–329.

Stitzer, M.L., Bigelow, G.E. and McCaul, C. (1983). Behavioral approaches to drug abuse. In M. Hersen, R. Eisler and P. Miller (Eds), *Progress in Behavior Modification*, vol. 14, Academic Press, New York.

Stollak, G.E. (1967). Weight loss obtained under different experimental procedures. *Psychotherapy: Theory, Research, and Practice*, **4**, 61–64.

Straw, M.K. and Terre, L. (1983). An evaluation of individualised behavioural obesity treatment and maintenance strategies. *Behavior Therapy*, **14**, 255–266.

Stuart, R.B. (1967). Behavioral control of overeating. *Behaviour Research and Therapy*, **5**, 357–365.

Stuart, R.B. (1971). A three-dimensional program for the treatment of obesity. *Behaviour Research and Therapy*, **9**, 177–186.

Stuart, R.B. (1975). Behavioral control of overeating: A status report. In G.A.Bray (Ed.), *Obesity in Perspective*, vol. 2, US Government Printing Office, Washington DC.

Stuart, R.B. and Davis, B. (1972). *Slim Chance in a Fat World: Behavioral Control of Obesity*. Research Press, Champaign Illinois.

Stuart, R.B. Mitchell, C. and Jensen, J. (1981). Therapeutic options in the management of obesity. In C. Prokop and L. Bradley (Eds), *Medical Psychology: Contributions to Behavioral Medicine*, Academic Press, New York.

Stunkard, A.J. (1980). The social environment and the control of obesity. In A.J. Stunkard (Ed.), *Obesity*. W.B. Saunders, Philadelphia.

Stunkard, A.J. and Brownell, K.D. (1980). Worksite treatment for obesity. *American Journal of Psychiatry*, **137**, 252–253.

Stunkard, A.J. and Kaplan, D. (1977). Eating in public places; a review of reports of the direct observation of eating behavior. *International Journal of Obesity*, **1**, 89–101.

Stunkard, A.J. and Rush, J. (1978). Dieting and depression re-examined: A critical review of untoward responses during weight reduction for obesity. *Annals of Internal Medicine*, **81**, 526–533.

Thompson, J.K., Jarvie, G.J., Lahey, B. and Cureton, K. (1982). Exercise and obesity: Etiology, physiology, and intervention. *Psychological Bulletin*, **91**, 55–79.

Van Itallie, T.B. and Vanderweele, D. (1981). The phenomenon of satiety. In P. Bjorntorp, M. Cairella and A.N. Howard (Eds), *Recent Advances in Obesity Research*, vol. 3, John Libbey, London.

Wadden, T.A., Stunkard, A.J. and Brownell, K.D. (1983). Very low calories diets: Their efficacy, safety, and future. *Annals of Internal Medicine*, **99**, 675–684.

Wadden, T.A., Stunkard, A.J., Brownell, K.D. and Day, S.C. (1984). Treatment of obesity by behavior therapy and very low calorie diet: A pilot investigation. *Journal of Consulting and Clinical Psychology*, **52**, 692–694.

Wilson, G.T. and Brownell, K.D. (1980). Behavior therapy for obesity: An evaluation of treatment outcome. *Advances in Behaviour Research and Therapy*, **3**, 49–86.

Wing, R. and Jeffery, R. (1979a). Outpatient treatments of obesity; a comparison of methodology and clinical results. *International Journal of Obesity*, **3**, 261–279.

Wing, R. and Jeffery, R. (1979b). The effects of two behavioral techniques and social context on food consumption. *Addictive Behaviors*, **4**, 71–74.

Wing, R., Epstein, L.H., Marcus, M. and Shapira, B. (1981). Strong monetary contingencies for weight loss during treatment and maintenance. *Behavior Therapy*, **12**, 702–710.

Wing, R.R., Epstein, L.H., Marcus, M.D. and Kupfer, D.J. (1984). Mood changes in behavioral weight loss programs. *Journal of Psychosomatic Research*, **28**, 189–196.

Wooley, S. (1972). Psychological versus cognitive factors in short-term food regulation in the obese and non-obese. *Psychosomatic Medicine*, **34**, 62–68.

Wooley, O. and Wooley, S. (1981). Relationship of salivation in humans to deprivation, inhibition, and the encephalisation of hunger. *Appetite*, **2**, 331–350.

Wooley, O., Wooley, S. and Turner, K. (1975). The effects of rate of consumption on appetite in the obese and non-obese. In A. Howard (Ed.), *Recent Advances in Obesity Research*, vol. 1, Newman Publishing, London.

Wysocki, T., Hall, G., Iwata, B. and Riordan, M. (1979). Behavioral management of exercise: contracting for aerobic points. *Journal of Applied Behavioral Analysis*, **12**, 55–64.

CHAPTER 4

Hunger, Satiety and Feeding Behaviour in Early Infancy

Peter Wright
University of Edinburgh,
Department of Psychology, 7 George Square, Edinburgh EH8 9JZ, UK

The overriding concern of all mothers, once they have established that their newborn baby is alive and well, is the establishment of a successful feeding relationship. Indeed a major justification in the UK for the routine practice of hospitalizing mothers and infants for periods up to 1 week following birth is to monitor and advise mothers in the care and feeding requirements of their babies. The mother will then embark on a prolonged period, especially if her baby is a firstborn, in which she will attempt to make sense of her baby's behaviour. From the birth itself, inevitably accompanied by the first vital statistic of birthweight, her concern, and the enquiries of family and friends, will be directed towards the growth and feeding progress of her infant. Most parents would probably confirm that they very quickly develop a distinct view of their children in terms of their expressed interest or disinterest in food. Indeed it is this very focus on the feeding situation which has made it such a fertile area of investigation for psychologists whose interests are rarely feeding *per se* but more the social interaction between mother and baby which the feed permits. It is also very easy when confronted with the vigour and intensity with which babies can suckle to understand the psychoanalytic emphasis on feeding experience being related to personality development.

What makes feeding in early infancy unique, compared with the preschool child and beyond, is that in one sense the opportunity for her child to eat is completely under the mother's control. Probably the most important influence on the availabiltiy with which milk is offered to the infant is the choice of feeding technique, that is, from the breast or from the bottle. But whichever method the mother adopts, it will be accompanied by advice — from health visitors, physicians, and from the manufacturers of the formula — as to appropriate schedules of feeding, and in the case of bottle-fed infants, appropriate amounts to be offered. This professional advice may or may not be compatible with the mother's perception of her infant's needs. The personality of the mother is an important influence — how anxious she is made by feeding demands; the parity of the baby is known to be important in determining how much milk is taken at a single feed — more experienced mothers provide larger feeds. There may be considerable differences in the ability and perhaps, more importantly, the avidity with which the infant signals its need for food. Conversely, the interpretation the mother makes of this behaviour and how far her beliefs and knowledge of the immediate feeding history alter her reading of such 'hunger signals' from the baby may vary considerably. In the UK with the decline of breastfeeding and the move away from the extended family, many mothers face the prospect of coping with their newborn infant with dismay, and requests for help with feeding problems and difficulties are commonplace for health visitors and GPs (MacKeith and Wood, 1977). In the last two decades there has been a shift in opinion from the era of the local baby shows where the biggest and most bouncy baby held the day to an outright rejection of the fat smiling baby as an ideal by nurses and midwives. This change in attitude is largely the result of surveys of infant feeding practice which have made both mothers and health professionals very aware of the risks of overfeeding in early infancy.

CRITICAL PERIODS IN EARLY INFANCY AND THE FAT CELL HYPOTHESIS

Considerable interest and concern about the feeding practices of infants arose from two distinct areas of research. The most obvious were a number of epidemiological studies in the early 1970s, many in the UK, which suggested that the problems of obesity and rapid weight gain were reaching alarming proportions. Possibly the most influential study was that of Shukla, Forsyth, Anderson and Marwah (1972), which surveyed 300 infants up to 1 year of age and born of normal pregnancies. Anthropometric measurement of the infants and their dietary histories were obtained from their mothers when attending local welfare clinics. A total of 16.7% were found to be clinically obese and a further 27.7% to be overweight. The authors identified the low incidence of breastfeeding and the fact that 80% of the sample has been introduced to solids before the age of 8 weeks as major contributory factors to the excessive weight gains. There was close agreement on the proportion of infants with weight problems to an earlier report (Eid, 1970) which had also claimed that rapidity of weight gain in infancy was a better guide to the risk of being overweight at the age of 6 or 8 years than was the weight of the parents.

There are clearly very different problems in assessing obesity in a fast growing infant compared to adults, and several methods are in widespread use. These include straightforward measures of weight; indices based on weight and height and using centile charts; skinfold thicknesses measured at various sites. Weight is commonly related to some standard for height and age, and in the UK with reference to the charts of Tanner, Whitehouse and Takiushi (1966), an individual whose weight exceeds 120% of ideal weight is classified as obese. There are inherent difficulties in all these methods, particularly with infants (Taitz, 1983). Percentage overweight measures excess weight above certain norms, but in infants weight deviations alone are very poor indicators of fatness because they do not take growth into account. Therefore percentile estimations do not necessarily assess degrees of fatness since they do not take somatotype into account. Weight gain can represent different compositions of total mass; for example, one infant may be fat and another muscular but not overfat. In addition the type of tissue gained varies not only between individuals but also according to age. During the first 6–9 months of life, the normal increases in fat are more marked than at any other period in childhood until puberty (see Kirtland and Gurr, 1979). To deal with these problems a bewildering variety of indices relating height and weight have been devised to correct for the effect of height and body mass. Taitz (1983) states that plotting of height and weight on centile charts adequately demonstrates discrepancies between these parameters and invariably means the infant is obese. Skinfold thickness measurements certainly overcome the problem of height, but they are notoriously difficult to obtain with any degree of reliability. Compared with adults, where about 30% of all fat is subcutaneous, in the newborn this is as high as 70–80% Lohman, 1981), and skinfolds are therefore a very good measure of total bodyfat. The problems of measurement are to do with the compressibility of the fat (more so in girls than in boys); the inter-observer variation; and whether to use single site or multiple site measurements (see Taitz, 1983 for discussion). It is thus no surprise to find that there is no generally accepted definition of obesity, and that because of the ease of measurement, the most widely used measures are those relating weight to height.

At about the same time that the reports of overfeeding in early infancy appeared in the medical literature, a second field of research, this time with animals, suggested that overfeeding and subsequent obesity could be achieved by two mechanisms, either a filling up to a maximum size of existing fat cells, or an increase in the number of these cells and their eventual filling.

Concern for the future of the obese infant was heightened when a functional explanation of why babies might become and remain fat as adults was provided by Hirsch and Knittle. Their experiments with rats indicated that a period of overfeeding restricted to the first few weeks of life led to permanent obesity and was accompanied by an increase in the number of fat cells in the adipose tissue. Subsequent restriction of food intake decreased the amount of bodyfat by reducing the fat contained in the adipose tissue cells, but did not change the number of these cells. They subsequently reported that human adults whose obesity appeared to begin in infancy had a higher fat cell number than a group of equally fat adults whose obesity was of more recent origin (Hirsch and Knittle, 1970). It was also reported (Grinker, Hirsch and Levin, 1973) that the psychological problems encountered in attempting to lose weight were more pronounced in those with early onset obesity. Hirsch and Knittle postulated that, since early nutritional experience determines both the size and number of fat cells in rats, a similar nutritional experience in man may be of prime importance in producing the hyperplasia and hypertrophy of adipose tissue in obese adults. Furthermore, the lack of success in treating obese adults might be due to the inability to affect any permanent changes in adipose tissue cellularity in adult life. They suggested that 'treatment of the disorder may, therefore, lie in its prevention early in life through the control of factors that influence adipose cell division and enlargment.' The final link in the story came with the report of Brook (1972) that children whose obesity had developed during the first year of life also showed an increase in both the number and size of their fat cells. Brook suggested that in human infants there was probably a sensitive period from approximately 30 weeks gestation to the age of 9 months during which the basic complement of fat cells is determined.

This 'fat cell hypothesis' was a most attractive idea, but the essential causal sequence that, during a critical period, overfeeding will lead to an increase in fat cell numbers and that this predisposes the adult to obesity now looks almost certainly incorrect. Firstly the idea of increase in cell number arising only in a critical period appears to be untrue, even in the rat. As Kirtland and Gurr (1979) have noted, the original experiments produced overfeeding in rat pups by altering the litter size, and then compared the fat cell counts in rats from either small or large litters. The assumption that a higher cell count in the small litters is due to overfeeding was unwarranted; it could equally have been the case that there was a reduction of cell numbers in rats suckled in large litters. In one experiment, which attempts to mimic a possible explanation for obesity in human infants, Czajka-Narins and Hirsch (1974) gave rat pups supplementary feeds in the preweaning period. Despite the experimental animals being heavier than the control group, there was no difference in fat cell numbers. This suggests that differing ways of producing overnutrition (decreased litter size vs supplementary feeds) can have very different effects on adipose cellularity. There are also considerable differences in fat cell size and number in such experiments according to the choice of experimental animal, and the choice of fat cell site may also bias the result with some sites showing increases and others little change in number.

Considerable argument has also centred on whether increase in cell number is due to a true genesis of new cells, or merely that pre-adipocytes, which because they are empty of fat and cannot therefore be detected by histological techniques, then fill up with fat and become visible. Enzyme methods can give a direct indication of cell division, and seem to suggest much more restricted periods of active cell synthesis in the rat epididymal pad than do the counting methods. Moreover, Kirtland and Gurr (1979) argue that rats which have only

2% of their bodyweight as fat at birth are not a very useful animal model and that in guinea pigs, with a similar percentage of fat at birth to man, the fat cell synthesis is largely complete. Adipocytes may even oscillate between being full and empty and thereby give the impression, with histological examination, of having fewer cells at times of leaness (Hager, 1977). The fat cell hypothesis is therefore largely rejected, and with this the notion of a critical period for physiological development of obesity. But this does not remove the possibility of infancy as a critical period in the psychological sense of learning appropriate feeding habits, or for the development of appropriate interactive behaviours between mother and infant which are related to somatic growth (Pollitt, Gilmore and Valcarcel, 1978).

EXPLANATIONS OF INFANT OBESITY

The explanations offered to account for obesity include inherited and environmental causes, and among the latter, diet and psychological factors have been given the most emphasis. Of those investigators who have found no correlation between obesity and birthweight, Taitz (1971) blamed the mother for overfeeding her baby with excess starch and sugary preparations. He suggested that overfeeding occurs for two reasons: the image that a healthy baby is a bonny baby, and the low resistance of mothers to crying infants with the feed as a ready solution. Oates (1973) certainly found that mothers were not making up their feeds according to the recommended proportions. He found that 22% of mothers attending a welfare clinic were preparing a milk formula more concentrated than the recommended strength. With the unmodified cow's milk formula available at that time, such milk feeds would contain excessive quantities of salts, and result in the baby becoming thirsty and therefore waking and crying. If the mother interprets the crying as hunger she would give the baby more milk, and hence set up a vicious circle and provide the baby with an excessive calorie intake. In many cases the high concentration of the feed may be deliberate, in that the mother may be concerned to ensure her infant sleeps as long as possible to counter expected delays in the clinic, and believe that the concentrated formula will help the baby sleep longer! Taitz (1971) therefore implies in his explanation that (1) excess in caloric intake always leads to obesity, (2) mother determines the intake, and the infant does not refuse excess food, (3) the infant manifests the same behaviour patterns whether hungry or thirsty, and (4) that the infant does not distinguish a milk feed from a need for water.

In both studies, the authors suggest the combination of early introduction of solids and overconcentration of the infant formula as the likely cause of rapid weight gain. The two studies identified bottle-fed infants as being at greater risk than breastfed babies, but did not demonstrate that it was the babies who received the overconcentrated formula who showed the rapid weight gain. Subsequently de Swiet, Fayers, and Cooper (1977) found no evidence that mixing of overstrength feeds, or the early introduction of solids leads to obesity. There is certainly good evidence (Taitz, 1977) that, as a result of an intensive campaign in the Sheffield region to stress the dangers of overconcentration of formula, the problem of rapid weight gain has receded, and there are corresponding increases in the proportion of mothers still breastfeeding at 6 weeks postnatally. The particular problem of excessive salt intake is now largely eliminated with the widespread introduction of modified cow's milk formula from the middle 1970s onwards.

Wolff (1955) had previously argued that, although obesity itself is acquired, it may be caused by an abnormal appetite-regulatory mechanism resulting from an inherited condition. This assumes that normally infants can regulate their intake and that they do this through the expression of appetite; infants know when they are hungry and when they are full. As an alternative hereditary explanation Heald and Hollander (1965) suggested that obesity in childhood occurs as a consequence of some inborn error in metabolism. They predicted that the expression of early-onset obesity should be manifest early in life, a prediction supported by the general finding that childhood obesity correlates with a rapid weight gain during the first year of life.

So Taitz only considers the nature of caloric intake as a cause, Wolff sees excessive intake occurring as a consequence of a faulty biological mechanism, and Heald and Hollander that excessive lipogenesis results from an inborn error in metabolism not necessarily related to quantity of caloric intake. An environmental cause is given by Taitz, while genetic or constitutional factors are suggested by Wolff and Heald and Hollander.

Of those investigators who report a correlation of obesity with birthweight and a familial predisposition of obesity, Shukla, Forsyth, Anderson, and Marwah (1972) suggest that there is probably some constitutional influence which may be related to factors operating during the antenatal period. They do not favour a pessimistically deterministic view since they propose that any constitutional influence merely places the child 'at risk', but if the child is not overfed then it will not develop obesity. This implies that some metabolic or biological factor is involved and that it can be modified during the antenatal period. However, these factors in themselves will not cause obesity so long as caloric intake is controlled. It would seem that the explanation is consistent either with a position that would suggest the regulating mechanism can be overcome externally, or in some metabolic process that has become disturbed during foetal life.

BREAST VERSUS BOTTLE-FEEDING

The issue of whether breastfeeding prevents rapid weight gain during infancy and protects against obesity in later childhood still remains unresolved. Poskitt and Cole (1977) re-examined about two-thirds of the original Shukla sample when these children were aged between 4 and 6 years, and found that, although in infancy 43% were overweight, now only 18% were still overweight using the Shukla index. They concluded that, if rapid weight gain in infancy is due to overfeeding, overfeeding in infancy seems to have little influence on childhood body size. Fomon (1980) compared children from birth to 8 years of age, and found that although by 120 days formula-fed infants were larger and heavier, by 8 years of age, fatness was unrelated to type of feeding during infancy. Most of these studies have used a cohort design, in which a group of newborn infants is followed to determine their later nutritional status. Such studies are susceptible, by virtue of the relatively low incidence of the outcome and small sample sizes, to Type II error, i.e. they may fail to detect a positive effect that really exists.

In one recent study Kramer (1981) attempted to correct such methodological flaws, and concluded that breastfeeding *does* provide a significant protective effect against later obesity. Two teenage populations were examined, 508 attending a local clinic and 389 of similar age at a local high school. The classification of obesity was based on both relative weight and skinfold criteria, and the use of the clinic population ensured the inclusion of a number of cases of obesity sufficient to avoid a significant Type II error. The decision to focus on an adolescent group was made because of the greater association between adolescent and adult obesity, but obviously meant that the early feeding experience was more remote for the mothers and therefore potentially unreliable data. To check on this, vigorous attempts were made to contact the physicians and clinics caring for each child in early infancy. This proved possible in about one-third of the sample and in all cases the mothers' account was found to be correct. A stepwise discriminant function analysis revealed that breastfeeding discriminated significantly between obese and non-obese subjects even after controlling for race, birth order, and socioeconomic status. Kramer argues that these results are the strongest evidence accumulated that breastfeeding may be a potent manoeuvre for preventing obesity, and that the protective effect is long lasting.

The legacy of the alarm generated by the increased incidence of rapid weight gain reported in the early 1970s is generally to support the notion that breastfeeding should be encouraged, not only because of its immunological benefits to the child, but because it will minimize weight problems. But it may be impossible ever to resolve conclusively the issue either way. In particular, retrospective studies are always problematical because of the problem of reliability of the information, and also because of the very different meanings attached by authors to the label 'breastfeeding'.

It is not sufficient to place an infant into the breastfeeding category on the basis of one week breastfeeding in hospital or even one month of breastfeeding. The experience of the long term breastfed infant is very different from the infant that is switched to bottle-feeding after a few days or weeks. Even in Kramer's (1981) study a child had to receive no more than one bottle-feed per day to qualify as 'being breastfed'; more stringent criteria may be necessary to detect relationships. Conversely it can be argued that, given the ever present advice to breastfeed, the mother who determines to bottle-feed from birth may be exceptional and not representative of bottle-feeders as a group (Wright, 1981).

The chief characteristic of breastfeeding which, it is felt, aids in minimizing obesity is the absence of any direct knowledge of intake on the part of the mother. The implicit assumption is that you cannot overfeed the breastfed baby because there is a limit to the milk available and the baby is able to refuse the breast when satiated. Deprived of any direct feedback on amount consumed, the mother who is breastfeeding might be expected to be more attentive or more observant of expressive behaviours indicating hunger and satiety in her baby. Dwyer and Mayer (1973) point out that it is precisely this very knowledge of intake which is available to the bottle-feeding mother and which, if she is anxious, may evoke her concern and lead her to overfeed. When mothers are asked in the first week following birth what criteria they use to decide when the baby has taken enough milk, Crow (1977) found that whereas 42% of breastfeeding mothers recognized falling asleep as a satiety cue, only 6% of bottle-feeding mothers cited such behaviour. A total of 32% of bottle-feeding mothers stopped feeding only when the baby spat out the teat compared with 4% of breastfeeders. There seem to be several stages in the process of terminating a feed: the baby's suckling decreases, it becomes drowsy, and if the mother continues to feed, the baby will refuse to open its mouth and will spit out the teat if forced into the mouth. If these stages are indicative of satiety, then some bottle-feeding mothers are more likely to ignore early satiety signals and be in a greater danger of overfeeding their infants.

Henning (1980) argues that it is milk availability rather than infant appetite which determines how much is ingested in breastfed infants, but Drewett and Wooldridge (1981) have shown in 5 to 7-day-old human infants that intake is curtailed by the baby and not limited by the mother's milk supply. However, as I shall discuss later on in this chapter, this will also depend on the time of day and on the age of the infant. There are very few direct comparisons of intake in breast- and bottle-fed infants, but again in the first week of life, whereas the daily milk intake will increase for the breastfed infant as lactation is established, the bottle-fed infant receives a fairly constant daily intake. If one of the aims of artificial feeding is to mimic as closely as possible the natural feeding pattern, then in a biological sense, bottle-fed babies already consumed too much milk on the third day of life (Crow and Wright, 1976).

Edelman and Maller (1982) favour breastfeeding, not only because of nutritional advantages, but because of the increased frequency of feeding, and the greater opportunity of the caretaker to learn and correctly interpret the infant's expression of hunger and satiety. They cite the increased feeding frequency of the breastfed infant and the increased lipogenesis from a few large meals compared with more small meals when caloric intake remains the same. Crow and Wright (1976) have found that babies whose mothers practise true demand feeding, i.e. will feed their infants very frequently, reflecting their own intuition rather than following guidelines offered by nursing staff, have a very similar 24-hour intake to those fed more conventionally. But if the babies are bottle-fed, then the increased feeding frequency significantly increases 24-hour intake compared with those fed every 4 hours. The second suggestion of Edelman and Maller, that breastfeeding provides greater learning opportunities for the mother, is equally true for the baby (Wright, Fawcett and Crow, 1980; Wright, 1981, 1982). The next section will review the evidence for potential signals in the behaviour of newborn infants and then explore the role of learning in early feeding experience.

EXPRESSIVE RESPONSES AS SIGNALS FOR HUNGER AND SATIETY

There are a number of reports on neonates which attempt to detail the behaviours associated with feeding, quiescent periods, and other levels of activity. An enduring theme is the interest in individual differences of temperament and how this will influence the mother in her caretaking behaviour. It would clearly be important to know whether the highly expressive and vocal infant succeeds in getting more attention during feeding, and whether this is associated with greater milk intake or more rapid weight gain. Unfortunately, most of the studies concentrate on the captive audience of neonates hospitalized in the first week of life, and there are very few observational studies of older infants in relation to behaviours observed before and after feeding. As one of the issues is not only whether there are behaviours clearly associated with hunger and satiety, but whether these are recognized as such and acted on by mothers, the concentration on the immediate postnatal period when the mothers are not in their own homes, may not be the most appropriate time for observation.

The expressive behaviours shown to be significantly related to feeding are those behaviours collectively known as oral behaviour and crying. Oral behaviours include mouthing, finger-sucking, and hand-face contacting, hand-mouth contacting, and sucking during the feed. Korner, Chuck and Dontchos (1968) studied 2 to 3-day-old infants and were particularly interested in which oral behaviours were associated with variations in levels of arousal and which were related to the time since the last feed. They scored the behaviour of the infants in one half-hour period before a feed and then in three half-hour periods following the feed. The two indexes of high arousal were the frequency of shifts in states of arousal and the duration of crying in the four half-hour periods. All four oral behaviours scored (mouthing, hand-face contacts, hand-mouth contacts, finger-sucking) were highly related to frequency in shifts in states of arousal but only finger-sucking, hand-face, and hand-mouth contacting were significantly related to crying duration. They suggested that while sucking, tongueing and all other forms of mouthing were associated with high arousal, mouthing did not partake in the more active or expressive aspects of high arousal which characterizes crying. Mouthing was the only oral measure significantly related to the frequency and duration of alert inactivity and the authors felt this further supported their impression that while mouthing was associated with high arousal, it lacks the more agitated attributes of the other oral behaviours. Mouthing was the only oral behaviour for which the decrease in occurrence following a meal and the increase before a meal was significant. This suggests that sucking, tongueing and all the other forms of mouthing are highly hunger related, whereas finger-sucking, hand-face, and hand-mouth contacting are not. Subsequently Korner (1973) has reported sex differences in the frequency of hand-to-mouth contacts. Girls are significantly more likely to engage in hand-to-mouth approach behaviour where the mouth is dominant. The definition for this behaviour was that the mouth approached the hand and scoring only occurred if the mouth opened when the hand was at a distance of at least 1½ inches (3¾ cm) or more from the face, the infant's head straining forward in an effort to meet the hand. When this particular behaviour was isolated and examined in terms of 'time since last feed' in both sexes it was found to be related to hunger, Korner's work does indicate that the neonate can use oral behaviours to signal hunger, but oral means specifically mouth activities if it can be assumed that a mouth-dominated hand approach is mouth-directed. The implications for understanding the nature of hunger in infants is that whereas mouthing is a reliable predictor, the other oral be- haviours indicate the individual's tendency to be generally active and vocal rather than the level of hunger. A noisy, active, expressive infant need not be more hungry than his less demonstrative fellow being. Richards and Bernal (1972) confirm this in their study of sleep patterns. It suggests that needs can be expressed either passively or actively depending upon the individual's tem- perament.

Kessen, Williams and Williams (1961) examined mouthing and hand-mouth contacts of infants aged between 1½ hours and 5 days, recording the be- haviours once each day, for a 5-min interval. They found stable and significant individual differences in the frequency of hand-mouth contacts and reliable individual differences in the duration of mouthing. No regular increase or decrease in occurrence appeared over the 5-day period for either behaviour, so experience did not appear to influence their occurrence. More importantly for the question of their possible signal value, there appeared to be no correlation between feeding experience and the duration of frequency of the behaviours. In a later study using slightly different procedures, Hendry and Kessen (1964) showed that the oral responses are relatively low only in a second period of observation (i.e. about 30 minutes after the feed) and found that mouthing was affected by age, being more frequent at 23 hours than at 71 hours of age. Although Kessen, Williams and Williams (1961) did not specifically analyse the relationship of these oral behaviours to hunger, they suggested that hunger is only reduced some time after the feed when physiological processes are complete.

It is therefore possible that the immediate satiating effects normally associ- ated with the end of a meal may be learned and that oral behaviours in the early neonatal period are ambiguous signals because of this time between the physiological states of deprivation and satiety which psychological processes later come to bridge. Overall, the occurrence of hand to mouth contacting is more reliable as a measure of individual differences and this must be borne in mind when claiming it has possible value as a hunger signal.

From these investigations it would seem that the very young infant can affect the nature of his interaction with his mother regarding feeding. A mother who has a very expressive infant is more likely to be in danger of considering that she has a very hungry baby. Whether it is also true that the satiating effect of the feed is learned during the first five days needs further elaboration, but it could follow, if this is a factor, that the expressive infant then determines his own destiny by stimulating his mother during the very early days to provide larger feeds than he really needs. However, if this is a factor in the development of obesity in infancy, it would also need to be shown that the rapid weight gainers are more expressive and take more food than the normal weight babies during these early days.

The spontaneous oral behaviour of sucking can be seen in both nutritive and non-nutritive forms (Wolff, 1968). The components that have been studied are sucking rate, time spent sucking, and sucking pressure. Bridger (1962) has shown that whereas the amount of sucking is related to hunger, infants will also suck as much when satiated but highly aroused; sucking rate is therefore a measure of arousal level rather than just hunger (see also Jensen, 1932; Kaye, 1967). The method of feeding also affects sucking performance; Dubignon and Campbell (1968) found that breastfed babies sucked less often over all the experimental trials they studied than did bottle-fed babies, and this was true for both nutritive and non-nutritive sucking. Bernal and Richards (1970) reported the precise opposite in their comparison of breast and bottle-fed infants' non-nutritive sucking. Their Ss were slightly older (8 days vs 3 or 4 days) and were a mixture of first and second borns compared with the second borns of the Dubignon and Campbell study. Because feeding in the human infant is an interactive process between mother and baby, this will obviously limit the usefulness of many experimental studies of what influences infant sucking patterns. Despite attempts to improve the proportion of mothers who choose to breastfeed, it remains very much tied to socioeconomic level in both the UK and the USA, with a higher proportion of social class 1 and 2 choosing to breastfeed than social classes 3, 4, and 5. This can often mean that even from birth there may be inherent differences between the infants which are related not so much to the technique of feeding, but more to maternal differences in personality, to perinatal complications, and to child care practices.

The important consideration for infant feeding behaviour, however, is how well these measures of sucking correlate with actual consumption. Dubignon and Campbell found no relationship between measures taken of non-nutritive sucking and the amount of milk taken, in contrast to the findings of Bell, Weller and Waldrop (1971). Infants of 3 to 4 days old were studied by both investigators. Bell and colleagues found that non-nutritive sucks correlated positively when the amount consumed in 14 feedings was divided by birthweight. The feedings/weight ratio was calculated to provide an index of appetitive behaviour freed from the influence of bodyweight. It proved to be highly consistent despite variations between tests used during bottle feeding and individuals feeding the baby. However, as Bell points out, the correlations are not strong enough to indicate an identity of function. But if the non-nutritive sucking rates include the initial onset rate, which Dubignon and Campbell did not record, then it is probably as good an index as when the sucking on an apparatus occasionally delivers a nutrient.

Where, however, the measures of sucking seem to be more clearly separated is in their response to satiation and fatigue. Dubignon and Campbell (1969) found that whereas nutritive sucking time and count were influenced by satiation and fatigue, the nutritive sucking rate was not. Babies who have had enough or who are tired will reduce the amount of time they spend sucking, but will not alter the rate at which they suck. It has been shown (Levin and Kaye, 1964) that non-nutritive sucking rates show little relaxation over periods as long as 10–15 minutes and recover after a 1-minute rest period. Dubignon and Campbell therefore suggest that the decrease in time spent sucking and sucking count can be attributed to both satiation and fatigure, as recovery following stops for winding occurred throughout the feed, not just at the beginning. Satiation, however, is independently expressed by refusal of the bottle. It looks therefore that when satiation is assessed, sucking is not the most reliable index because it becomes confused with fatigue and the level of arousal. In direct observation of breastfeeds at 1 week, 1 month, and 2 months a reliable and significant change in the rate of sucking is observed at all ages, with babies sucking faster towards the end of the feed at each breast (Wright, Fawcett and Crow, 1980). These changes probably reflect a decrease in milk supply and together with changes in the state of the baby (becoming more drowsy) bring about a switch to a non-nutritive sucking pattern and hence a faster rate. The expressive behaviour showing an apparently uncontaminated functional relationship with feeding is refusal of the nipple (see Wright and Crow, 1982 for further discussion on this point).

Another reason for suggesting that measures of the pattern of sucking have multiple behavioural correlates is because sucking also has a quieting effect on the infant. Kessen, Lentzendorff and Stoutenberger (1967) have found that apparently babies will quiet when they suck non-nutritively very soon after birth. The pacifier rightly takes it name from this suckling–quieting response. It appears to take advantage of a congenitally organized phenomenon. Any study concerned with the satiation properties of food using sucking pattern would need to take into account this general effect on activity level.

It thus appears that the presence of spontaneous sucking behaviour in the 3 to 4-day-old infant is as much an expression of his general level of arousal as of this hunger. Mothers successful in arousing their infants will stimulate sucking whether or not the infant is really hungry. However, where the infant can have his say is in whether he is prepared to accept the bottle or breast in the first place. Either he can refuse to open his mouth or it may be that he will reject the food. Again it seems that interaction during feeding is a two-way process, and experience on the part of the caretaker is a major determinant of how much milk will be consumed at a single bottlefeed (Thoman, 1975).

The other behaviour that has been closely linked with feeding is crying. Its duration, quality, and intensity have been studied in some detail. Wolff (1969), in a study of 18 bottle-fed babies observed in the natural home setting, found that crying can occur because the infant is hungry, because it appears that the taste or texture of food is unpleasant or because the feed was interrupted. However, not all these responses were shown to occur in the very young infant. Four-day-old babies cry more when hungry than satiated and do not stop until they are fed; not surprisingly, holding will not quieten them. But it is not until the second week that the infant will respond consistently to an interruption of feeding. The most vocal protest occurs when the feed is removed after the infant has taken only an ounce. The frequency of crying continues to increase during the third and fourth week. By the fifth week, however, unless the infant is very hungry, no protest occurs following an interruption. This decline in protest is paralleled by a growing alertness and interest in things going on around during the meal. Both Bernal and Richards (1970) and Wright and Crow (1982) reported increased frequency of crying at one week in breastfed compared with bottle-fed infants, but the latter found that crying episodes remained high during bottle-feeds and tended to disappear for breastfeeds between 2 and 6 months. They interpreted the crying as a frustration response to mother-initiated interruptions in the course of feeds. Such breaks in the feeds were initiated by mothers on 80% or more occasions for the bottle-fed infants, compared with 25% for the breastfed infants (Wright, Fawcett and Crow, 1980).

From Wolff's (1969) observations therefore infants certainly seem able to express their hunger vocally, as any mother knows. But the developmental events suggest that their ability to control what goes on during the feed only appears after about the first 2 weeks of life. It starts with a demand to continue eating if disturbed and then involves the actual choice of food. With the introduction of mixed feeding Wolff found that infants show an obvious preference for puréed fruits in contrast to a dislike of cereal. The cereal produced grimacing and subsequent crying when it was tasted, whereas puréed fruits left the infants quietly expectant. Since cereal is subsequently accepted with enjoyment, then the fussing and crying that occur when it is first given either indicate an initial strong dislike, which is then rapidly modified by experience, or simply are responses to novelty. In view of the reported trend of starting cereals between 3 and 4 weeks (Oates, 1973), possibly following the addition of rusks or cereals to the bottle as early as 2 days, it seems unlikely that infants are born to dislike cereal. Perhaps the developmental achievement is the ability to recognize and respond to change rather than reflexively reject or accept the nutrient. It is possible that the taste of the feed given within the first 2 weeks could set the pattern for subsequent months if an inexperienced mother only gave the baby what it 'liked'. As long as she kept to milk and started weaning late the baby would be slow to accept the change and may be old enough to regulate the amount. But if she started very young then the information in the 'change' of taste or texture would not be available for pick up (Gibson, 1966).

In summary, it would seem that hunger has recognizable expressive components in both oral behaviour and crying which are present by 2–3 days of age. Frequency of mouthing is a reliable predictor, but other oral behaviours say more about the individual's tendency to be generally active and vocal than to indicate the level of hunger. There is, however, disagreement as to how these responses change with age, and no information on their relationship to measures of growth. Decreases in sucking are not good measures of satiation because they are easily confused with level of arousal and with fatigue, and refusal of the nipple/teat is a more unambiguous signal. There is one study in which mothers of both normal weight and obese 6-month-olds were retrospectively questioned about their attention to such expressive signals (Dubois, Hill and Beaton, 1979). They found no evidence that maternal disregard for infant hunger and satiety signals or maternal use of food in response to signals of non-nutritional needs had contributed to the obesity of the group of 47 infants. But as there was no attempt to confirm the mother's answers with direct observation of the feeds, it is likely that a strong halo effect will have operated in both groups and may have obscured any real differences between them.

Because of the need to understand more about how mothers interpret such behaviours in older infants, we are currently investigating how aware mothers are of variation in their infant's degree of hunger across the day. We have decided to study infants from 2 months of age and who are being entirely breastfed as we have good evidence (see p.97) that at this age there is a reliable change in the amount of milk taken at different times of the day. The mothers are first asked a series of questions to find out whether they feel there is a time in the day when their infant is most or least hungry, and they are also asked whether they feel their own milk supply varies across the day. We then ask them to test-weigh the infants before and after each breastfeed and to keep a record of how much milk is consumed at each feed. The preliminary results are intriguing as they suggest that mothers are more likely to report being aware of variation in hunger if they have a girl (see Table 1(a)) and this may therefore support Korner's earlier observation (Korner, 1973) that certain hunger-related behaviours (hand to mouth contacts) were more frequent in girls a few days after birth. We have deliberately not attempted to define what is meant by hunger, but if the mother gives a positive answer, we ask what behaviours lead her to make that decision. After each feed, and before the mother reweighs the infant, we ask her to rate how hungry she felt the infant was during the feed, using a visual analogue scale. We can then compare for each mother-infant pair, the agreement between the prior statements and the actual measures of milk and rated hunger (see Table 1(b)). If her statements are based on amount of milk taken at a breastfeed then less than one-third of the mothers were apparently correct in their judgements, and this is equally true when we use the

Table 1(a). Prior awareness of hunger variation. Mothers' initial statements about whether they felt their baby was more or less hungry at particular times in a 24-hour period.

	Yes	No
Male	13	7
Female	16	0

$\chi^2 = 4.89$, $p<0.05$.
$n = 36$.

Table 1(b). Correctness of mother's statements about hunger. For the intake measure, the mothers' stated beliefs (see Table 1(a)) are compared with actual measures of intake at different times over a 4-day period, and scored as either correct or not. The same procedure is repeated but this time using the ratings of hunger obtained immediately after a feed. If, for example, a mother stated that her baby was more hungry in the middle of the day, and the ratings she had given for feeds at this time of day were consistently high, this would be judged as correct.

Yes	No
10	26 (intake)
11	25 (ratings)

$n = 36$.

ratings as a measure of hunger. So it looks as if what a mother believes to be the case about hunger in her 2-month-old infant is not very often correct.

LEARNING EXPERIENCES IN BREAST- AND BOTTLE-FED INFANTS

There is increasing discussion of the potential importance that learning plays in the control of the amount eaten at a meal in adult humans (Booth, 1977; Stunkard, 1975) and of anticipatory strategies in the initiation of feeding. The techniques of bottle- and breastfeeding result in very different experiences for the babies and there has been considerable interest in how this may affect their social development (Ainsworth and Bell, 1969; Richards and Bernal, 1972; Dunn, 1975). If learning plays any role in experiencing hunger and satiety as was suggested by Hebb (1949), we might also expect to find differences in food regulation between breast- and bottle-fed babies later in development. Whereas it is clear that the capacity to express hunger is innate, as judged by the appearance of rooting reflexes (Peiper, 1961; Korner, Chuck and Dontchos, 1968), there is some evidence of learning of satiety in very early infancy (see p. 86). Regulation is fundamentally the ability to adjust intake according to requirements. Can babies regulate their intake from birth and is there any difference between bottle- and breastfed infants?

The often quoted reason for the major advantage of breastfeeding in minimizing the risk of obesity is that control of milk intake rests with the baby rather than the mother and, of course, the mother remains in ignorance as to the exact amount consumed. In contrast, the bottle-feeding mother always has immediate feedback as to how much milk has been taken from the bottle. But what if she was unaware as to the true nature of the formula, and had no explicit instructions concerning the appropriate amount to offer at a feed? Would bottle-feeding mothers under these circumstances allow their infants to determine intake and would the babies alter their intake to compensate for changes in the strength of the feed? This issue has been investigated by Fomon and colleagues in a series of experiments in which they studied small groups of bottle-fed infants from 8 to 111 days of age and provided their mothers with a plentiful supply of made-up formula in prepackaged bottles, but of varying strength. In a study with male infants (Fomon, Filer, Thomas, Rogers and Proksch, 1969) they compared intakes when formula of either 67 or 133 kcal/100 ml were provided; and later with female infants (Fomon, Filer, Thomas, Anderson and Nelson, 1975) they compared the intakes of either 54 or 100 kcal/100 ml strength formula. Mothers were told to feed the infant until satisfied and no information on the calorie concentration of the formula was provided. A supply of formula sufficient for 3–4 days was weighed and delivered to the families, and then collected at the end of 24 hours and reweighed to calculate the volume consumed. When they examined intakes and growth over the first 6 weeks of life, the volume of formula taken per day was always significantly greater when fed the less concentrated formula (see Tables 2 (a) and 2 (b)). It was also the case that infants fed the more concentrated formula consumed significantly more calories per day, and in consequence gained weight more rapidly. However, over the second age period from 6–16 weeks there appeared to be some compensation. Although the volume consumed continued to be significantly greater on the weaker formula, the calorie intakes were no longer significantly different for infants receiving differing strengths, and this was also the case when adjusted for the weight of the infant.

Unfortunately, the authors do not provide full details of the advice offered to mothers at the start of the study, as it would be surprising if the mothers had not expressed some anxiety about the quantities consumed. They do comment that a ceiling effect may have operated for the infants offered the more dilute formula in the first 6 weeks, and that the mothers' perceptions about what is the correct intake could influence consumption.

As Fomon (1980) puts it, 'the babies found out what was going wrong, and they fixed it'. These studies have been widely taken to imply that the infant has the capacity to regulate after about 6 weeks of age (Taitz, 1977; Pollitt, Consolazio, and Goodkin, 1981; and Birch, present volume). If the regulation revealed in the experiments of Fomon and colleagues is by the infant rather

Table 2(a).   Comparison of milk intake with concentration of formula in male infants (after Fomon, Filer, Thomas, Rogers and Proksch, 1969)

	8–41 days		42–112 days	
	dilute	concentrated	dilute	concentrated
Volume of intake (ml per day)	675 (84)	* 445 (61)	851 (92)	* 526 (149)
Intake of calories kcals/day	451 (56)	* 593 (84)	572 (63)	680 (201)

* Significant difference at $p<0.05$.
Dilute = 67 kcal/100 ml, concentrated = 133 kcal/100 ml.
The figure in brackets is the standard deviation.

Table 2(b).   Comparison of milk intake with concentration of formula in female infants (after Fomon, Filer, Thomas, Anderson and Nelson, 1975)

	8–41 days		42–112 days	
	dilute	concentrated	dilute	concentrated
Volume of intake (ml/day)	735 (111)	* 540 (126)	939 (127)	* 582 (86)
Intake of calories kcal/day	393 (59)	* 538 (90)	521 (74)	572 (81)

* Significant difference at $p<0.05$.
Dilute = 54 kcal/100 ml, concentrated = 100 kcal/100 ml.
The figure in brackets is the standard deviation.

than the mother, we still do not have any information on how this has been achieved. Are the infants adjusting intake by varying the number of meals each day, or by the amount taken at each meal? And, if the latter, are the mothers perhaps attending to cues earlier in the satiety sequence because of their lack of guidance on appropriate intake each day, rather than feeding to the point of final satiety indicated by spitting out the teat?

Wright, Fawcett and Crow (1980) asked 132 bottle-feeding mothers and 58 breastfeeding mothers in the postnatal wards to keep a 3-day diary of their baby's milk intake in the first week of life. The original intention of the study was to examine the relationship between meal size and meal intervals in a large population of infants ostensibly feeding 'on demand'. We found, however, that because of the various constraints which operate in maternity wards, and despite the prevailing regime being one of demand-feeding, nurses advise

Table 3.   Relationship between meal size and long meal intervals. Long intervals: 5.2–8.5 hours, mean = 6.4 hours.

	Preceding meal larger	Following meal larger	No difference
Breast	7	17	5
Bottle	11	7	29

df 2, χ^2 = 18.73, $p<0.001$.

mothers to approximate roughly to a 4-hour rule, i.e. if the baby sleeps longer than 4 hours he should be woken to feed, and if he cries before this time, he is not necessarily hungry. We argued that the regulatory process might be more apparent in mothers who are not following informal rules, and allow their babies, for whatever reason, to go without food for a relatively long period of time, i.e. a natural deprivation experiment. Accordingly, we selected from our data all instances of relatively long intervals between meals (76 long intervals, mean = 6.4 hours range 5.2–8.5). If the meals at either side of the interval differed by less than 15g, they were classified as not different, if greater than 15g, we classified whether the preceding or the following meal was larger. The results are shown in Table 3. Clearly around long intervals of time, the treatment of bottle- and breastfed babies is very different. Bottle-fed babies tend to receive the same amount of food either side of such long intervals, whereas breastfed babies tend to take larger meals *following* the long interval. When the same analysis is carried out around short inter-meal intervals (Table 4) the treatment of bottle- and breastfed babies is seen to be identical, and the preceding meal tends to be larger for both techniques of feeding.

The reasons for this difference may be that in the case of breastfed babies, more milk is present after long intervals and therefore baby takes more, or baby is hungrier and therefore baby sucks more. In the case of short intervals, all mothers may be operating under informal rules, or baby is not hungry. The question of availability of milk in the breastfed infant makes interpretation of

Table 4.   Relationship between meal size and short meal intervals. Short intervals: 0.5–3.0 hours, mean = 2.3 hours.

	Preceding meal larger	Following meal larger	No difference
Breast	17	8	13
Bottle	23	10	14

df 2, χ^2 = 0.25, NS.

these results problematic. There is some evidence to indicate that in the first week, breastfed infants are more hungry than those bottle-fed (Bernal and Richards, 1970). Over these first few days the 24 hour intake of bottle-fed infants is constant, whereas the breastfed infant experiences a gradual increase in intake from day to day (Crow and Wright, 1976; Crow, 1977). The present results suggest that the breastfed baby under mild deprivation conditions experiences a matching between long intervals without food and a large meal following that interval, an experience which is much rarer for the bottle-fed baby.

What is especially interesting about these data is that they do not agree with one of the commonest beliefs that mothers have about the relationship between amount consumed and sleeping, i.e. the more the baby takes the longer will the baby sleep. It would seem that: the longer you have slept, then the more milk will be consumed if breastfed. There is no evidence that this belief is true for bottle-fed infants either.

Composition of Milk as a Satiety Cue

In the case of breastfed infants, Hall (1975) has suggested that the changes in composition of human milk during the feed are associated with the development of an appetite-control mechanism, and in particular that changes in the composition and presumably the taste of the milk might act as a satiety cue for the breastfed infant. She suggests that the baby ends feeding from the first breast with milk rich in fat and protein and is able to start on the second breast with thin watery milk, satisfying hunger and thirst. Such compositional cues are clearly unavailable to the bottle-fed infant and Hall speculates that this might well account for the increased risk of obesity and rapid weight gain in bottle-fed babies. This is an appealing hypothesis and it has been widely quoted in the medical literature (Taitz, 1983: Pollitt, Consolazio and Goodkin 1981; Edelman and Maller, 1982), but the identity of a potential signal is more easily recognized than the demonstration that it is available for use (Gould, 1975). Smart (1978) has pointed out that the rate of milk flow may be the important variable determining the rate of the suckling response. This alternative to Hall's notion of the high-fat milk taste inhibiting feeding and the low-fat milk disinhibiting the feeding response would simply be that the baby stops feeding from the first breast when his sucking is insufficiently rewarded and resumes sucking on the second side because the ready milk flow sustains his feeding responses.

Two experiments purport to explicitly test the Hall hypothesis. The first (Chan, Pollit and Leibel, 1979) gave 5-week-old babies a series of five daily tests in which they were presented with two different formulas at a single feed in a counterbalanced design. The three formulas used were a control commercially available formula, and two isocaloric experimental formulas — one high lipid, the other high carbohydrate. The aim of the experiment was to not only test the Hall hypothesis that increase in lipid density during the course of a feed will depress intake, but whether elevated nutrient content *per se* is sufficient to depress intake, i.e. whether high carbohydrate will have the same effect as high lipid density. There was no support for the Hall hypothesis, or for the alternative that change in caloric density acts as a meal-ending signal. The authors' rationale for choice of 5-week-old infants was because of the reported greater weight of bottle-fed compared to breastfed infants of this age (citing Taitz, 1971). 'It was therefore assumed that 5-week-old infants should be responsive to nutrient cues if the lipid change hypothesis is valid.'

The second study by Wooldrige, Baum and Drewett (1980) used a similar method, comparing intake from two bottles presented at a single feed and separated by a brief winding session. This time the feeds were of human breast milk previously fractionated into a high- or low-fat composition, the difference in lipid content being of the same order as that reported to occur in the duration of a normal breastfeed. The infants (this time 4–9 days of age) were provided with one of three conditions: either high/low (simulating the changes at the breast); or one of two control conditions, low/low (control for no change in lipid density); and high/low (to control for change *per se*). None produced any significant differences in intake, and in addition analysis of the sucking patterns showed that change in milk composition did not influence sucking. The crucial factor which influences sucking pattern seems to be the flow rate of the milk, and the authors point out that changing from a high to very low flow rate in bottle-fed infants mimics the changes in sucking pattern seen at the beginning and end of breastfeeds. Since at the breast the high flow rate coincides with the low-fat milk and the low flow rate to the high-fat content, it looks as if flow rate is the more important signal.

Despite the lack of support from either of the above experiments, it could be argued that the Hall hypothesis might still be correct. Both experiments are confounded by the use of subjects who are already bottle-feeding, and for whom there has been no previous experience of variation in the nature of the milk. As the composition cue is likely to be learned and such learning presumably will take some time, the Wooldridge study may not provide sufficient experience for the infants to respond to the change in composition of the milk. It might also be argued that the ability to respond to such cues would not be present in such young infants. This objection cannot apply to the older infants of the Chan, Pollitt and Leibel (1979) study and, because they were given five trials, there was adequate opportunity for learning to occur. However, the age is still problematical in view of Fomon's experiments, which would suggest that infants aged 6 weeks or above might be more appropriate. Although Wooldridge and Drewett did not observe any variation in the sucking pattern with the high versus low-fat milk, Johnson and Salisbury (1975) had previously reported differences in the temporal pattern of sucking in babies aged 1–10 days according to whether they were bottle-fed cow's milk or expressed human milk. They considered that it was the nature of the milk being sucked and not the use of the feeding bottle which modifies the sucking bahaviour.

Faulty Learning Experiences

With a unique biological and psychoanalytic viewpoint, Bruch (1974) argues persuasively from the basis of individual case studies of patients with severe eating disorders, that whether the problem is of anorexia or overeating, the common factor is an inability to identify hunger correctly or to distinguish it from other states of bodily need or emotional arousal. She maintains that the recognition of the experience of hunger is not innate, but something that contains important elements of learning. 'It gradually became apparent that something had gone wrong in the experimental and interpersonal processes surrounding the satisfaction of nutritional and other bodily needs of these later patients, and that incorrect and confusing early experiences had interfered with their ability to recognize hunger and satiation, and to differentiate "hunger", the urge to eat, from other signals of discomfort that have nothing to do with "food deprivation", and from emotional tension states aroused by the greatest variety of conflicts and problems.' (p. 45)

This distinction between the physiological state of nutritional depletion and the psychological processes involved in perceptual and conceptual awareness of the nutritional state is one which has been commented on by other clinicians (Stunkard and Koch, 1964) and which was used as a basic tenet of Schacter's influential external/internal dichotomy (Schachter, 1971). Bruch argues that this ability depends on 'correct' learning experiences being provided by the mother, such as offers of food in response to signals indicating hunger. As pointed out earlier (Wright and Crow, 1982), her theory assumes that right from birth there are clear signals indicating biological needs and recognized as such by the mother. Bruch therefore interprets the reason for rapid weight gain in the Ainsworth and Bell (1969) study as being due to faulty learning experiences provided by the mother. Ainsworth and Bell were primarily interested in attachment behaviour and viewed the feeding interaction as important because the baby's experience in influencing his mother's behaviour through his own activity would, they argue, influence the nature of his attachment to her. The degree to which the mothers allowed their babies to regulate their own feeding schedule, to be an active participant during the feed, and whether the mothers responded appropriately to various signals were used as measures of sensitivity. Successful development, i.e. normal weight and ability to sustain brief separation from the mother at 1 year were found to relate to the sensitivity with which the mother responded to the baby's signals. In six out of 26 mother–infant pairs, the baby became overweight because it was said that their mothers overfed them (no measures were reported). This overfeeding was ascribed to an overconcern either to gratify the child, and in consequence treating too broad a spectrum of cries as signals indicating hunger; or to make the children sleep for a long time. They did not consider the possibility of the baby's signals being inappropriate.

An alternative explanation to Bruch's comes from the results of a study by a group of workers who were also interested in the consequences of mother–

infant interaction during feeding, but who focus on more specific aspects of behaviour (Sander, 1962; Burns, Sander, Stechler and Julia, 1972). They recorded whether feeding was on a fixed nursery schedule or by demand, and then observed to what degree an infant became distressed during a feed when the caretaker was changed. Distress was measured by the amount of grimacing, turning away from the nipple, or spitting out, fussing and crying. This ability to show distress was considered as providing evidence of the abiity of an infant to respond to change in the caretaking environment and it was suggested that this ability points to an establishment of expectactions of key features in the environment. It was found that infants who were fed on demand in the first 10 days of life, and thus received individualized and special care, were capable of responding in this way. Burns, Sander, Stechler and Julia (1972) consider that an important component of regulation in feeding may, therefore, be this capacity of the infant to signal that something is wrong. For the development of successful feeding what may matter is that the infant is allowed to use this signalling system, otherwise it will be 'turned off' or will drop out, and so lead to a failure to thrive. Not responding to infants rather than, as Bruch proposed, reinforcing incorrect behaviour is what really matters. Brody (1956) found that satisfactory weight gain was correlated with mothers who were 'sensitive, consistent and attentive . . . conspicuous for their ability to accommodate to the needs of their infants'. This also suggests that in feeding the important thing is to allow the *infants* to respond appropriately.

A second series of case studies is again supportive of the importance of satisfactory learning experiences associated with feeding. Dowling (1977) describes seven infants with an oesophageal atreria, making normal functioning of the oesophagous impossible. (The oesophagous is not fully formed, and sometimes the section which is necessary is so long that surgery to correct the fault cannot be performed until the infant is considerably older.) The infants need to receive all their food requirements through a tube directly into the stomach from birth until surgery to correct the fault can be performed between 6 months and 3 years of age.

Because of the risk of pneumonia from aspirated saliva, an opening is made from the upper part of the oesophagus to the side of the neck. In those infants who were fed via the gastric tube alone, and who were given little or no opportunity to suck or receive food through the mouth, there was noticeably deficient motor development. Dowling considers that the physical act of oral feeding provides an important stimulus and organizing force for a variety of developmental accomplishments. For the babies where oral feeding was permitted as an accompaniment to the essential gastric feeding, development was essentially normal. But for all parents, there was a tendency to disregard hunger and satiation as signals for beginning and ending a feed as illustrated in the example of a case report below. While confusion due to the unusual mode of feeding contributed to parental failure to seek and utilize obvious signals, unwillingness to give up control to the infant appeared to be a far more important factor.

Case report 'Mrs B. did not regularly recognize Matt's hunger cry at 8 weeks, although other cries, including a gas-pain cry and fussy cry, relieved by holding, were recognized as specific signals. This failure to recognize a hunger cry did not seriously distress Mrs B. as she knew she could provide adequate nourishment through her control of food intake. Furthermore, she judged the amount of milk to be given by the tension of the infant's abdomen rather than by his experience of satiation. By 10 weeks, encouraged by Matt's excellent weight gain, Mrs B. became more comfortable in stopping gastronomy feeding when Matt stopped the oral feeding. By 12 weeks, Matt had a distinct hunger cry which initiated feedings. He now effectively controlled both onset and termination of feeding. In this instance, autonomy of hunger-satiation perceptions in controlling onset and termination of feeding was firmly established only after repeated opportunities to experience the association of onset of feeding with hunger cry, and termination of feeding with satiation.' (p. 233)

Developmental psychologists have stressed the importance of opportunities for the infant to initiate and control actions in cognitive and perceptual development (Bower, 1977) and the cases described by Dowling may be extreme instances of the importance of the feeding context for such learning to occur.

Size of Feeds Across the Day

As the baby ages, the pattern of feeds will change such that there is established a distinction between night and day, with the gradual elimination of feeds in the early hours of the morning. At least, this is the pattern preferred in the UK, and must in part be culturally determined, as the assumption that infant feeding involves the same behaviour throughout the world whenever indigenous societies retain the traditional practice of breastfeeding is unlikely to be correct. We have been particularly interested in the developmental changes which occur in the size of milk feeds over a 24-hour period, because a comparison between the two techniques of feeding should aid our understanding of the role of learning. To collect this kind of information requires the active collaboration of the mother, as it is hardly feasible to become a round the clock guest, in the home of the baby during the period of observation! Accordingly we ask mothers, recruited shortly after the birth of their baby to keep a careful record of their baby's feeding behaviour over a 3-day period. They record the size of each milk feed, its duration, and the time when the feed was initiated. If breastfeeding, then the infant is weighed immediately before and after each feed in order to obtain a measure of the milk consumed. Because feeding is such a cause of concern to mothers, they are strongly motivated to take part in these studies, and we have always found their records to be carefully kept and reliable.

At the ages of 1 week and 1 month, in both breast- and bottle-fed infants, the sizes of meals throughout the day are very similar. For the purposes of analysis we have grouped feeds and plotted the mean meal size at the traditional feeding

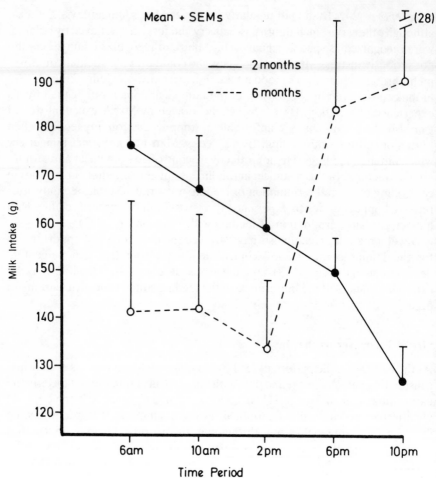

Figure 1.   Diurnal variation in meal size in breastfed infants at two months and six months of age

times of 2, 6, 10 am and 2, 6, 10 pm, such that a feed initiated between midnight and 4 am contributes to the mean meal size plotted at 2 am, and so on throughout the 24-hour period. For the breastfed infants (see Figure 1) at 2 months of age a pronounced diurnal variation in meal size has developed with the largest meal appearing at 6 am and then subsequent meals decrease in size throughout the day. At this age many of the infants in our sample were regularly sleeping through the early morning hours, and this first feed of the day may therefore follow a long night fast of between 6 and 8 hours. This same response, as we have noted earlier, is already more apparent in breastfed infants than in bottle-fed infants in response to a long inter-meal interval in anarchic mothers in the first week of life. We can characterize the 2-month-old infant as essentially responding to a deficit signal and compensating for the long night interval without milk. By 6 months the pattern of responding seems to be reversed, with the same infants now taking their largest breastfeed at the end of the day and before the long night fast, and this we have characterized as anticipatory responding.

These infants may not be very representative, as relatively few breastfeeding babies are still feeding at the breast when aged 6 months, and of course all have now been introduced to solids, which was not the case for the younger age group. We have no indication from this study that these changes represent a conscious strategy on the part of the mother, and the mothers did not have any awareness of this change in pattern of meal size. Indeed informal observation at the time suggested that mothers are not very good at judging how much milk has been taken at a particular feed. Could this be a response on the part of the infant to either changes in availability of milk or to variation in the composition of the milk across the day? Although diurnal variation in milk composition is well known for the young baby (Gunther and Stainer, 1949) there is no indication that this varies with age of baby or stage of lactation (Prentice, Prentice and Whitehead, 1981). The availability of milk is more problematical, as many mothers comment that their breasts feel more engorged and heavy first thing in the morning, and this might well change with the usual decreased frequency of suckling that occurs with age of infant.

However, we do have some evidence that these explanations in terms of composition or amount of milk available are unlikely to be correct. For one infant (see Figure 2) I was able to obtain continuous records of meal size from birth until about 6 months of age. Although this infant (SMW) was breastfed initially, his feeding was switched to bottle milk because of medical complications with the mother. However, unlike most bottle-fed infants, he was fed from the bottle in a true demand breastfeeding style, i.e. a bottle was always offered when the mother judged him to be hungry, and he was always offered a second bottle if the contents of the first were consumed. So for SMW there were no restrictions on availability of milk and no variation in composition of milk across the day, yet he nevertheless developed the same pattern of feeds when older as seen in Figure 1 for the entirely breastfed group of infants. Therefore the changes in the diurnal pattern of meal size are likely to have been determined by the infant, and could be a result of learning to cope with the period of night starvation by anticipating the absence of food, and taking a large meal ahead of the long fast period.

A final example of how the technique of feeding may have both an immediate and long-term influence on behaviour is the interaction of feeding and sleeping. For reasons which remain unclear, bottle-fed infants begin to sleep through the night and establish a more socially acceptable pattern of feeding at an earlier age than breastfed infants. This has been found both in a longitudinal direct observation study (Wright, 1981) and using a retrospective interview (Wright, Macleod and Cooper, 1983). Previous investigators have suggested a relationship with birthweight, that is, the heavier infants drop night feeds earlier (Campbell, 1958) and a possible relationship with the earlier introduction

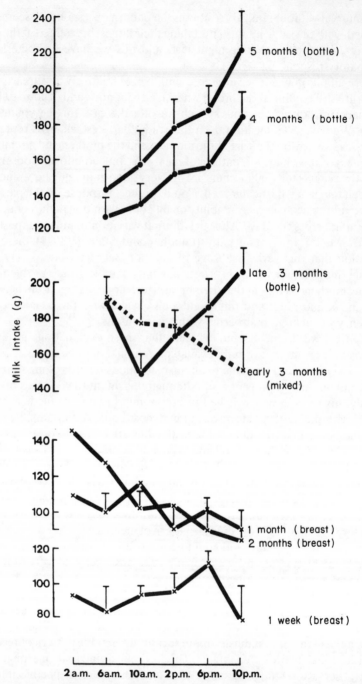

Figure 2. Diurnal variation in meal size in an individual infant from birth to six months of age

of solids. Beal (1969) reported that earlier solid food introduction did not influence night feeding, and neither was there any relationship with birth-weight, sex or weight increment over the first 3 months. This is obviously information which breastfeeding mothers should be aware of. For the mother, sleeping through the night is a definite milestone in development. However, the breastfeeding mother is likely to see the children of her bottle-feeding friends reaching this milestone before her own child. Health care professionals then should be able to assure the breastfeeding mother that the difference which she sees between the behaviour of her child and that of the bottle-fed child is perfectly normal.

The present finding is especially significant for the advice on introduction of solids which is offered to mothers. Generally physicians and health profes-sionals advise delaying the introduction of solid food until the infant is at least 3–4 months of age. Despite this advice, bottle-feeding mothers consistently introduce solid feeds earlier than do breastfeeding mothers (Martin, 1978). As most bottle-fed infants will have developed a pattern of sleeping through the night by at least the age of 3 months, disruption of this pattern by resuming night waking will be viewed by the mother with dismay and interpreted, rightly or wrongly, as the infant needing food other than milk. It is therefore hardly surprising that bottle-feeding mothers disregard the advice offered in the face of a far more persuasive argument, namely the changed behaviour of their infant. Because such a pattern of consistent sleeping is not so likely to be present in the breastfed infant at this age, the advice to delay the introduction of solids is entirely compatible with the infant's behaviour.

The long-term effects are that we found a clear association of continued problems in night waking occurring at the time of interview with method of feeding in early infancy (Wright, McLeod and Cooper, 1983). Out of 76 mothers who had breastfed and were interviewed when their children were aged between 2 and 4 years of age, about 25% reported persistent waking during unsocial hours of the night. Only one mother out of the 48 who had bottle-fed their infants reported night waking to be a problem at this age. It is tempting to explain the spontaneous night waking on the part of the previously breastfed infants as an indication of continued and more marked internal determination of behaviour, assuming that the night waking is a product of hunger and that this is more likely to be registered and responded to by the breastfeeding mother than the mother who had bottle-fed. But the argument is implausible when applied to a 3-year-old, and it was rarely the case in our sample that the children who were still waking at night were being given anything to eat or drink. Neither did we find any evidence that these night wakers were taking a larger breakfast, or were breakfasting earlier in relation to their bedtime. Our tentative explanation is analogous to that already proposed to account for the earlier introduction of solids by the bottle feeding mothers. In general terms, events which parents deem to be a 'problem' will depend on their past experience of their child's behaviour. If an infant who has previously settled into a pattern of sleeping through the night begins to wake again, then a problem will be perceived (the child is hungry?) and a solution sought in the introduction of solid feeds. If, on the other hand, the child has not settled into a pattern of sleeping through the night, continued disturbed nights will not be a cause of anxiety. Therefore, night waking is more probable in a setting in which mother (and father) are less likely to perceive its occurrence as a problem. On this basis the bottle-feeding mother is more likely to perceive early episodes of night waking as a situation desirous of a solution, and be more ready and able than the breastfeeding mother to apply any necessary negative reinforcement.

The demands placed on the bottle-feeding mother are, by and large, less than those placed on the breastfeeding mother over the initial period of their infant care and feeding. Because of this, the bottle-feeding mother is more likely to view her response to the behaviour of the child in a problem/solution framework, and to attempt (however unconsciously) to control the infant's behaviour and change it to a more acceptable pattern. Early experience of breastfeeding, however, being rather more demanding of physical effort and time on the part of the mother, is likely to promote a more liberal and permissive attitude, with a set of circumstances being tolerated for longer before a 'problem' is identified about which something should be done.

SUMMARY

In this chapter I have described some of the issues which influence the contemporary research into infant feeding behaviour. The earlier theory that there might exist a critical period in early development when the number of fat cells becomes fixed, and which would then predispose the fat infant to become the fat child and ultimately the fat adult appears untrue. Although some restrospective studies suggest that fat adults are often also overweight as children, prospective studies do not indicate that fat babies will inevitably continue to have weight problems in early childhood (Poskitt and Cole, 1977). Despite the uncertainty of the long-term outcome of rapid weight gain in early infancy, it is the case that health professionals remain at pains to minimize its incidence. The widespread belief that breastfeeding *per se* minimizes the risk of excessive weight gain is difficult to prove, largely because of the many confounding variables associated with the decision to breastfeed (social class, prior expectations, etc.), but when attempts have been made to control for these (Kramer, 1981) the evidence supports a protective role for breastfeeding.

A case has been presented for the essential difference between the breast- and bottle-feeding techniques as the establishment of control over the nature and frequency of feeds by the baby rather then the mother. Breastfeeding mothers are more likely to be aware of variation in their babies' hunger as the size of breastfeeds changes across the day in the course of development. These changes in diurnal pattern may represent a gradual movement from the infant responding to a deficit signal and feeding accordingly, to adopting an antici- patory strategy of planning ahead and taking larger meals before the overnight fast characteristic of the older infant. As similar changes can appear in a bottle-fed infant, provided there are no restrictions on the availability of milk, this suggests that they are baby rather than mother-determined, and are not to be understood in terms of a passive response to biochemical differences between breast milk and formula milk.

The interaction established between mother and infant in these first months may therefore produce expectancies on the part of the mother such that she may view her infant with respect to feeding as being possibly either very hungry or fairly indifferent. How far such views extend into later childhood and how far there is continuity between the early feeding experience and that of the older child is not clear. That bottle-feeding leads to earlier loss of night feeds, and apparently to less likelihood of waking at night in the preschool years, suggests that there will be lasting influences of the early feeding period.

REFERENCES

Ainsworth, M.D. and Bell, S.M. (1969). Some contemporary patterns of mother-infant interaction in the feeding situation. In A. Ambrose (Ed.), *Stimulation in Early Infancy*. Academic Press, London, pp. 133–170.

Beal, V.A. (1969). Termination of night feeding in infancy. *Journal of Paediatrics*, 75, 690–692.

Bell, R.G., Weller, G.M. and Waldrop, M.F. (1971). Newborn and preschooler: organisation of behaviour and relations between periods. *Monographs of the Society for Research into Child Development*, 36, (1–2).

Bernal, J. and Richards, M.P.M. (1970). The effects of bottle and breast feeding on infant development. *Journal of Psychosomatic Medicine*, 14, 247–252.

Booth, D. (1977). Satiety and appetite are conditioned reactions. *Psychosomatic Medicine*, 39: 76–81.

Booth, D.A. (ed.) (1978). *Hunger Models*. Academic Press, London.

Bower, T.G.R. (1977). *A Primer of Infant Development*. Freeman, San Francisco.

Bridger, W.H. (1982). Ethological concepts and human development. *Recent Advances in Biological Psychiatry*, 4, 95–107.

Brody, S. (1956). *Patterns of Mothering*. International Universities Press, New York.

Brook, C.G.D. (1972). Evidence for a sensitive period in adipose-cell replication in man. *Lancet*, 2, 624–627.

Bruch, H. (1974). *Eating Disorders, Obesity, Anorexia Nervosa and the Person Within*. Routledge and Kegan Paul, London.

Burns, P., Sander, L.W. Stechler, G. and Julia, H. (1972). Distress in feeding: short term effects of caretaker environment of the first ten days. *Journal of the American Academy of Child Psychiatry*, 11, 427–439.

Campbell, I. (1958). Duration of night feeding in infancy. *Lancet*, 1.

Chan, S., Pollitt, E. and Leibel, R. (1979). Effects of nutrient cues on formula intake in 5-week old infants. *Infant Behaviour and Development*, 2, 210–208.

Crow, R.A. (1977). An ethological study of the development of infant feeding. *Journal of Advanced Nursing*, 2, 99–109.

Crow, R.A. and Wright, P. (1976). The development of feeding behaviour in early infancy. *Nursing Mirror*, 142, 57–59.

Crow, R.A., Fawcett, J.N. and Wright, P. (1980). Maternal behaviour during breast- and bottle-feeding. *Journal of Behavioural Medicine*, 3, 259–277.

Czajka-Narins, D.M. and Hirsch, J. (1974). Supplementary feeding during the pre-weaning period. Effect on carcus composition and adipose tissue cellularity of the rat. *Biology of the Neonate*, **25**, 176–185.

De Swift, M., Fayers, P. and Cooper, L. (1977). Effect of feeding habit on weight in infancy. *Lancet*, **1**, 892–894.

Dowling, S. (1977). Seven infants with osophageal atreria: a developmental study. *Psychoanalytic Study of the Child*, **32**, 215–256.

Drewett, R.F. and Wooldridge, M. (1981). Milk taken by human babies from the first and second breast. *Physiology and Behaviour*, **26**, 327–329.

Dubignon, J. and Campbell, D. (1968). Intraoral stimulation and sucking in the new-born. *Journal of Experimental Child Psychology*, **6**, 154–166.

Dubignon, J. and Campbell, D. (1969). Sucking in the newborn during a feed. *Journal of Experimental Child Psychology*, **7**, 282–298.

Dubois, S., Hill, D.E. and Beaton, G.H. (1979). An examination of factors believed to be associated with infantile obesity. *American Journal of Clinical Nutrition*, **32**, 1997–2004.

Dunn, J. (1975). Consistency and change in styles of mothering. In *Ciba Symposium 33, Parent-Infant Interaction*. Elsevier, Amsterdam, pp. 155–170.

Dwyer, J. and Mayer, J. (1973). Overfeeding and obesity in infants and children. *Bibliography of Nutrition and Diet*, **18**, 123–152.

Edelman, B. and Maller, O. (1982). Facts and fictions about infantile obesity. *International Journal of Obesity*, **6**, 69–81.

Eid, E.F. (1970). Follow-up study of physical growth of children who have excessive weight gain in the first six months. *British Medical Journal*, **2**, 74–76.

Fomon, S.J. (1980). Factors influencing food consumption in the human infant. *International Journal of Obesity*, **4**, 348–350.

Fomon, S.J. Filer, L.J., Thomas, L.N., Rogers, R.R. and Proksch, A.M. (1969). Relationship between formula concentration and rate of growth of normal infants. *Journal of Nutrition*, **98**, 241–245.

Fomon, S.J., Filer, L.J., Thomas, L.N., Anderson, T.A. and Nelson, S.E. (1975). Influence of formula concentration on caloric intake and growth of normal infants. *Acta Paediatrica Scandinavica*, **64**, 172–81.

Gibson, J.J. (1966). *The Senses Considered as Perceptual Systems*, Houghton, Boston.

Gould, J.L. (1975). Honey bee recruitment: The Dance-Language Controversy. *Science*, **189**, 685–693.

Grinker, J., Hirsch, J. and Levin, B,. (1973). The affective response of obese patients to weight reduction: a differentiation based on age at onset on obesity. *Psychosomatic Medicine*, **35**, 57–63.

Gunther, M.. and Stanier, J.E. (1949). Diurnal variations in the fat content of breast milk. *Lancet*, **2**, 235–237.

Hager, A. (1977). Adipose cell size and number in relation to obesity. *Postgraduate Medical Journal*, **53**, 101–107.

Hall, B. (1975). Changing composition of human milk and early development of an appetite control. *Lancet*, **1**, 779–781.

Hebb, D.O. (1949). *Organisation of Behaviour*. McGraw-Hill, New York.

Hendry, L.S., and Kessen, W. (1964). Oral behaviour of newborn infants as a function of age and time since feeding. *Child Development*, **35**, 201–208.

Henning, S.J. (1980). Maternal factors as determinants of food intake during the suckling period. *International Journal of Obesity*, **4**, 329–332.

Hirsch, J. and Knittle, J.L. (1970). Cellularity of obese and non-obese human adipose tissue. *Federation Proceedings*, **29**, 1516–1521.

Jensen, K. (1932). Differential reactions to taste and temperature stimuli in newborn infants. *Psychology Monographs*, **12**, 363–479.

Johnson, P. and Salisbury, D.M. (1975). Breathing and sucking during feeding in the newborn. *Ciba Symposium 33, Parent-Infant Interaction*. Elsevier, Amsterdam, pp. 119–128.

Kaye, H. (1967). Infant sucking behaviour and its modification. *Advances in Child Development and Behavior*, **3**, 2–52.

Kessen, W., Lentzendorff, A. and Stoutenberger, K. (1967). Age, food-deprivation, non-nutritive sucking and movement in the human newborn. *Journal of Comparative Physiology and Psychology*, **63**, 82–86.

Kessen, W., Williams, E.J. and Williams, J.P. (1961). Selection and test of response measures in the study of the human newborn. *Child Development*, **32**, 7–24.

Kirtland, J. and Gurr, M.I. (1979). Adipose tissue cellularity: a review. The relationship between cellularity and obesity. *International Journal of Obesity*, **3**, 15–55.

Knittle, J.L. and Hirsch, J. (1970). Effect of early nutrition on the development of rat epididymeal fat pads: cellularity and metabolism. *Journal of Clinical Investigation*, **47**, 2091–2098.

Korner, A.F. (1973). Sex differences in newborns with special reference to differences in the organisation of oral behaviour. *Journal of Child Psychology and Psychiatry*, **14**, 19–29.

Korner, A.F., Chuck, B. and Dontchos, S. (1968). Organismic determinants of spontaneous oral behaviour in neonates. *Child Development*, **39**, 1145–1157.

Kramer, M.S. (1981). Do breast feeding and delayed introduction of solid foods protect against subsequent obesity? *Journal of Pediatrics*, **98**, 883–887.

Levin, G. and Kaye, J. (1964). Non-nutritive sucking by human neonates. *Child Development*, **35**, 748–758.

Lohmon, T.G. (1981). Skinfolds and body density and their relation to body fatness: a review. *Human Biology*, **53**, 181–225.

Mackeith, R. and Wood, C. (1977). *Infant Feeding and Feeding Difficulties*, 5th edn. Churchill Livingstone, Edinburgh.

Martin, J. (1978). *Infant Feeding 1975*. Office of Population Censuses and Surveys, Social Survey Division SS 1064, HMSO, London.

Oates, R.K. (1973). Infant-feeding practices. *British Medical Journal*, **2**, 762–764.

Peiper, A. (1961). *Cerebral Functions in Infancy and Childhood*. Pitman Medical London.

Pollitt, E., Gilmore, M. and Valcarcel, M. (1978). Early mother-infant interaction and somatic growth. *Early Human Development*, **1**, 325–336.

Pollitt, E., Consolazio, B. and Goodkin, F. (1981). Changes in nutritive sucking during a feed in two-day and thirty-two days old infants. *Early Human Development*, **5**, 201–210.

Poskitt, E.M.E. and Cole, T.J. (1977). Do fat babies stay fat? *British Medical Journal*, **1**, 7–9.

Prentice, A., Prentice, A.M. and Whitehead, R.G. (1981). Breast-milk fat concentrations of rural African women and long-term variations within a community. *British Journal of Nutrition*, **45**, 495–503.

Richards, M.P.M. and Bernal, J. (1972). Mother-infant interaction. In N. Blurton-Jones (Ed.), *Ethological Studies of Child Behaviour*. Cambridge Univeristy Press, Cambridge.

Sander, L.W. (1962). Issues in early mother child interaction. *Journal of the American Acedemy of Child Psychiatry*, **1**, 141–166.

Schachter, S. (1971). Some extraordinary facts about obese humans and rats. *American Psychologist*, **10**, 107–116

Shukla, A., Forsyth, H.A., Anderson, C.M. and Marwah, S.M. (1972). Infantile over-nutrition in the first year of life: A field study in Dudley, Worcestershire. *British Medical Journal*, **4**, 507–515.

Smart, J.L. (1978). Human milk fat and satiety: an appealing idea revisited. *Early Human Development*, **2**, 395–397.

Stunkard, A.J. (1975). Satiety is a conditioned reflex. *Psychosomatic Medicine*, **37**, 383–389.

Stunkard, A.J. and Koch, C. (1964). An interpretation of gastric motility: I. Apparent bias in the reports of hunger by obese persons. *Archives of General Psychiatry*, **11**, 74–82.

Taitz, L.S. (1971). Infantile overnutrition among artificially fed infants. *British Medical Journal*, **1**, 315–316.

Taitz, L.S. (1977). Obesity in pediatric practice: infantile obesity. *Pediatric Clinics of North America*, **24**, 107–115.

Taitz, L.S. (1983). *The Obese Child*. Blackwell Scientific, Oxford.

Taitz, J.M. and Whitehouse, R.H. (1962). Standards for subcutaneous fat in British children. *British Medical Journal*, **1**, 446–450.

Tanner, J.M., Whitehouse, R.H. and Takiushi, M. (1966). Standards from birth to maturity for height, weight, height velocity, weight velocity; British Children, 1963 *Archives of Diseases in Childhood*, **41**, 454–470.

Thoman, E.B. (1975). Development of synchrony in mother-infant interaction in feeding and other situations. *Federation Proceedings*, **34**, 1587–1592.

Wolff, P.H. (1968). The serial organisation of suckling in the young infant. *-aedoatrics*, **42**, 943–956.

Wolff, P.H. (1969). The natural history of crying and other vocalisations in early infancy. In B. Foss (Ed.), *Determinants of Infant Behaviour*, **4**, 81–109.

Wooldridge, M.W., Baum, J.D. and Drewett, R.F. (1980). Does a change in the composition of human milk affect sucking patterns and milk intake? *Lancet*, **2**, 1292–1294.

Wright, P. (1981). Development of feeding behaviour in early infancy: implications for obesity. *Health Bulletin*, **39**, 197–206.

Wright P. and Crow, R.A. (1982). Nutrition and feeding. In P. Stratton (Ed.), *Psychobiology of the Human Newborn*. Wiley, New York. pp. 339–364.

Wright, P., Fawcett, J. and Crow, R.A. (1980). The development of differences in the feeding behaviour of bottle and breast-fed human infants. *Behavioral Processes*, **5**, 1–20.

Wright, P., Macleod, H.A. and Cooper, M.J. (1983). Waking at night: the effect of early feeding experience. *Child: Care, Health and Development*, **9**, 309–319.

CHAPTER 5

The Acquisition of Food Acceptance Patterns in Children

Leann Lipps Birch
Department of Human Development and Family Ecology,
University of Illinois, Urbana, Illinois 61801, USA

Patterns of food acceptance in humans are largely acquired and a great deal of the acquistion process occurs during the early years of life. Children must learn what to eat, when to eat, and, I would argue, how much to eat. This includes the acquisition of affective reactions to foods — conditioned preferences and aversions — as modulators of intake, as well as knowledge about the meanings of food and the purposes of eating. Learning the act of eating, *per se*, is relatively trivial; the appearance of motor movements required for chewing and swallowing solid foods is limited by maturation, but with practice appear in all the normal members of the species. What is of interest is the acquisition of stimulus control of eating.

This stimulus control of eating behaviour is acquired largely as a result of transmission from one generation to the next and among members of a cohort. How does this transmission occur? An analysis of intergenerational transmission has been suggested by Galef (1976) in the context of his elegant research on social transmission of feeding patterns from one generation of rats to the next, and proves useful in viewing the human case as well. First, transmission may occur as a result of endogenously organized genetically preprogrammed propensities for behaviour. Second, similar food acceptance patterns across generations may be the result of similar exposure to and experience with food across generations. These similar exposures are due to social constraints on food experience. These constraints limit what foods children are exposed to, and in what contexts the exposure occurs. Third, transmission of behaviour can result as a consequence of direct social interaction among individuals of a social group. In man, the third form of transmission frequently involves an individual who acts as an agent of socialization in the culture, transmitting cultural rules to the child.

Such a framework for viewing social transmission and the acquisition of food acceptance patterns does not insure uniformity across generations or within a generation, although the factors that contribute to variation across and within generations are different. Lack of uniformity across generations can result from the disruption of the three transmission processes described above and to changes over time in the physical and cultural environment (e.g. the appearance of 'fast foods' on the scene). Lack of uniformity within a generation can result from differences in what is transmitted to different members of the cohort: differences in genetically determined predispositions, differences in the social constraints that limit exposure to and experience with food, and differences in the cultural/social patterns that are transmitted.

This view, in which the acquisition of food acceptance patterns results from three non-independent types of social transmission, will be used to organize this review of the relevant literature. It will become apparent that there are currently large gaps in our knowledge at the descriptive level with respect to what children are acquiring; we have less information regarding the acquisition processes that produce children's food acceptance patterns, although the lack of data will not prevent speculation on the question. Much of the evidence to be presented provides examples of instances of the second and third categories of social transmission: social constraints on experience with food, which provide limits on opportunities for learning; and direct social interaction with others. The interdependence of the three forms of social transmission will be apparent in the review; many of the studies illustrate acquisitions that involve more than one form of social transmission.

GENETICALLY PREPROGRAMMED BEHAVIOURAL PROPENSITIES

There is a great deal of evidence indicating an innate preference in humans for the sweet taste. The human newborn prefers sugar solutions to water (cf. Crook, 1978; Desor, Maller and Turner, 1973), and even to formula (Desor, Maller and Greene, 1977). LeMagnen (1977) has viewed the sweet taste as an unconditioned stimulus for ingestion and Rozin (1982), among others, has pointed to the adaptive value of such a preference because the sweet taste tends to signal a safe, carbohydrate-rich source of calories.

With respect to innate responses to other basic tastes, Steiner (1977), among others, has presented data on infant facial expressions to support the view that the newborn also shows distinct unlearned responses to sour, bitter, and salty tastes as well as to the sweet taste; and that the facial expressions elicited by sour and bitter are adaptive because they include facial and mouth movements that tend to eject such tastants from the mouth.

The infant's innate, unlearned facial expressions that occur in response to tastes can function in combination with reflexive sucking, rooting, and crying in the newborn to form the basis for communication and attachment to the caregiver (Chiva, 1982). Although a discussion of the development of attachment is outside the scope of this contribution, I would like to emphasize the fact that during the first months of life the majority of the infant's alert/awake interactions with the caregiver occur during feeding. It is, therefore, surprising that there have been so few investigations of mother–infant interactions during feeding, either as they affect feeding behaviour or the quality of the attachment relation. Ainsworth and Bell (1969) did investigate infant feeding patterns during the first three months of life. They reported that individual differences in the infant's innate characteristics (such as regularity, rhythmicity, sensory thresholds, reactions to novel stimuli, etc.) influenced the feeding patterns that developed, as did the mother's sensitivity and responsiveness to infant–initiated indications of need. These early mother–infant interactions provide a central context in which the child learns about food and eating.

Results of research on infant perception have made it clear that the infant comes into the world with innate predispositions to attend to some stimuli and ignore others. Newborns are capable of both operant and respondent forms of learning and both forms may be centrally involved in producing change through the second and third forms of social transmission. Due to the lack of research in the area, it will often prove difficult to know whether food acceptance patterns reflect a genetic predisposition or are primarily a result of learning.

The research on intake regulation in infants and young children illustrates this problem. For example, Clara Davis (1928, 1939), conducted a 'natural experiment' with 15 infants of weaning age, 6 to 11 months old, who had no experience with solid foods at the beginning of the experiment. She used subjects of this age because they had no previous experience with food and, she believed, could not yet be influenced by others' preconceptions, biases, and preferences. These infants were then allowed to self-select their diets without adult intervention over a period of from 6 months to several years, and the studies provide valuable descriptive data on intake patterns of infants under these circumstances. In conducting the research Davis (1928) hoped to obtain information on several questions, including: (1) whether infants could, in the absence of adult intervention, choose a diet adequate to maintain health and growth; (2) whether the infant had 'any *instinctive* means of handling either qualitatively or quantitiatively the problem of . . . optimal nutrition . . .'. With respect to her first question, it can be answered by the descriptive data, which included the children's consumption patterns and indices of nutritional status, growth, and health. She reported that the health and nutritional status of the children was outstanding and that they showed no evidence of the feeding problems often reported for this age group. With respect to her second question, she also argues that the data provide evidence for 'the existence of some innate, automatic mechanism . . . that regulates appetite' (Davis, 1939).

However, Davis's data do not clearly support her contention that the results provide evidence for our first form of social transmission. Although her 'natural experiment' effectively ruled out the operation of our third form of social transmission, the second form of transmission, social constraints on food experience leading to similar transactions with the physical environment, cannot be ruled out.

Her description of the children's behaviour during the early phases of the study is consistent with the idea that what is innate is the capacity to learn; that is, to learn about the consequences of eating particular foods through the associative conditioning of food cues to physiological consquences of eating those foods. This form of learning can be conceptualized as fitting within the second form of social transmission, which occurs as a result of similar trans-actions with foods. Even Davis's observations point to the importance of this experience with food. When first presented with the arrays of foods, '. . . there was not the faintest sign of "instinct" . . . they tried not only foods but chewed hopefully on the clean spoon, dishes, the edge of the tray . . . all of the articles on the list . . . were tried by all . . . and most . . . (foods were) tried several times, but within the first few days, they began to reach eagerly for some and to neglect others so that *definite tastes grew under our eyes*. Patterns were shown to develop on the basis of sensory experience, i.e. taste, smell, and doubtless the feeling of comfort and well-being that followed eating.' Davis also discusses what she refers to as the 'trick' of the experiment that allowed the infants to regulate their intake so successfully: the selection of the set of foods to be presented to the infants was made by the adult caretakers. Although Davis interpreted her results as evidence for the existence of an innate regulatory mechanism, the research is more accurately viewed as an illustration of the second form of social transmission in which adults of the group limit the young's experience to only certain foods. The processes brought into play at this point are those discussed in the section on the second form of social transmission.

Other evidence on the question of self-regulation of food intake early in life comes from Fomon's (1974) research on infant feeding patterns. Although he reports that intake is determined in large part by the attitude of the caretaker, his results also demonstrate that the infant plays a very active role in intake regulation. By about 40 days of life, infants adjusted their volume of intake to compensate for differences in the caloric density of formulas; infants fed relatively dilute diets (53 kcal/100 ml) consumed greater volumes of formula, while infants receiving calorically dense formulas (100 kcal/100 ml) consumed smaller quantities. In fact, this adjustment of intake was such that the caloric intake per unit body weight was nearly identical for these two groups to the intake per unit body weight for infants consuming standard formulas (67 kcal/100 ml), providing evidence for the infants' ability to modify their intake in response to differences in caloric density. Fomon also suggests that there is an innate mechanism that makes such intake adjustment possible, although he does not speculate on its form. Again, since these regulatory abilities develop gradually and do not appear to be fully functional before about 40 days after birth, it can be argued that what may be innate is the ability to learn to associate food cues with the consequences of ingesting the nutrient loads paired with those cues, allowing the organism to learn to anticipate those consequences and adjust intake accordingly. Unfortunately, Fomon's between-subjects designs do not provide direct evidence on this point. Again, although we have descriptive data on early food acceptance patterns, the results do not provide evidence regarding the type of social transmission that may be responsible for the behaviour.

Davis (1928, 1939) and Fomon's (1974) research indicates that infants and young children have some capacity to adequately regulate both the quantity and variety of foods ingested. In both cases evidence for self-regulation comes from situations that involved repeated experience with eating foods and hence opportunities for associative conditioning to occur. Therefore, rather than providing clear evidence for relatively fixed, prewired behavioural regulatory mechanisms that might include unlearned taste preferences as modulators of intake, the available data suggest an innate capacity to learn about the consequences of eating particular foods. The infant comes into the world with a set of behavioural reflexes related to feeding (sucking, rooting, crying), with the tendency to attend to some aspects of the environment rather than others, and with the ability to learn certain types of associations. These innate predispositions place constraints on the organisms' experiences with both the physical and social environments, and innate differences in temperament including reactivity to stimuli (Milstein, 1980) will produce individual differences in the effects of social transmission of food acceptance patterns.

SOCIAL CONSTRAINTS ON EXPERIENCE WITH FOOD

For the young child, adult caretakers severely limit experience with food. Middle-class American parents purchase only a very small subset of the foods available in supermarkets, and only some of these foods are seen as appropriate to feed to young children. For example, Jerome (1977) notes that in the USA young children are not typically fed lobster or caviar; coffee is not seen by USA parents as appropriate for children; and Rozin and Schiller (1980) point out that even in cultures where hot, spicy foods play a central role in the diet, such foods are not fed to very young children. Further, a society's rules of cuisine also limit the time of day as well as the time in the lifespan when particular foods are eaten; at least in affluent western cultures certain foods are 'for breakfast' or 'for dinner' (Rozin, 1981; Birch, Billman and Richards, 1984). Culture, as Rozin (1976) points out, accounts for the largest proportion of variance in what individuals eat.

In a manner analogous to the mother rat exposing her pups to food present in a particular location (Galef, 1976), culture, as mediated by parents and caretakers, exposes children to foods limited by the rules of cuisine of the culture. Once we conceptualize the child is being exposed to a limited, socially determined, cuisine-appropriate set of foods, we can ask what happens during that exposure that leads to the acquisition of food acceptance patterns. 'Mere exposure' may lead to the reduction of neophobia, and associative conditioning of food flavour cues to the consequence of eating those foods may occur.

Although conventional wisdom and much of the research on food acceptance patterns in children has tended to view these patterns as resulting from either innate predispositions or from direct social interaction, there is increasing evidence for the central role played by this second form of social transmission in this acquisition process. Some of the evidence for the relative importance of this non-social, direct experience with food comes from research completed in our laboratory.

To determine the extent to which children's food preferences were related to those of their parents, we obtained preference orders on foods from 120 children and their parents (Birch, 1980a). When the rank orders given by the children were correlated with those of their parents, only 10% of the mother-child and 6% of the father-child correlations were significant. When the children's preference orders were correlated with parents of other children attending the same preschool programmes, an equivalent proportion of the correlations was significant overall (8%). Further, when the distribution of correlations for mother–child, father–child, and stranger–child pairs was examined, all three distributions contained a preponderance of low but positive correlations: 68% of the mother–child pair correlations are positive, 60% of the father–child pairs, and 56% of the stranger–child pairs, providing evidence for some commonality of preference across generations. If parental modelling was particularly important relative to other forms of social transmission, we would expect to see stronger relationships between parent–child than between stranger–child pairs. The obtained pattern suggests that social transmission is accomplished in part by limiting exposure to foods by a particular cultural group.

When we began the investigation of factors influencing the development of food preferences in children several years ago, I assumed that intrinsic organoleptic characteristics of foods, as well as their visual characteristics, would be important determinants of preference. Our initial research was designed to check the reliability and validity of preference measures and to reveal the dimensions or attributes of foods that were most salient for young children in determining food acceptability (Birch, 1979a). To investigate this issue, we obtained preference data from 2½ to 5-year-old children on sets of foods. Results of the multidimensional scaling analyses of these data revealed two nearly equally salient dimensions that consistently accounted for a total of 55–60% of the variance in the preference data. One of these dimensions was identified as sweetness, while the second dimension was intepreted as 'familiarity.' Familiarity is not an intrinsic characteristic of a food but a function of the individual's experience with the food. The results were particularly dramatic because the exposure dimension accounted for essentially the same proportion of variance as sweetness, a very powerful determinant of acceptability, which has been discussed as an unconditioned stimulus for ingestion (cf. LeMagnen, 1977).

A dimension that was labelled 'familiarity' or 'degree of exposure' emerged repeatedly in the multidimensional scaling analyses of the preference data obtained in subsequent studies with different foods and different samples of children (Birch, 1979b; 1980a). Beauchamp and Maller (1977) and Rozin (1976) have both discussed the central role played by experience in the formation of food preferences in adults and other animals, and Rozin (1976) cites numerous examples illustrating the salience of the novelty–familiarity dimension and the role of neophobia in determining food selection in other animals. Our findings indicated that experience with food is also a very important determinant of food acceptance patterns in young children.

Other indirect evidence on the role of experience in determining food acceptability in children also comes from the work of Desor, Maller and Greene (1977), who noted age and race differences in preferences for sucrose and salt solutions varying in concentration. Heritability estimates based on studies of twins in the sample provided no support for the hypothesis that preference for sucrose or salt concentration was under genetic control. They speculated that differential experience with sweet and saltiness might be responsible for the observed differences. More recently, Beauchamp and Moran (1982) investigated the relationships between dietary intake of sweets and the effect of intake on the appetite for sweet tastes in human infants in a short-term longitudinal correlational study. They obtained taste preference for simple sucrose solutions from 140 infants at birth and at 6 months of age. At 6 months, mothers provided 7-day diet records and based on these records, children were divided into those who were and were not fed sweetened water. They found a relationship between feeding sweetened water and preference for sweet; infants not fed sweetened water showed a decline in intake of sucrose solutions from birth to six months, while those fed sweetened water maintained their level of consumption. The data suggest that experience with sweetened water maintains the preference for sucrose whereas an absence of experience results in a decline in preference.

We have recently conducted experiments that provide direct evidence on the causal relationship between frequency of exposure and food preferences in 2-year-old children (Birch and Marlin, 1982). In two experiments, children received 20, 15, 10, 5, or 2 (or 0) exposures of five initially novel foods during a 26-day series of familiarization trials in which one pair of foods was presented per day. After the familiarization trails, children were given ten choice trials, comprising all possible pairs of the five foods. As shown in Figure 1, preference is an increasing function of exposure frequency. The data are consistent with the 'mere exposure' hypothesis (Zajonc, 1968), as well as with the literature on the role of neophobia in food selection of animals other than man.

In its basic form, the 'mere exposure' hypothesis makes no statement regarding the underlying mechanism(s) that may be responsible for the

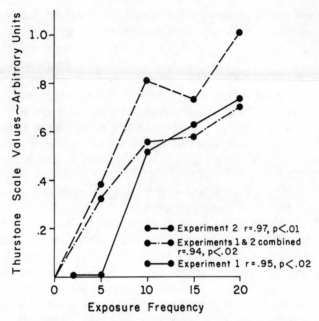

Figure 1.   The relationship between exposure frequency and preference

exposure effect. However, other investigators (cf. Berlyne, 1974; Harrison, 1977; Stang, 1975) have addressed this point. Most of these interpretations, including the response competition, arousal formulations (cf. Berlyne, 1974), and two factor theories incorporating learning and satiation components (Stang, 1975), rely very heavily on posited cognitive processes in accounting for exposure effects on affect. Such cognitively laden formulations seem poorly suited to the data obtained from 2-year olds who do not yet possess the requisite cognitive capacities required by these formulations.

An alternative interpretation of these exposure effects can be found in the literature on food selection in animals other than man (Domjan, 1977; Rozin, 1976), in which the importance of neophobia in food selection is well-documented. According to this interpretation, the organism fears and actively avoids new foods because the ingestion of a novel substance is risky and potentially dangerous. Successive exposures to the new substance that do not result in negative consequences reduce the negative affect, resulting in enhanced liking.

Minimal neophobia for foods would be adaptive during the postweaning period when the child is being introduced to many new foods and the child's acceptance of these foods is essential to growth and health. The relatively high incidence of accidental poisoning among preschool children provides some support for minimal neophobia among this age group. The danger to the child presented by minimal neophobia is countered to some extent by the fact that childrearing practices include the close monitoring of the young child, reducing the possibility that the child will ingest a harmful substance. The declining salience with age of the familiarity dimension underlying the food preferences of 3- and 4-year-old children (Birch, 1979a) suggests that children may be becoming less susceptible to exposure effects as they near the end of the preschool period.

Short-term Changes in Food Acceptability with Consumption

The research discussed above has indicated that over days, weeks, and months changes in children's food acceptance patterns occur with exposure to food. Momentary changes in acceptability occur during the course of eating a food, with indicators of acceptability declining as amount consumed increases or foods eaten showing decreased preference relative to foods not eaten (cf. Rolls, Rolls, Rowe and Sweeney, 1981; Cabanac, 1971), at least for adult subjects. Debate has continued regarding the extent to which such effects are due to changes in internal state or to food specific sensory effects. Such changes in acceptability provide a mechanism for regulating the quantity of food consumed and to the extent that they are food-specific can provide a mechanism for insuring variety in the diet when an array of foods in available to the organism.

Despite a large literature on alliesthesia effects and the effects of variety on intake in adults and rats, there are no data that provide evidence that such short-term changes in preference, either food-specific or non-specific, contribute to intake regulation in children. In fact, in the only studies reported in the literature that used children as subjects, Rolls (Rolls, Rolls and Rowe, 1982) reports negative results. However, Rolls' data from a similar study with adult subjects in which only flavour or colour alone was varied in an otherwise constant food medium also failed to produce the variety effect; such a manipulation does not result in increased intake.

There are many open questions regarding self-regulation of intake in children (e.g.: Do children show patterns of responsivenes to sensory and post-ingestive cues that are similar to those shown by adults? If so, are these patterns influenced by learning and experience with food and eating?). We have essentially no information on the contributions made by innate predispositions and learning and experience to the development of intake regulation during the early years of life.

It was argued in the previous section that the data of Davis (1928, 1939) and Fomon (1974), which the authors interpreted as evidence for innate mechanisms, can also be interpreted as evidence for the role of learning in intake regulation. We have recently begun a series of experiments designed to look at children's ability to regulate their intake in response to preloads of different caloric density. These experiments examine children's affective reactions and intake in response to these differing loads. Some of the experiments are designed to provide situations in which there is no opportunity for learning to occur or be manifest in performance. Others are explicitly designed to provide many opportunities for experience and learning to occur. The results will provide initial information on the role of learning in children's regulation of food intake.

In the first study, recently completed, we investigated the extent to which children showed direct satiety effects in the absence of opportunities for learning. We designed the experiments to provide data on the extent to which any changes in children's food acceptance from before to after eating was affected by the caloric density of the food eaten and the extent to which any changes in preference were specific to the foods eaten. Four- and 5-year-old children gave us preferences for a set of six foods (chocolate, vanilla, butterscotch pudding, marshmallows, cheese crackers, and animal crackers) before immediately following, and 20 minutes after consumption of approximately 4 oz by volume of chocolate pudding. Each child was seen for two indentical sessions, which differed only in that in one session the chocolate pudding contained approximately 180 kcal, and in the other 50 kcal.

The preference data obtained from the children in this experiment are presented in Figure 2. The results indicate clear food-specific effects: the only declines in acceptability were for the chocolate pudding; none of the other foods showed a decline. Evidence against children having an unlearned ability to respond to differences in post-ingestive cues generated by the different caloric loads is reflected in the total lack of interaction between caloric load and the time of assessment; the pattern of preference change over time is essentially identical for the high and low caloric load conditions. The fact that acceptability

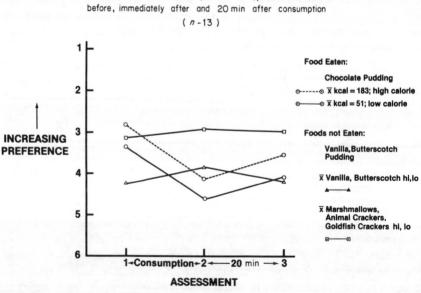

Figure 2.   Preference for food eaten (Hi/Lo calorie), foods not eaten = before immediately after, and 20 min after consumption

is lowest immediately following consumption, showing a slight recovery at 20 minutes, also provides evidence against the children's sensitivity to post-ingestional cues. In the absence of any opportunities for learning about the physiological consequences of eating these foods, preschoolers are not responsive to such differences in caloric loads.

The results of the initial experiment are promising for it has allowed us to test procedures and measures, and has given us a set of data that provides no evidence for unlearned direct responsiveness to the consequences of eating, allowing us to explore the possible contributions made by the associative conditioning to food acceptance patterns in children. The data indicate that responsiveness to whatever satiety signals may be present does not occur for our young subjects in the absence of opportunities for associative conditioning. We have begun a series of experiments to see whether children can learn about the nutrient consequences of eating by associating distinctive food cues with distinctive physiological consequences of consuming those foods, which differ in carbohydrate density (Birch and Deysher, 1985).

In the initial experiment, nine 3- and 4-year olds received a series of six pairs of training snacks, two per week for six weks. Within each pair of snacks, one flavour of pudding (vanilla or chocolate) was paired with a high (155 kcal/4 oz) or low (40 kcal/4 oz) starch load. Following these loads, the children had the opportunity to eat snack foods to satiety and their consumption was recorded. After the completion of the six pairs of training trials, and 'extinction' test pair of trials was given that was identical to the training trial pairs except that both flavours of pudding were of intermediate density (95 kcal/4 oz). Consumption of snack foods following the preloads across the six pairs of training trials and the extinction test trails are presented in Figure 3. During training the children showed direct caloric compensation, eating more following the low calorie load than the high calorie load, and this difference becomes more pronounced over trials. In the extinction test trials, children ate significantly more following the flavour previously paired with low starch than following the high starch load, providing evidence for associative conditioning of flavour cues to the nutrient consequences of eating. If given repeated experience with eating foods, young children can learn to associate the flavour cues in those foods with the consequences of ingestion, at least under these circumstances (Birch and Deysher, 1985).

This finding is of both theoretical and practical significance. It suggests that such a mechanism can function and contribute to the self-regulation of intake in children as young as 3 years, and provides one piece of information that contributes to our understanding of the development of intake regulation in humans. Parents of preschoolers are often very concerned about the quantity and quality of their children's diets and they frequently resort to a variety of control techniques in their attempts to regulate the child's intake (see the subsequent section on direct social interaction for a discussion of the specific effects of these practices). These techniques, including the use of contingencies to increase the child's intake above baseline, 'cleaning the plate', and fixed mealtimes that do not occur in response to child indicated need, create an

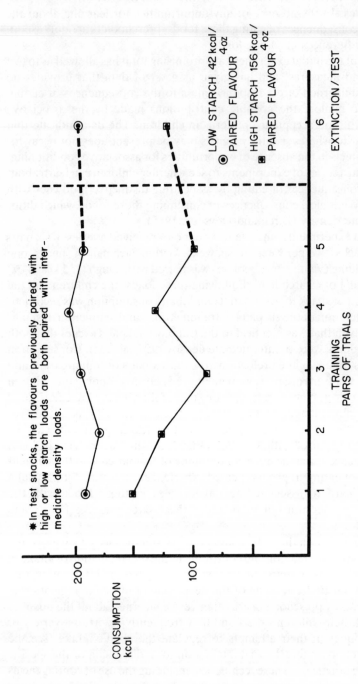

Figure 3. Conditioning of flavour cues to consequences: Consumption during training and extinction test *snacks following high and low starch loads

* In test snacks, the flavours previously paired with high or low starch loads are both paired with inter-mediate density loads.

LOW STARCH 42 kcal/4oz
PAIRED FLAVOUR

HIGH STARCH 156 kcal/4oz
PAIRED FLAVOUR

CONSUMPTION kcal

200

100

1   2   3   4   5   6

TRAINING
PAIRS OF TRIALS

EXTINCTION / TEST

eating environment that is not an optimal one to allow the child to learn about the nutrient consequences of eating foods and regulate consumption in response to any such internal cues that are perceived.

A similar point is made by Bruch (1961) in the context of discussing parent–child interactions and the development of childhood obesity. She reached the conclusion that hunger awareness is not innate but is the outcome of learning experiences early in life. Based on her extensive case history information, she posited that failure of parents to give appropriate responses to child-initiated cues was of primary importance in the development of deficits in the self-regulation of food intake. She states: '. . . the outcome of such learning is the inability to recognize distinctly the need to eat, to recognize hunger and satiation and to differentiate hunger from signals of bodily discomfort which have nothing whatsoever to do with the nutritional state of hunger. . . . When a mother learns to offer food in response to signals indicating needs, the infant will develop the engram of "hunger" as a sensation distinct from other tensions or needs. However, if the mother's reaction is continuously inappropriate, be it neglectful, oversolicitous, inhibiting or indiscriminatingly permissive, the outcome for the child will be perplexing confusion . . . he will not be able to recognize whether he is hungry or . . . suffering from some other discomfort. . . . Such a person needs outer criteria to know when to eat and how much to eat' Bruch, 1961, p. 467).

More recently, in discussing psychological factors contributing to the aetiology of obesity, Rodin (1981) commented, 'It is likely that some features of responsiveness (to external cues) can be learned or modified during early childhood and animal data suggest that neonatal feeding experiences related to the unpredictable availability of food lead to the development of an animal analogue of external responsiveness.' Although there is no direct evidence that indiscriminate presentation of food in response to a variety of needs impedes learning to discriminate various need states, such as hunger, we know that indiscriminate parental responding to children's needs does have negative effects on the development of the child's sense of security, competence, and internal control over the environment (cf. Ainsworth and Bell, 1969).

The best known and most thoroughly studied examples of associative conditioning of food cues to consequences are conditioned aversions, in which the organism eats a food and then suffers nausea and/or vomiting after eating. In these conditioned aversions the organism learns to associate food cues with the negative physiological consequences that follow ingestion and the food's acceptability declines (cf. Garcia, Hankins and Rusiniak, 1974). Much of the research has been generated by investigators primarily interested in learning rather than feeding because of the unusual characteristics of conditioned aversions from a learning theorist's point of view: these aversions appear after a single trial, with long CS-UCS intervals, are very long-lasting, and some particular CSs are much more readily associated with the UCS than others. In one of the few human studies, Garb and Stunkard (1974) reported a great many aversions formed during childhood, and this may be related to the fact that gastrointestinal upsets are relatively common during the early years of life. The lack of human data is due in part to ethical considerations and, in fact, the existing research on conditioned aversions in children has been done with children receiving chemotherapy for cancer. Bernstein and her colleagues (cf. Bernstein, Webster and Bernstein, 1982) have demonstrated the phenomenon in children, providing direct evidence that children do show this form of associative conditioning.

Conditioned aversions occur in children and can account for why one or a few foods are not accepted by a given individual, but they make a relatively minor contribution in accounting for day-to-day food acceptance and intake patterns. It has been suggested by several investigators that associative conditioning plays a more central role in modifying food acceptability and intake patterns by contributing to the regulation of how much as well as which foods are consumed by the individual through the conditioning of preferences, appetite, and satiety (LeMagnen, 1955; 1971; Stunkard, 1975; Booth, 1977). Although it is possible to speculate that such conditioning is particularly crucial during the early years of life when children are being introduced to many new foods and can begin to learn about the consequences of eating those foods in establishing food acceptance patterns, we have very little evidence on this point.

Earlier, the analogy was drawn between the mother rat, who exposes her pups only to food in a particular location, and cultural rules of cuisine that limit the child's exposure and experience with food in a number of ways, including restricting the foods that are purchased, how they are prepared, who eats them, and when they are eaten. In affluent western cultures, we have a set of rules of cuisine that specifies that certain foods are appropriate only at certain mealtimes and occasions. For example, in the USA, people typically do not eat pizza and green salads at breakfast and cold cereal and orange juice at dinner. Children are exposed to these constraints from the time they begin to be exposed to the adult diet of their culture, although they are often not so rigidly applied to children as to adults. We were interested to see whether young children had knowledge of these rules and whether restricting eating of foods to particular times of day of 'temporal locations' produced patterns of acceptance that shifted systematically with time of day (Birch, Billman and Richards, 1984). That is, does a food's acceptability change as a function of the degree to which the food is seen as appropriate or inappropriate for consumption at a particular time of day?

To obtain information on these questions, adults and 3- to 5-year-old children were first asked to give us preference rankings on a set of foods, which varied in the time of day for which they were appropriate. The same subjects were also asked to categorize of the foods as 'for breakfast' or 'for dinner.' All subjects were seen for two indentical sessions, one near breakfast time and one near dinner time.

The results provide evidence that children as young as 3- to 5-year-olds already possess knowledge regarding when foods are appropriate. The propor-

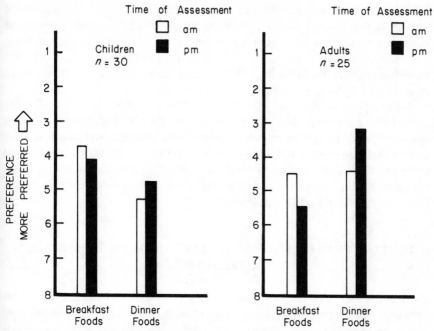

Figure 4. Summed preference ranks for three breakfast and three dinner foods, obtained am and pm, children and adults

tion of children categorizing scrambled eggs, orange juice, and Cheerios as 'for breakfast' were 0.70, 0.73, and 0.93, respectively, and the proportions categorizing pizza, green beans, and macaroni and cheese as 'for dinner' were 0.87, 0.95, and 0.75. There was no difference in the foods' categorization with time of day. As shown in Figure 4, both the adults and the preschool children showed the predicted preference shifts with time of day: breakfast foods were more preferred in the morning than in the afternoon, while the reverse was true for the dinner foods. There was no age difference in the pattern of preference shifts; the same pattern of preference shifts is shown from morning to afternoon for adults and children: a decrease in preference for the breakfast foods and an increase in preference for the dinner foods from morning to afternoon. The one age difference in these data is that the children have a clear preference for breakfast foods over the dinner foods at both times of day, while the adults tended to show an overall preference for the dinner foods.

These results indicate that cultural rules of cuisine that restrict the temporal 'location' of foods influence their acceptability, with foods being more preferred at the appropriate mealtime. These changing affective reactions, shown to shift in ways consistent with the culture's rules of cuisine, can function to reinforce and perpetuate these rules. When one cultural group is integrated into another, the cuisine of the group is often maintained even after other aspects of the culture have all but disappeared (e.g. Jerome, 1977). The affective component may be primarily responsible for the persistence of cuisine; the individuals eat foods consistent with their rules of cuisine, not just because they know what is appropriate, but also because what is appropriate has become the most acceptable and is preferred in the appropriate context. Surprisingly, the affective shifts noted in the present study are already apparent in children as young as 3 years.

With respect to the form of social transmission primarily responsible for these patterns, casual observation and discussions with parents and children suggest that although direct social interaction and parental teaching may contribute, children are not, by and large, explicitly taught these rules of food appropriateness: in most cases they are inferred by children from repeated experience with foods in a particular mealtime context that results from the meal patterns generated by parents.

SOCIAL TRANSMISSION RESULTING FROM DIRECT SOCIAL INTERACTION

Particularly for young children eating is a social occasion, which can involve not only other eaters but also adults who are attempting to regulate what and how much the child eats. The research reviewed below includes studies of social learning, e.g. the effects of peer and adult models, and the effects of particular child feeding practices designed to control the child's consumption and/or behaviour in general on the acquisition of food acceptance patterns.

In an early study Duncker (1938) investigated: . . . '(1) the objective reasons why, in a social group, certain likes and dislikes rather than others become dominant and traditional, and (2) the psychological mechanisms by which such likes and dislikes are instilled into the individual member of the group.' To explore these general social-psychological questions he chose to attempt to modify experimentally through 'social suggestion' the food preferences of young children, which he felt were 'especially fit for investigation.' In one experiment, he exposed preschool children to others who were making food choices. Based on prior information about their choices in the absence of social influence, the choices were arranged so that the children observed others making choices that were different from their own. Duncker then noted the food choices made by the observers following their exposure to the peers' choices and compared these to those made prior to social influence and investigated whether the degree of social influence was related to (1) the difference in age among the children, (2) the absolute ages of the children, and (3) the relationship among the children. He also investigated the effectiveness of the adult 'predecessor' and fictional predecessors. He noted clear evidence for social influence; the children's choices changed in the direction of others' choices. The effects were greater for younger children down to a lower limit of about 2 years 8 months, and were greater when the children were friends or when a more powerful child was the predecessor. Surprisingly, he found that an adult stranger was not effective in influencing the children's choices among the familiar foods. Fictional heroes were also effective agents of social transmission. He concluded that social influence was dependent upon the relationship among the individuals and individual characteristics, that influence tended to survive beyond the original situation, and that the influence was effective because it '. . . came to affect the sensory qualities of the food.' Although there is no direct support in his data for this last statement, the issue should receive attention. When a food preference is acquired as a result of experience, does it reflect (1) a change in the meaning of the object for the individual or (2) the discovery of favourable qualities or characteristics in the food itself? This issue is related to a question that has arisen in the context of associative conditioning: should the (food) CS be viewed (1) as a signal or a predictor of the UCS, or (2) as having acquired some of the qualities or characteristics of the UCS. (See Rozin, 1982 for a discussion of this point in the context of conditioned aversions and preferences for food.)

In a subsequent study, Marenho (1942) replicated Duncker's work with fictional heroes as models and investigated the long-term time course of the social influence procedures on young children's food preferences. She demonstrated that social influence effects were related to whether or not children had clear initial preferences, and the persistence of the social influence effects was also related to the strength of the initial preference.

More recently, we have extended Duncker's work (Birch, 1980b) in a study on the effects of peer models on young children's food preferences and eating behaviours. To investigate the effects of social learning on the acquisition of food acceptance patterns, we constructed social influence situations within the natural context of the preschooler's lunch programme. Specifically, the influence of peer models' food selections and eating behaviours on preschooler's food preferences for familiar vegetables were assessed and seating at lunches was arranged based on these preferences. A target child who strongly preferred vegetable 'A' to vegetable 'B' was seated with three or four other children who preferred 'B' to 'A.' Children were served these pairs of vegetables in a series of four consecutive lunches and were asked to choose a vegetable. On the first day, the 'minority' child chose first, followed by peers, which gave us a check on the preference data as a predictor of food choice. On the following three days, the target child chose last, following peers' selections. The target children showed a significant shift from choosing their preferred vegetable on day 1 to choosing their non-preferred food by day 4; consumption data corroborated these results. In post-influence preference assessments, the target children showed an increased preference for the initially non-preferred vegetable, while their peers did not. These data provide clear evidence that acceptability of familiar foods can be altered by social learning through exposure to peer models.

In one of few studies on the effects of social learning on children's food acceptance, Harper and Sanders (1975) investigated the effectiveness of adult models in inducing young children to ingest novel foods. They offered novel foods to children of two age groups (14- to 20-month-olds and 42- to 48-month-olds) under two conditions: the adult offered the food to the child, or the adult ate the food while offering it to the child. The results indicated that more children ate the novel foods in the 'adult eating' condition than in the 'offer only' condition, and that younger children were more affected than the older ones. In analysing the form of observational learning that occurred, the authors attribute the results of simple social facilitation, which they refer to as the most basic form of social learning, in which the actions of the model arouse a similar action in the observer. It is not a case in which new behaviour is acquired, but rather a situation in which a change in the stimulus control of behaviour has been induced. This social facilitation provides a mechanism for initiating ingestion of the novel food. Once the child ingests the food, feedback on palatability and associative conditioning of food cues to the social contexts and physiological consequences of eating will contribute to whether or not the food becomes an accepted part of the diet. This view is similar to that presented by Galef (1976), in which he sees direct social interaction as a means for giving the young organism an initial experience with a new food, bringing into play the mechanisms that produce change in affective reactions with exposure. Thus, the results of the studies on social learning effects on food acceptance patterns may be best viewed as arising from a combination of the second and third forms of social transmission; social interaction only provides initial opportunity for experience with the food.

We have continued to investigate the effects of social experience with food on food acceptance (Birch, Zimmerman and Hind, 1980; Birch, 1981; Birch, Birch, Marlin and Kramer, 1982; Birch, Marlin and Rotter, 1984). In these studies we have begun to look more closely at how the nature of the social interactions that occur during child feeding can influence acceptance patterns. The studies just described can be viewed as examples in which social interaction provides a mechanism for initiating contact with a food. In addition to this initiating function of social interaction, we believe that the specific type and effective tone of interactions that occur during feeding influence the acquisition of patterns of acceptability during childhood. We began to consider this possibility as a result of examining child feeding practices currently in use in our culture. To explore this possibility, our general strategy has been to reproduce these practices in the laboratory, and, by monitoring children's preferences and consumption patterns before, during, and after the use of such practices, have assessed their impact on food acceptability.

Parents of preschool children frequently underestimate the adequacy of their young children's diets (Beal, 1957; Dierks and Morse, 1965; Sabry, Ford, Roberts and Wardlaw, 1974). In their concern regarding this perceived inadequacy, parents often employ contingencies in order to effect increases in consumption (Kram and Owen, 1972). In order to increase the child's consumption of peas above a very low baseline level, eating peas becomes the instrumental activity in a contingency, e.g., 'Eat your peas and then you can . . . engage in an attractive activity such as watching TV, playing outside, or eating chocolate ice cream' (more will be said below on the effects of the use of palatable foods in the reward component of contingencies). Unlike the case of social learning, there does not seem to be an animal analogue of this form of social transmission; to my knowledge 'mom' rats have not been known to make pups stay at the food cup until they have finished all their pellets.

We investigated whether the use of such contingencies had effects on the acceptability of foods consumed instrumentally (Birch, Birch, Marlin and Kramer, 1982). To obtain initial data on this question, 12 preschool children's preferences for seven fruit juices and seven play activities were assessed twice, before and after the imposition of a series of contingency schedules in which the children drank juice in order to gain access to the play activity.

The results indicated that nine of 12 children decreased their preference for the instrumentally consumed juice; the other three children showed no change. For the total sample the negative shift in acceptability was significant, indicating that the repeated association of the food with the instrumental eating context had decreased the food's acceptability.

A second experiment on the effects of instrumental eating was conducted to replicate these results under different conditions and to obtain information on the psychological processes that might be responsible for the observed effects (Birch, Marlin and Rotter, 1984). To obtain information on the psychological processes contributing to changes in acceptability each child was randomly assigned to one of four contingency groups or one of two controls, matched for age, sex, and beverage preference. The four contingency conditions were generated by crossing two variables, each of which had two levels: type of reward (tangible or positive verbal feedback) and amount consumed (baseline or baseline plus an additional amount). The selection of type of reward as a variable was based on the extrinsic motivation literature (cf. Lepper and Greene, 1978), which indicates that, while tangible rewards for the performance of activities reduces the attractiveness of those activities, providing feedback regarding the quality of performance does not. Positive verbal feedback has the effect of focusing the child on the activity that the adult wants the child to perform. In contrast, the use of salient tangible rewards focuses the child on the reward rather than on the instrumental activity. The other variable (amount consumed) was included to determine whether negative effects on preference noted previously were attributable, not to the contingency *per se*, but to having the child consume more of a food than his or her ideal preferred amount of that food. As indicated above, we hypothesized that this overconsumption of the food might, in and of itself, be aversive and account for the negative shifts in preference noted. A series of eight contingency or control sessions was given. The results indicated significant negative shifts in acceptability in all four instrumental conditions and slight increases in acceptability in the control groups. These changes in acceptability can be viewed as a result of associative conditioning in which food cues become associated with perceived social context cues present during eating. Depending on the affective tone of these social contexts, the food's acceptability increases or declines. There is direct evidence that children see this instrumental eating context in a negative light. Lepper, Sagotsky, DaFoe and Greene (1982) reported that when children were told stories involving the eating of two imaginary foods (called 'Hupe' and 'Hule'), in which one food was in the instrumental component and the other in the reward component of a mealtime contingency, the children indicated that they would prefer the food used as a reward over the food eaten instrumentally.

Additional evidence on the central role of associative conditioning to social contexts in determining food acceptability during early childhood also comes from our work on the use of foods as rewards. We repeatedly presented one food to each child in one of four social contexts: as a reward for the performance of a prosocial behaviour (e.g. sharing, helping, responding to a request); non-contingently, paired with positive adult attention; at snacktime, along with other foods as a control for exposure effects; or in a non-social context (Birch, Zimmerman and Hind, 1980). The series of 20 presentations was integrated into the ongoing preschool programmes over a 6-week period; teachers were trained to present the foods to the children. Results showed a significant increase in the acceptability for the foods presented as rewards or paired with positive adult attention, and these increases in acceptability were maintained for at least six weeks following the cessation of the presentation procedures. The basic findings were replicated and the changes in acceptability resulting from such associative conditioning were found to generalize to foods perceived as similar to the presented food (Birch, 1981).

Taken together, the results provide evidence for associative conditioning of food acceptability during early childhood. The results of the work on the use of foods in contingencies suggest that these child feeding practices have effects opposite to those intended by parents when they use these practices. In the case of instrumental eating, parents employ this strategy to increase children's consumption. Our data indicate that instrumental eating results in reduced acceptability, making it less likely that the food will be consumed when the contingency is removed. On the other hand, increases in acceptability result from the use of foods as rewards. There is a confounding of food and function in these contingencies, with highly palatable foods typically serving as rewards. Our data indicate that the use of these foods (frequently sweets) as rewards increased the acceptability of those foods. Parents who use sweets as rewards are frequently the same parents who express concern that their child's consumption of sweets is too high (Kram and Owen, 1972). More generally, parental use of contingencies implicitly denies that the child has the ability to regulate intake adequately in response to internal, physiological cues of hunger and satiety.

SUMMARY AND CONCLUSIONS

Patterns of food acceptance in humans are acquired, and a great deal of learning about food and eating occurs early in life. What is acquired includes the control of what is eaten and how much is eaten, as well as when eating occurs. This control is mediated largely by hedonic responses to food. These acquisitions can be viewed as a result of three non-independent forms of transmission: genetically preprogrammed predispositions, social constraints on experience with food, and direct social interaction. The view presented is that genetic predispositions, social constraints on experience, and direct social interaction determine the quantity and quality of the child's experience with food and provide the context for associative conditioning and other forms of learning to occur.

At this point the available data provide descriptive information and we have little evidence that suggests the nature of the learning mechanisms that result in food acceptance patterns, or more specifically, how experience with the physiological consequences and the social contexts of eating combine to produce these emerging food acceptance patterns during early childhood.

It has been assumed that these early food acceptance patterns are important because they are reflected in food acceptance patterns later in life. There are currently no prospective or longitudinal data with human subjects to provide support for this assumption. Whether or not this assumption is ultimately supported by the data, the acquisition of these early acceptance patterns are of interest because they contribute to our understanding of the development of food intake regulation during the early years of life. Such information also has direct application to child feeding practices which, in turn, influence children's nutritional status, growth, and health.

REFERENCES

Ainsworth, M.S. and Bell, S.M. (1969). Some contemporary patterns of mother-infant interaction in the feeding situation. In A. Ambrose (Ed.), *Stimulation in Early Infancy*, Academic Press, New York.

Beal, V. (1957). On the acceptance of solid foods and other food patterns of infants and children. *Pediatrics*, **61**, 448–457.

Beauchamp, G. and Maller, O. (1977). The development of flavor preference in humans: A review. In M.R. Kare and O. Maller (Eds), *The Chemical Senses and Nutrition*, Academic Press, New York. pp. 292–315.

Beauchamp, G.K. and Moran, M. (1982). Dietary experience and sweet taste preference in human infants. *Appetite*, **3**, 139–152.

Berlyne, D. (Ed.) (1974). *Studies in New Experimental Aesthetics: Toward an Objective Psychology of Aesthetic Appreciation*, Hemisphere, Washington.

Bernstein, I.L., Webster, N.M. and Bernstein, I.D. (1982). Food aversions in children receiving chemotherapy for cancer. *Cancer*, **50**, 263–265.

Birch, L.L. (1979a). Dimensions of preschool children's food preferences. *Journal of Nutrition Education*, **11**, 91–95.

Birch, L.L. (1979b). Preschool children's preferences and consumption patterns. *Journal of Nutrition Education*, **11**, 189–192.

Birch, L.L. (1980a). The relationship between children's food preferences and those of their parents. *Journal of Nutritional Education*, **12**, 14–18.

Birch, L.L. (1980b). Effects of peer models' food choices and eating behaviours on preschoolers' food preferences. *Child Development*, **51**, 489–496.

Birch, L.L. (1981). Generalization of a modified food preference. *Child Development*, **52**, 755–758.

Birch, L.L., Billman, J. and Richards, S. (1984). Time of day influences food acceptability. *Appetite*, **5**, 109–112.

Birch, L.L., Birch, D., Marlin, D. and Kramer, L. (1982). Effects of instrumental eating on children's food preferences. *Appetite*, **3**, 125–134.

Birch, L.L. and Deysher, M. (1985). Conditioned and unconditioned caloric compensation: Evidence for self-regulation of food intake by young children. *Learning and Motivation*, **16**, 341–355.

Birch, L.L. and Marlin, D.W. (1982). I don't like it; I never tried it: Effects of exposure on two-year-old children's food preferences. *Appetite*, **3**, 353–360.

Birch, L.L., Marlin, D. and Rotter, J. (1984). Eating as the 'means' activity in a contingency: Effects on young children's food preference. *Child Development*, **55**, 431–439.

Birch, L.L., Zimmerman, S. and Hind, H. (1980). The influence of social affective context on preschool children's food preferences. *Child Development*, **51**, 856–861.

Booth, D. (1977). Satiety and appetite are conditioned reactions. *Psychosomatic Medicine*, **39**, 76–81.

Booth, D., Lee, M. and McAleavey, C. (1976). Acquired sensory control of satiation in man. *British Journal of Psychology*, **67**, 137–147.

Bruch, H. (1961). Transformation of oral impulses in eating disorders: A conceptual approach. *Psychiatric Quarterly*, **35**, 458–481.

Cabanac, M. (1971). Physiological role of pleasure. *Science*, **173**, 1103–1107.

Chiva, M. (1982). Taste, facial expression and mother-infant interaction in early development. *Baroda Journal of Nutrition*, **9**, 99–102.

Crook, C.K. (1978). Taste perception in the newborn infant. *Infant Behavior and Development*, **1**, 52–69.

Davis, C.M. (1928). Self-selection of diet by newly weaned infants. An experimental study. *American Journal of Diseases of Children*, **36**, 651–679.

Davis, C.M. (1939). Results of the self-selection of diets by young children. *The Canadian Medical Association Journal*, 257–261.

Deci, E.L. (1971). Effects of externally mediated rewards on intrinsic motivation. *Journal of Personality and Social Psychology*, **18**, 105–115.

Desor, J., Maller, O. and Greene, L. (1977). Preference for sweet in humans: Infants, children and adults. In J.M. Weiffenback (Ed.), *Taste and Development the Genesis of Sweet Preference*. United States Department of Health, Education and Welfare, Bethesda, MD, pp. 161–172.

Desor, J., Maller, O. and Turner, R. (1973). Taste acceptance of sugars by human infants. *Journal of Comparative and Physiological Psychology*, **84**, 496–501.

Dierks, E.C. and Morse, L.M. (1965). Food habits and nutrient intakes of preschool children. *Journal of the American Dietetic Association*, **47**, 292–296.

Domjan, M. (1977). Attenuation and enhancement of neophobia for edible substances. In L.M. Barker, M.R. Best, and M. Domjan (Eds), *Learning Mechanisms in Food Selection*, Baylor University Press, Houston, Texas, pp. 151–180.

Duncker, K. (1938). Experimental modification of children's food preferences through social suggestion. *Journal of Abnormal Social Psychology*, **33**, 489–507.

Fomon, S.J. (1974). *Infant Nutrition*, 2nd edn, Saunders, Philadelphia.

Galef, B. (1976). Social transmission of acquired behavior. In J.S. Rosenblatt, R.A. Hinde, E. Shaw and C. Beer (Eds), *Advances in the Study of Behavior*, vol. 6, Academic Press, New York.

Garb, J.L. and Stunkard, A.J. (1974). Taste aversions in man. *American Journal of Psychiatry*, **131**, 1204–1207.

Garcia, J., Hankins, W.G. and Rusiniak, K.W. (1974). Behavioural regulation of the milieu interne in man and rat. *Science*, **185**, 823–831.

Harper, L.V. and Sanders, K.M. (1975). The effect of adults' eating on young children's acceptance of unfamiliar foods. *Journal of Experimental Child Psychology*, **20**, 206–214.

Harrison, A.A. (1977). Mere exposure. In L. Berkowitz (Ed.), *Advances in Social Psychology*, vol. 10, Academic Press, New York.

Jerome, N.W. (1977). Taste experience and the development of a dietary preference for sweet in humans: Ethnic and cultural variations in early taste experience. In J.M. Weiffenback (Ed.), *Taste and Development*: The Genesis of Sweet Preference, U.S. Government Printing Office, Washington, pp. 235–248.

Kram, F.M. and Owen, G.M. (1972). Nutritional studies on United States preschool children: Dietary intakes and practices of food procurement, preparation and consumption. In S.J. Fomon and T.A. Anderson (Eds), *Practices of Low-income Families in Feeding Infants and Small Children with Particular Attention to Cultural Subgroups*, Department HEW Publication No. 72–5605, U.S. Government Printing Office, Washington.

LeMagnen, J. (1955). Surle mechanisme d'establissament des appetits caloriques. *Comp. Perd. Acad. Sci.*, **240**, 2436–2438.

LeMagnen, J. (1977). Sweet preference and the sensory control of caloric intake. In J.M. Weiffenbach (Ed.), *Taste and Development: The Genesis of Sweet Preference*. United States Department of Health, Education and Welfare, Bethesda, Maryland.

LeMagnen, J. (1971). Advances in studies on the physiological control and regulation of food intake. In E. Stellor and M.M. Sprague (Eds), *Progress in Physiological Psychology*, vol. 14, Academic Press, New York.

Lepper, M. and Greene, D. (Eds). (1978). *The Hidden Costs of Reward? New Perspectives on the Psychology of human motivation*. New Jersey: Lawrence Erlbaum Associates.

Lepper, M., Sagotsky, G., Dafoe, J.L. and Greene, D. (1982). Consequences of superfluous social constraints: Effects on young children's social inferences and subsequent intrinsic interest. *Journal of Personality and Social Psychology*, **42**, 51–65.

Marenho, H. (1942). Social influence in the formation of enduring preferences. *Journal of Abnormal Social Psychology*, **37**, 448–468.

Rodin, J. (1981). Current status of the internal-external hypothesis for obesity. What went wrong? *American Psychologist*, **36**, 361–372.

Rolls, B.J., Rolls, E.T. and Rowe, E.A. (1982). The influence of variety on human food selection and intake. In L.M. Barker (Ed.), *The Psychobiology of Human Food Selection* AVI Publishing, Westport, Connecticut. pp. 101–122.

Rolls, B.J., Rolls, E.T., Rowe, E.A. and Sweeney, K. (1981). Sensory specific satiety in man. *Physiology and Behavior*, **27**, 137–142.

Rozin, P. (1976). The selection of foods by rats, humans, and other animals. In J.S. Rosenblatt, R.A. Hinde, E. Shaw and C. Beer (Eds), *Advances in the Study of Behaviour*, Academic Press, New York, pp. 21–76.

Rozin, P. (1982). Human food selection: The interaction of biology, culture and individual experience. In L.M. Barker (Ed.), *Psychobiology of Human Food Selection*, AVI Publishing, Westport, Connecticut, pp. 225–254.

Rozin, P. and Schiller, D. (1980). The nature and acquisition of a preference for chili pepper by humans. *Motivation and Emotion*, **4**, 77–101.

Sabry, J.H., Ford, D.Y., Roberts, M.L. and Wardlaw, J.M. (1974). Evaluative techniques for use with children's diets. *Journal of Nutrition Education*, **6**, 52–56.

Stang, D. (1975). The effects of mere exposure on learning and affect. *Journal of Personality and Social Psychology*, **31**, 7–13.

Steiner, J.E. (1977). Facial expressions of the neonate infant indicating the hedonics of food-related chemical stimuli. In J.M. Weiffenbach (Ed.), *Taste and Development: The Genesis of Sweet Preference*, United States Department of Health, Education and Welfare, Bethesda, Maryland, pp. 173–188.

Stunkard, A.J. (1975). Satiety is a conditioned reflex. *Psychosomatic Medicine*, **37**, 383–389.

Zajonc, R.B. (1968). Attitudinal effects of mere exposure. *Journal of Personality and Social Psychology Monograph Supplement*, **9**, 1–27.

Eating Habits
Edited by R.A. Boakes, D.A. Popplewell and M.J. Burton
© 1987 John Wiley & Sons Ltd

CHAPTER 6

Palatability: Concept, Terminology, and Mechanisms

Jacques Le Magnen
*Laboratoire de Neurophysiologie Sensorielle et Comportementale,
College de France, 11 Place Marcelin Berthelot, 75231 Paris Cedex 05, France*

Descartes recommended 'les idées claires et distinctes' which are such only if the exact meanings of words are defined. He also recommended going into all matters 'du simple au complexe'. Historically, at least since Aristotle, it was thought, and noted in accord with common experience, that the sensory perception of food, its 'taste', and the like and dislike for various foods were the main subjective components of eating behaviours and eating habits. In addition, Aristotle mentioned that a food, which is pleasant when we are hungry, becomes unpleasant when we are satiated and well nourished. These casual observations and notions have been repeated throughout the centuries. However, science, that is to say, experimental investigations on animal models and humans, has not really clarified the matter. Why is a food liked or disliked depending on both 'taste' and the person's hunger? What relationships are there between the sensory and nutritive properties of foods, between eating habits and an effective feeding of the body? One of the reasons for the relative failure to answer this question is the lack of consensus among experimenters on basic concepts and on terminology.

PALATABILITY: CONCEPT AND TERMINOLOGY

What is meant by the 'palatability of foods'? It is not the activity of solid or liquid food on cephalic sensory receptors. It is the ingestive response (acceptance or refusal) and the amounts eaten in a defined condition as they are mediated by this sensory activity.

The sensory signature of each particular food item results from a complex pattern of activity of the material on various sensory modalities stimulated prior to and during eating the food. Outside the mouth it is the visual aspect and location of the food and its odour. When the food is accepted, it is its gustatory, olfactory, mechanical, and thermal properties which are perceived during chewing and swallowing. In addition to this pattern of a successive and/or simultaneous action on different sensory modalities, food items may act on different systems of qualitative discrimination within each sensory apparatus. The same compounds present in the food may be both sweet and bitter, or salty and sour. The particular odour of a food is the result of a tremendous number of pure odorous compounds, each of which can be discriminated as a pure olfactory stimulus, but is not generally recognized in the mixture.

This sensory 'oral' analysis of food permits one to 'individualize' practically all possible food items, and therefore to distinguish each of these items one from another. Even different sweet substances, sugars and sweeteners, and similarly different types of bitter substances, can be discriminated by humans and animals after some training (Dugas du Villard, Her and MacLeod, 1981; Faurion, 1982). The unique exception is probably represented by the two salts which are exclusively and only salty, sodium chloride and lithium chloride (Boudreau, Hoang, Oravec and Do, 1983). However, a sensory discrimination of families of stimuli is superimposed on the possible 'individualization' of each product. These groupings are based upon either sensory resemblances or the existence of a common stimulus within a series of food products. Liquid and solid items, though differing widely in their various other sensory properties, are discriminated as fluids and solids. Sweet products are known as such, despite their differences due to associated stimuli.

Before proceeding further a clarification of terminology is needed. The combined sensory properties of a food product are designated its 'flavour'. However, according to different authors and even to different glossaries, the term 'taste' in English, as in French, is highly equivocal and, because it is used with different meanings, is a source of confusion. Taste is used to designate either the gustatory property only or a series of undefined sensory properties synonymous with flavour. In addition, 'taste of . . .' is not distinguished from 'taste for . . .', i.e. the sensory activity from the palatability.

Here, several major points must be emphasized. The complex sensory activity of foods is entirely dependent on the response of sensory receptors to their contents. This sensory pattern is not at all dependent on the nutritive or non-nutritive properties of a food. Some sugars are sweet; but equal intensities and sweetness of various sugars are provided by various concentrations and therefore by different calorific densities. Other carbohydrates are not sweet. Artificial sweeteners are sweet and some of them are highly toxic. Lithium chloride can not be discriminated from sodium chloride, but is a poison. Many bitter compounds are not toxic (Kratz, Levitsky and Lustick, 1978; Aravich and Sclafani, 1980). Similarly, in the case of the smell of food, that is, olfactory activity, which, as noted earlier, is due to traces from a great variety of odorous compounds, its quality and intensity are unrelated to the nutritive properties of the food. Carbohydrates, fats, and proteins do not have a specific odour which would permit their identification as such (Larue, 1978). As families of products, they can be discriminated only by permanently associated non-nutritive stimuli or by other common sensory characteristics, such as texture.

Sensory activity is therefore only dependent on the activation of sensory receptors by a food and not on its nutritive properties. In addition, this sensory activity is independent of the person's nutritional state and needs. Contrary to some early assertions (Goetzl and Stone, 1947), sensory thresholds, the stimulus-intensity suprathreshold relationship, and the quality of the perceived sensation are not influenced by hunger and satiety. In satiated as in hungry subjects sweet is sweet and the perceived intensity remains the same (Berg, Pangborn, Roessler and Webb, 1963; Furchtgott and Friedman, 1960). Recordings of chorda tympani nerve discharges and of peripheral olfactory receptors give no indication of a change in responding resulting from variations in nutritional states such as the level of blood glucose or of food deprivation (Pfaffmann and Bare, 1950). Old theories, which re-emerge periodically, ascribe changes of specific appetites to various metabolic disturbances of the sensory input. This is not supported by experimental data (Pfaffmann and Hagstrom, 1955; Richter, 1941; Richter, 1957).

Although sensory properties are not correlated with nutritive properties, the palatability of a food, that is, the eating response to these sensory properties, is generally correlated with its nutritive properties and with the person's nutritional state. Palatability is related, but sensory activity is unrelated, to nutritive properties. Therefore (it is a syllogism), palatability is also relatively independent of the nature of the sensory pattern to which it is the response. A sweet solution, which is genetically palatable, may be rendered unpalatable or aversive.

CHARACTERISTICS OF PALATABILITY

Palatability, as a response to cephalic stimuli from foods, is the 'sensory specific stimulation to eat'. Various characteristics of food palatabilities and of their role in feeding behaviour and nutritional homeostasis may be described as follows.

Palatability Depends on Central Processing of Peripheral Inputs.

The palatability of each particular food results from central processing of the specific pattern of sensory input generated peripherally by this particular food item. It is thus dependent on the discriminated quality and intensity transmitted by the afferent pattern. But its level for different foods and its fluctuations, as determined by central processing, are independent of peripheral sensory activities. However, there are some well-known prewired and genetically programmed ingestive responses to gustatory cues, such as preferences for sweet substances and aversions to bitter compounds (Desor, Maller and Turner, 1973; Steiner, 1973; Pfaffmann, 1936). Unlearned responses to specific olfactory cues also have been reported (Burghardt, 1970; Steiner, 1977). Nevertheless, these initial predetermined responses to specific sensory cues can be modified or reversed. Differential responses to sugar and saccharin solutions, high palatability of bitterness and low palatability of sweetness can be established (Rozin, and Kalat, 1971; Le Magnen, 1971).

Palatability is Learned

As recalled earlier, the sensory and nutritive properties of food items are not correlated. In the learning of palatability, and therefore in the central processing of sensory information, responses to food become dependent on, and correlated with, the nutritive properties of foods.

Harris, Clay, Hargreaves and Ward (1933) were the first to demonstrate that a specific appetite adapted to a particular metabolic need (vitamin B) was learned by rats and could be based on an odour arbitrarily chosen and added to the diet. We have demonstrated that the differential palatability of two versions of the same diet, which were distinguished by adding two different odour markers, could be learned if the intake of one of the two versions was supplemented by post-prandial glucose injections (Le Magnen, 1959). Rats so treated eat a lesser quantity of the supplemented version as if it were of a higher caloric density. This differential palatability adjusted to caloric density has been further studied and elegantly confirmed by Booth (1972).

As a result of a process of learning, palatability as a determinant of acceptance and refusal, and of amounts eaten, becomes adjusted to the nutritive properties of foods because, and in as much as, the primary reinforcer is the repletion of a metabolic deficit. Just as recovery from an illness has been demonstrated to be a positive reinforcer to induce a taste preference (Green and Garcia, 1971; Hasegawa, 1981; Zahorik, Maier and Pies, 1974), recovery from hunger and post-prandial satiety are primary reinforcers of sensory-specific appetite, or palatability, for foods, adjusted in accord with their caloric properties. The relief of illness or malaise resulting from protein, vitamin or mineral deficiencies also seems to cause the palatability of a food to be related to its protein, vitamin, and mineral content (Booth and Simson, 1974; Simson and Booth, 1973). Unconditioned stimuli, or primary reinforcers, other than factors associated with satiation, act to establish and to modulate higher or lower palatabilities. Psychotropic drugs in dependent animal and human subjects act to reinforce sensory-specific palatabilities (Marfaing-Jallat and Le Magnen, 1982; Marfaing-Jallat and Le Magnen, 1984; Parker, Failor and Weidman, 1973). Toxic post-ingestive effects condition a lowering of palatability (Rozin and Kalat, 1971; Le Magnen, 1971).

Palatability is a Continuum

This evident notion has been known for a long time, but is still obscured by the apparently conflicting terminology of 'preferences' and 'aversions'. Preferences and aversions are understood as palatabilities which are higher and lower, respectively, than those of another food taken as reference. Unfortunately, except for solutions in which water is generally the reference, this reference is not defined. Thus, a particular response to a food may be taken either as a preference or an aversion depending on the food used for a comparison. A food item or solution refused even in a maximal hunger stimulation is at palatability 0.

The unpalatability of a food, or relative aversion towards it, leading to its refusal before or after eating something else, must be distinguished from active rejection. Such rejection may be considered as a food-specific stress reaction, in as much as it includes specific defensive reactions such as nausea and vomiting, and involves particular brain mechanisms (Borison and Wang, 1953). Subjective experience indicates that the unpalatability of a food developing during a meal as a result of satiation is different from nausea generated by an intake beyond a satiety level or spontaneously elicited by non-edible materials. We propose to reserve the term 'aversion' or 'true aversion' for such active rejection. The unpalatability of a food that develops towards the end of a meal is not a true aversion.

The decline in palatability throughout a meal, its rate, and its specificity to the food eaten (Duclaux, Feisthamer and Cabanac, 1973; Rolls, Rowe and Rolls, 1982) apparently result from conditioning (Booth and Davis, 1973). But this conditioning of the specific satiating power of the oral qualities of food and of gastrointestinal satiating actions cannot be compared to conditioned taste aversion. Aversion induced by pairing intake of a food with a cholecystokinin (CCK) or lithium chloride (LiCl) injection does not demonstrate that CCK or LiCl are physiological factors of satiation (Deutsch and Hardy, 1977; Bernstein and Goehler, 1983; Booth, personal communication). This dissociation of mechanisms underlying levels of palatability in relation to hunger and satiety from true aversion is consistent with the findings of Berridge and Grill (1983). When a mixture of sugar and quinine is injected into a rat's mouth, it alternates between the oral expression of acceptance and rejection. The central processing of taste messages is such that in a mixture of basic tastes (sweet and bitter) a qualitative discrimination of the two components is maintained, despite a reciprocal compensation of their intensities (McCutcheon and Brown, 1983). In as much as two different pathways are involved in acceptance and active rejection, an alternation of the two responses is exhibited by rats rather than an intermediate response. In many states of disease or during pregnancy, some or all foods are not unpalatable, they are aversive, that is, offensive.

Palatability as a continuum has been verified experimentally. A LiCl-induced aversion was attenuated or blocked by an intracranial stimulation at low and strong intensity, respectively. Conversely, preference conditioned by association of a flavour with rewarding brain stimulation is attenuated in a dose-dependent manner by LiCl (Ettenberg, Sgro and White, 1982). These authors subscribe to the classical notion whereby preference is considered as positive and aversion as negative palatability. However, they argue in favour of an algebraic summation of preference and aversion, and therefore of a continuum.

New evidence for this notion of a palatability continuum will be provided in the experimental part of this chapter.

Palatability is Hunger Dependent

The sensory-specific stimulation to eat is dependent on the systemic or metabolic stimulation to eat. The role of palatability in determining the magnitude of eating responses in terms of amount eaten in a bout of eating or in a meal is masked by experimenting with a constant and familiar food. However, when various foods are compared and rats, for instance, are offered different foods in a given state of deprivation (for example, 6 hours), it is commonly observed that 0 or 6–8 g of food are eaten until satiation (Le Magnen, 1983). The different amount eaten is dependent on, and measures, the differential palatability of the offered foods, but the amount eaten of any one of these foods, whatever its intrinsic palatability, is also dependent on the degree of food deprivation at the time of testing. A food which has a low palatability when tested in 3-hour deprived rats may show a high palatability when tested after 12 hours of deprivation. In other words, an obvious additivity, or synergy, exists between internal and external stimuli to eat. Through the learning of palatability, oral sensory cues are 'conditioned stimuli to eat' and eating is a state-dependent 'conditioned response'.

Many experimental data argue in favour of the notion that systemic blood-born hunger signals have a permissive and modulating action in the triggering and mediation of feeding by the external sensory input (Le Magnen, 1983). The convergence in the lateral hypothalamus and amygdala of gustatory, olfactory, vagal, trigeminal, and visual afferents and the responsiveness of lateral hypothalamic sites to blood-borne signals seem to provide the neuroanatomical substrate of these hunger-palatability relationships (Kogura, Onada and Takagi, 1980; Norgren, 1976; Ricardo and Koh, 1978; Oomura, 1976; Saper, Loewy, Swanson and Cowan, 1976). This hypothesis has been supported by recordings from single units in the monkey's lateral hypothalamus. Units were found which responded to the sight of an object known by the monkey as food, but not to another object and only when the monkey was hungry (Burton,

Mora and Rolls, 1975; Burton, Mora and Rolls, 1976; Burton and Mora, 1976). The same processing, which, however, is not observed at the level of peripheral receptors, has been recognized to be effective at the level of sensory afferent pathways (Pager, Giachetti, Holley and Le Magnen, 1972; Chaput and Holley, 1976). Multi-unit discharges in the mitral cell layer of the olfactory bulb in rats and rabbits are modulated by hunger and satiety and are only evoked by a food-related stimulus (Pager, 1974). Eating the food or inflating a balloon in the stomach abolishes this selective response of the olfactory bulb to a food odour (Chaput and Holley, 1976). In the nucleus of the solitary tract (NST), single unit responses to sweet, but not to bitter, stimuli are attenuated by inflating a balloon in the stomach (Glenn and Erickson, 1976). Centrifugal pathways to the olfactory bulb and interactions between gustatory and vagal input in the NST are responsible for these effects.

Such electrophysiological recordings in the brain support the learning of palatability. A cell in the lateral hypothalamus, unresponsive in the hungry monkey, when presented with an unknown food object becomes responsive when the object has been experienced as food (Mora, Rolls and Burton, 1976). Likewise, mitral cells of the olfactory bulb, unresponsive to an odour not related to food, become responsive to that odour in the hungry rat when familiarized to its food flavoured by the odour (Pager, 1974). A CTA paradigm will reverse this palatability response of the olfactory bulb and also change the response to a sweet stimulus in the NTS (Pager and Royet, 1976; Chang and Scott, 1984; Aleksanyan, Buresova and Bures, 1976).

The Palatability Effect is a Sensory-Specific Reward

The concept of food reward has been obscured and biased by studies of operant conditioning. The delivery of food pellets is often considered to be the reward in instrumental learning (Mackintosh, 1974). As a reward for the conditioning of lever-pressing, for example, the food acts, not as a primary reinforcer through its post-ingestive action, but as 'secondary reinforcer' of the eating response, that is to say, through its palatability. This has been amply demonstrated. Reinforcement of the operant can be obtained by drops of a sweet solution, the reinforcing value of which depends on its sweetness (Guttman, 1953). The sight of inaccessible food is reinforcing (Wike and Casey, 1954) and so on. Thus, instrumental learning may be considered to be a form of 'second-order conditioning' in which stimuli from the lever are substituted for oral cues and pressing the lever substituted for the oral motor pattern of eating. However, from a physiological point of view, food as a sensory cue is the current reward, not of an artificially interposed instrumental response, but of the oro-motor pattern of ingestion. To say that a food is palatable, is rewarding or has a given hedonic value is to say the same thing. This terminology is the one commonly used in animal studies. The subjective correlate of palatability in humans is 'pleasantness-unpleasantness' or 'like-dislike'. Again, this dual terminology for the operational and the subjective aspects of the same phenomenon is a source of confusion and misunderstanding.

The theory that the so-called 'brain rewarding systems' involved in intra-cranial self-stimulation are also involved in food reward, and therefore in palatability, is supported by various experiments. One pertinent find-ing is that the association of electrical stimulation of brain rewarding sites with the intake of a saccharin solution enhances the palatability of this solution (Ettenberg, 1980). Similarly, lines of rats selected as high lateral hypothalamus (LH) self-stimulators were shown to be high-intake drinkers of a sweet saccharin solution (Ganchrow, Lieblich and Cohen, 1981).

Palatability and the Size of Meals

A very large proportion of research on feeding behaviour, particularly during recent years, has dealt in fact with the determinants of amounts eaten in a bout of eating from the initiation to the spontaneous end of this unitary intake, or meal. Such research is often (erroneously) described by their authors as studies of the 'mechanisms of satiety'. They are in fact studies of the balance between stimulating positive feedback and the satiating negative feedback in determin-ing meal size. Confused discussion is routinely found about the role of the oral activity of food passing the mouth and therefore of palatability, this role being either emphasized or denied. The latter point of view is often based upon experiments showing that loads or tube feeding in the stomach suppresses or abolishes oral intake or, on the contrary, that sham feeding does not induce satiation (Le Magnen, 1985). In fact, both types of experiment prove the opposite, that is to say, the fact that the mouth provides the positive feedback. This supports an enormous meal in the absence of a post-oral negative feedback. This also explains the fact that a direct manipulation of this negative feedback abolishes the oro-sensory stimulation to eat. Because palatability is hunger-dependent, satiation, which is the progressive abolition of hunger, also shifts progressively from palatability to unpalatability during the period from the initiation to the end of the meal (Cabanac, 1979). Whatever the site of the satiation mechanism (stomach, intestine or beyond), the oral intake and the time course of its evolution until the end of the meal are governed by the change in palatability occurring during the meal. How the balance between the strength of the initial palatability and the strength of the gastrointestinal feedback leads to the amounts eaten, which vary as a function of the former, is still obscure.

Another point is questionable and open to discussion. It is represented by the cumulative effects of food at the oral level as a contribution to the negative feedback. The contribution of food accumulating in the stomach and of stomach emptying is not in question (Deutsch, Gonzalez and Young, 1980; Deutsch and Gonzalez, 1980; Deutsch, this volume; Le Magnen, 1983). However, the contribution of the oral level also seems to depend on 'sensory variety'. We demonstrated this phenomenon, also termed 'sensory-specific satiety' some twenty-five years ago (Le Magnen, 1956; Le Magnen, 1960). It has been re-examined and confirmed recently by various experimenters

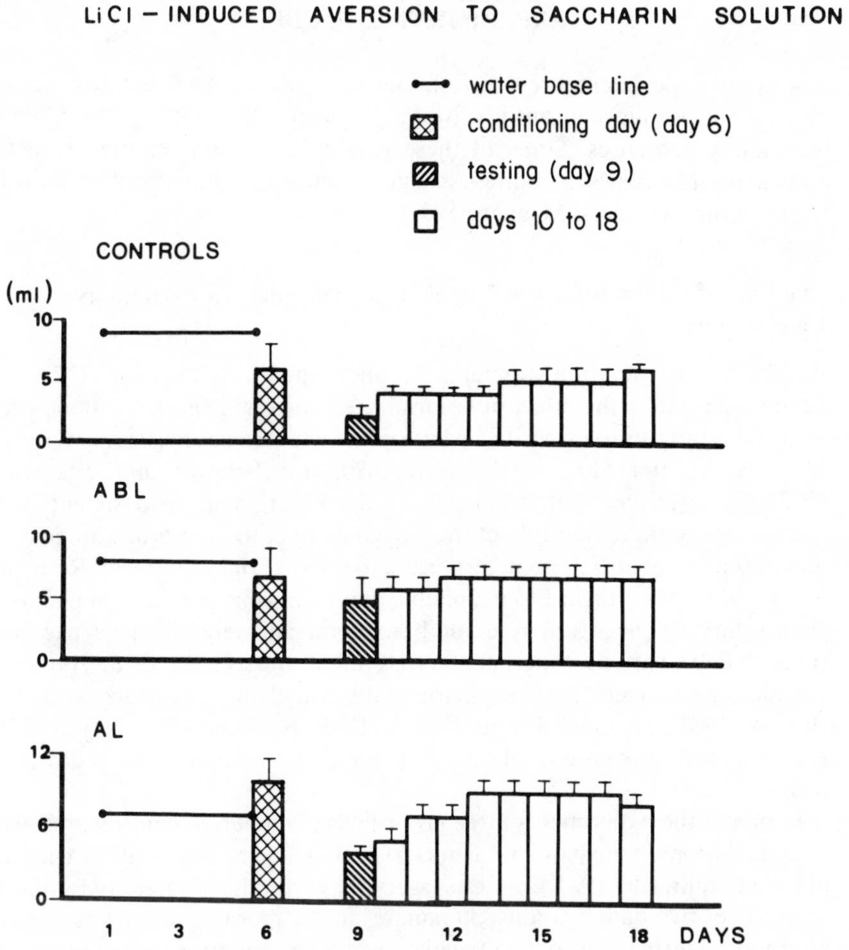

LiCl — INDUCED AVERSION TO SACCHARIN SOLUTION

●—● water base line
▨ conditioning day (day 6)
▨ testing (day 9)
☐ days 10 to 18

Figure 1.   Baso-lateral (ABL and lateral amygdala (AL) lesions abolish the neophobic response to a saccharin solution. Baso-lateral lesions suppress the LiCl-induced aversion, but this illness-induced aversion is not altered after lateral lesions

(Treit, Spetch and Deutsch, 1983; Rolls, Van Duijvenvoorde and Rowe, 1983). Since changing only the odour labelling of a food restores eating in rats previously satiated by eating the same food, it is clear that part of the satiation process is dependent on a cumulative action of specific oral cues during intake; but, since successive presentations of differently flavoured versions are progressively less efficient at restoring eating, it is also clear that the post-oral accumulation of food in the gastrointestinal reservoir provides another, and presumably the main, contribution to satiation. At the neuronal level in the brain a LH unit, no longer responsive in the monkey satiated by a food, is again responsive when the presentation of another food stimulates eating (Burton, Mora and Rolls, 1975).

EXPERIMENTAL STUDIES

A series of experimental results from our laboratory gives some new insights into the various mechanisms involved in the acquisition and manifestation of palatability responses. Some of these results have been reported in detail elsewhere (Kolakowska, Larue-Achagiotis and Le Magnen, 1984; Bellisle, Lucas, Amrani and Le Magnen, 1984).

The Role of the Baso-Lateral Nuclei of the Amygdala in Palatability Conditioning

A role for specific brain structures in conditioned taste aversion (CTA) has been suggested by the effect of lesions. Area postrema and LH lesions affect the capacity of rats to associate gustatory cues with toxicosis (Berger, Wise and Stein, 1973; Ritter, McGlove and Kelly, 1980; Roth, Schwartz and Teitelbaum, 1973; Schwartz and Teitelbaum, 1974). However, many experiments have focused attention on the role of the amygdala in both the acquisition and the manifestation of differential responses to food (Fonberg, 1969; Rolls and Rolls, 1973). With regard to neophobia and CTA (phenomena claimed to be closely linked), a critical role for basolateral and lateral nuclei has been supported by various experimenters (Kemble and Nagel, 1973; Aggleton, Petrides and Iversen, 1981; Aggleton and Passingham, 1982; FitzGerald and Burton, 1981; FitzGerald and Burton, 1983; Nachman and Ashe, 1974). Recent research from our laboratory extends these findings, as is described below.

In one of the experiments three groups were compared: controls, rats with bilateral lesions in the basolateral nuclei (A-BL), and rats with bilateral lesions in the lateral nuclei (A-L). After surgery they were habituated to a drinking schedule of two daily sessions: 30 minutes in the morning and 2 hours in the afternoon. During five consecutive days water consumption during the morning was measured and taken as baseline. On Day 6, rats were presented with a 0.25% saccharin solution during the 30-min morning session and their intake was followed by a LiCl injection, in accordance with the usual CTA paradigm. On Days 7 and 8 water was again presented during the morning session. From Day 9 and throughout a 10-day 'extinction' phase, the saccharin solution was presented.

As shown in Figure 1, on Day 6 control rats exhibited a neophobic response to saccharin solution in that intake was reduced in comparison to the water baseline. This neophobia was absent in A-BL rats, whereas A-L rats showed a preference for the sweet solution. When consumption on Day 9 (testing day) was compared to that on Day 6 (conditioning day) control rats showed the classical results of toxicosis, in that consumption was well below the baseline and this was maintained during the rest of the extinction phase. In rats lesioned in the baso-lateral nuclei (ABL) the conditioning by LiCl of a lower palatability of the saccharin solution was attenuated. On Day 9 and the following days the

SUCROSE SOLUTION

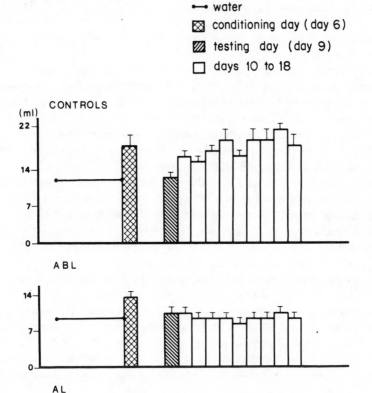

• ── • water
▨ conditioning day (day 6)
▨ testing day (day 9)
☐ days 10 to 18

Figure 2. Baso-lateral amygdala lesions (ABL) abolish the progressive increase in the intake of a daily presented sucrose solution or conditioned-taste preference for this solution. This progressive increase is maintained after lateral lesions of the amygdala (AL)

response to saccharin did not differ statistically from the response of other controls which had also been lesioned in the baso-lateral nuclei, but were injected with NaCl instead of LiCl on the conditioning day. This impairment of conditioning could be ascribed to the absence of an initial neophobia, according to the notion that a novel stimulus and neophobia are a prerequisite for learning (Archer and Sjoden, 1979; Braveman and Jarvis, 1978). This notion was ruled out by the results from the A-L group. Despite the initial preference for saccharin in this group, a LiCl-induced aversion was obtained as in the control, unlesioned rats.

In a second experiment, three groups of control, basolateral and lateral lesioned rats received a 20% sucrose solution to drink during the morning session according to the same timing of daily presentations as above. On Day 6, consumption was not followed by injections.

As shown in Figure 2, unlesioned rats drank a large volume of the sweet solution even on the first presentation. From Day 9 this intake increased progressively from a level initially lower than on Day 6. This increase obviously reflects a taste preference, or enhanced palatability, conditioned by the post-ingestive caloric action of the sweet solution, since control rats which received a saccharin solution under identical conditions did not show this progressive increase in intake (see Figure 3). The conditioning of a taste preference for sucrose was not affected by lateral lesions and was even more conspicuous in the A-L group than in the controls. However, no such trend was found in the animals given baso-lateral lesions. Over the 10-day period this group (A-BL) continued to drink an amount of sucrose solution equal to the daily amounts of water they had previously drunk during the initial baseline phase. Thus, they did not show the progressive increase of intake exhibited by the unlesioned and laterally lesioned rats during the same period. This cannot be an effect of the lower water intake in these baso-laterally lesioned rats, since

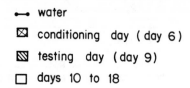

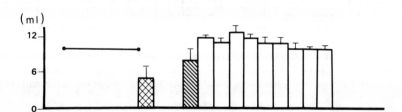

Figure 3.   In unlesioned rats successive daily presentations of a saccharin solution produce a maintained or diminished intake, after the initial neophobic response has disappeared. This is unlike the effect of sucrose shown in Figure 2

this reduced water intake was also exhibited by laterally-lesioned animals. Rats in the A-BL group drank no more sucrose solution over the 10-day test period than water during the previous six baseline days and considerably less than unlesioned and laterally lesioned rats during the same test period.

In summary, the baso-lateral nucleus of the amygdala appears to be a critical site in the neuronal circuitry involved in palatability learning. It is involved, not only in the conditioning of lower palatability known as aversion, but also and identically in the physiological conditioning of increased palatability or preference brought about by the post-ingestive nutritive properties of the food. This supports the notion of a continuum and of common mechanisms for the conditioning of the ingestive response in two opposite directions.

Brain Opioids and Sensory Food Reward

Many investigators have reported that the opiate antagonists, Naloxone and Naltrexone, suppress the 24-hour *ad libitum* intake of food by rats (Frank and Rogers, 1979). A considerable number of agents and drugs alter food intake. This alone is not, of course, evidence for their physiological involvement in feeding mechanisms. In order to show a physiological action these agents must be shown to act, or these drugs to interfere, with mechanisms already known to govern food intake.

It has been amply demonstrated that cumulative intake results from the interaction of separate mechanisms, stimuli, and brain targets which control meal initiation and meal size, respectively (Le Magnen, 1983). Meal initiation after a time of spontaneous no eating or satiety, or after food deprivation, is strictly dependent on, and brought about by, body energy imbalances, and in particular by a deficit of glucose supply to tissue. It is profoundly affected by the storage and/or the mobilization of body fats controlled by a specific and autonomous mechanism. This makes it *a priori* doubtful that brain opiates might be involved in meal initiation, since their release and their targets are not related to those metabolic factors which are demonstrated to be effective (Morley, Levine, Yim and Lowy, 1983). Food deprivation has been shown to be a stressor (Bodnar, Brutus, Glusman and Kelly, 1978; Bodnar, Kelly, Spiaggia and Glusman, 1978) and, as such, elicits endorphin release (Akil, Mayer and Liebeskind, 1976; Madden, Akil, Patrick and Barchas, 1977). However this, as well as the pharmacological action of various agonists and antagonists of κ or β opiate receptors, gives no evidence for the action to these receptors and their ligands in the response to food deprivation, i.e. eating food without delay.

We have been the first to suggest, and to provide experimental evidence, that opiate antagonists reduce food intake by antagonizing expression of the palatability of foods. Naloxone reduces acutely both the high palatability of a sweet solution and the low palatability of a quinine or ethanol solution in rats (Le Magnen, Marfaing-Jallat, Miceli and Devos, 1980). The suggestion of brain opiate release as a substrate for food reward has been recently confirmed. The intake of a saccharin solution indeed produces a depletion of beta endorphin in the hypothalamus (Dum, Gramsch and Herz, 1983). In addition, it has been shown by other investigators that, as expected, a chronic intake of saccharin solution by rats induced a state of opiate tolerance (Cohen, Lieblich and Granchrow, 1982; Lieblich, Cohen, Granchrow, Blass and Bergmann, 1983). Following such a chronic intake, rats exhibit a reduced analgesic action of exogenous morphine.

In two series of experiments we have obtained evidence for the role of brain opioids in brain rewarding systems underlying sensory food reward, as is summarized below.

Rats received during their first spontaneous meal of the nocturnal period either their familiar stock-diet or this diet adulterated by addition of the non-toxic bitter compound, sucrose octo-acetate. In successive tests, they took various amounts of either of the two diets until satiety. Thirty minutes after the end of the meal, they were submitted to a test of analgesia. The degree of analgesia was found to be proportional to the amount of food eaten and dependent on the palatability of the food eaten. Figure 4 illustrates the linear correlation which was obtained between the size of the meal and post-prandial analgesia and the difference betwen the two diets. A naloxone injection, which was given 15 minutes prior to the analgesic test, abolished food-induced analgesia and elicited hyperalgesia. This post-prandial analgesia, and its proportionality to the cumulative sensory activity of the food within the meal, strongly suggest that palatability and its level involve a release of endogenous opiates. It also suggests that brain rewarding systems underlying and current reinforcement of food intake involve brain opioids and opiate receptors in their synaptic transmission, in addition perhaps to other neurotransmitters such as dopamine (as suggested by Wise, 1982).

In another experiment, we have demonstrated that a chronic intake of high palatability foods by rats given what is known as a 'cafeteria regimen' (Sclafani and Springer, 1976; Rolls, Rowe, Rolls, Kingston, Megson and Gunary, 1981) induced a state resembling an opiate dependence, which appears to be a state of dependence on the release of endogenous brain opiates. Rats were placed for 15 days and more on a cafeteria regimen, i.e. a choice of highly palatable foods which were changed every day. Rats in this condition eat daily 50 to 100% more than their previous intake of the stock diet or the intake of controls maintained on the familiar diet. We have shown previously that this hyperphagia is not due to the high-fat diet selected by rats in their choice of the offered diet (Louis-Sylvestre, 1983). Hyperphagia and the resulting obesity are also induced by a choice of foods which mimic the stock diet in terms of their nutritional contents and which are made highly palatable by non-nutritive additives (Louis-Sylvestre, 1983). It has also been shown that the hyperphagia is entirely due to huge meals stimulated by the variety and successive intake of the offered diets during the meal and therefore to 'sensory specific satiety' (Rogers and Blundell, 1980; Le Magnen and Devos, unpublished).

After this chronic and palatability-induced hyperphagia developed, rats injected with naloxone exhibited a precipitated morphine withdrawal as if they

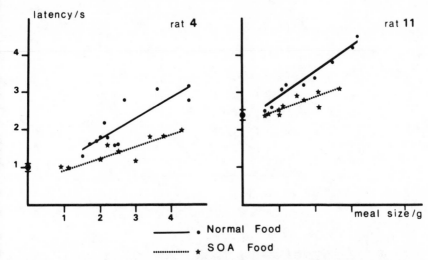

Figure 4. Post-prandial analgesia, tested by tail-flick latencies, is proportional to the amount of food eaten and to the palatability of the offered food, which was either their familiar diet (normal) or this diet adulterated with the bitter compound, sucrose octo-acetate (SOA)

were morphine-dependent. Some behavioural signs were observed: piloerection, lordosis, head shakes, whole body shakes, teeth chattering, and polypnea. The same rats prior to the cafeteria regimen and controls maintained on the stock diet did not display this typical syndrome under naloxone.

Thus, much evidence is now available implicating a role for brain opiates released by the sensory activity of foods supporting the palatability response to, and hedonic value of, food sensory stimuli. Furthermore, this last experiment suggests that a chronic elicitation of this system by high palatability foods produces in rats a state of morphine-like tolerance and dependence.

Hunger and Palatability in Man

A technique has been developed in our laboratory which permits the quantitative assessment of the microstructure of human meals. Equipment that is not disturbing to subjects allows the experimenter to record graphically the chewing and swallowing pattern during a test meal. At the time of their ordinary meal, subjects are offered pieces of bread of a constant size and asked to eat freely until satiety. A layer of various flavoured items on pieces of bread gives them different palatability. In previous work, it was shown that various indices of the chewing-swallowing pattern represent a measure of the palatability level or its inter-individual differences and intra-individual development during the meal. Chewing duration of each mouthful and number of masticatory movements of each bit of food at the beginning of the meal were correlated in each subject with a previous rating of their like or dislike of the food by visual analogue scaling (Bellisle, 1979; Bellisle and Le Magnen, 1981).

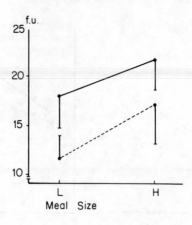

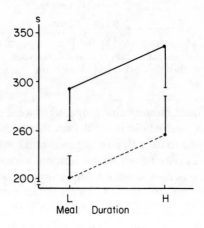

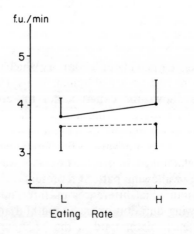

Figure 5.   Meal size, meal duration and eating rate during human meals of either high (H) palatability or low (L) palatability food

They were also positively correlated to meal sizes. Finally, when the indices were compared during the first and the last quarters of the meal, it was observed that these palatability indices decreased from the beginning to the end of the meal.

This technique has been used to test the hunger-palatability relationship. Eight subjects were tested with two flavours chosen as being of high or low palatability value by each subject in an initial visual analogue rating. The chewing-swallowing pattern for each of the two items was recorded under two different conditions of previous food deprivation. Subjects were tested at noon, either 4 hours after their ordinary breakfast or, omitting their breakfast, 15 hours after their last meal (Bellisle and Le Magnen, 1981).

Meal sizes and palatability indices at the beginning of the meal clearly indicated the additive effects of palatability and duration of food deprivation at the time of the meal. Fifteen hours compared to 4 hours of food deprivation increased by the same degree the high and low palatability food in the continuum of palatability levels. In terms of meal size, amounts eaten were in the order: low palatability–low hunger; low palatability–high hunger; low hunger–high palatability; high hunger–high palatability (see Figure 5). These hunger-palatability relationships indicated by indices of chewing and swallowing of each piece of food at the beginning of the meal were no longer apparent during the last quarter of the meal. This suggests that whatever the difference of palatability and of the strength of hunger at the initiation of the meal, palatability differences are suppressed and tend to zero during the onset of satiety (Bellisle and Le Magnen, 1981).

GENERAL DISCUSSION

The above conceptual discussion and experimental findings lead to the following conclusions.

Animals and human beings exhibit ingestive responses to various foods each of which manifests a sensory-specific stimulation to eat, i.e. a given level of 'palatability' for each food. This orosensory stimulation of eating and its strength mediate meal initiation and the rate of eating at the beginning of the meal. It is both state-dependent and sensory-specific. It is dependent on a systemic stimulus to eat and on the central state of hunger promoted by this systemic signal for most external sensory cues, for example, sweet tastes, food odours and textures. Palatability can be dependent on other states; for example, sodium depletion changes the effect of sensory stimuli such as a salty taste.

This permissive action of the internal state on the sensory mediation of eating is sensory-specific and, according to the stimulus concerned, is either genetically programmed or learned. It is unlearned: (1) when, and in as much as, the activity of the food on the sensory apparatus is due to a nutritionally active component of the food, and (2) when, and in as much as, this activity leads to a qualitative discrimination, specific to the particular nutritional property. These two conditions hold for sweet tasting compounds as long as they are carbohydrates, the palatability of which is promoted by hunger. These conditions also apply to salty compounds, the palatability of which is promoted by sodium depletion.

All other sensory-specific palatability levels based upon sensory activity arising from non-nutritive properties of the food are learned. From the first days of life in animals and humans, this learning of the palatability of foods (also called 'taste preferences') occurs by association between the pattern of oropharyngeal sensory activities of the food passing the mouth and post-ingestive relief or recovery from the systemic depletion. During the acquisition of palatability or flavour preference the post-ingestive primary food reinforcement or reward is transferred to the associated external stimuli as secondary reinforcer, as in the case of all forms of learning. This sensory food reward cannot be distinguished from the food's palatability and also, in man, from its subjective properties: hedonic value and pleasantness. This process of learning involves the brain reward systems identified by intracranial electrical self-stimulation. One particularly important system consists of the neuroanatomical connections between the baso-lateral nuclei and amygdala and the lateral hypothalamus, plus the sensory afferents to these two brain sites. We have provided evidence that neurochemical brain opioids and brain opioreceptors are critically involved in the brain mechanisms underlying sensory food reward.

Palatability level, as measured in animals and humans by initial rate of eating, is a continuum from 'unpalatability' (i.e. the lack of stimulation) up to some maximal level. Aversion (that is, the property of some stimuli to antagonize palatability and to actively inhibit the ingestive response) is a separate phenomenon. Genetically programmed and unlearned aversions are based upon sensory stimuli such as acid and bitter stimuli, in as much as they are due to offensive or deleterious components of the food. Other aversions are acquired by the process called 'conditioned taste aversion'. In a learned taste aversion illness or metabolic imbalances act as the post-ingestive UCS. However, in humans, social reinforcers and cognitive factors may produce aversions to non-tasted foods (Birch, this volume). During the acquisition, but not necessarily in the maintenance of those learned aversions, the lateral hypothalamus and the baso-lateral amygdala are involved. In addition, the area postrema seems to be specifically involved in the learning of genuine defensive reactions against intoxication and malnutrition (Berger, Wise and Stein, 1973; Ritter, McGlove and Kelly, 1980).

Following some initial level of sensory-specific stimulation, consumption of a food, and the subsequent cumulative action on oropharyngeal receptors and gastrointestinal sensors, gives rise to a peripheral satiation process which counteracts the initial stimulation, as a kind of negative feedback action. After a given amount of food has been eaten, the onset of satiety results from the balance between the respective strengths of the positive and negative feedbacks. Satiation is the progressive suppression of hunger throughout a meal. Since the palatability of a food is hunger-dependent, satiation is accompanied by the progressive suppression of palatability. This is well reflected by the pattern of chewing and swallowing described above in man. The shift from the beginning to the end of a meal is a shift from palatability to unpalatability, and not to a true aversion. A true aversion, accompanied by nausea and vomiting, seems to occur beyond satiation; for example, as a result of forced intake beyond the onset of physiological satiety.

Much evidence exists that the satiating action of eating a food, like its initial palatability level, is learned. This orally-induced and learned oral satiation is sensory and therefore food-specific. As a result, it appears, two separate processes of learning exist, one for the initial stimulating and one for the later inhibiting effects, some foods can be both palatable at the beginning of the meal and also strongly satiating, and vice versa. How these two distinct processes of learning occur is unclear. However, it was suggested long ago that this peripheral satiating action of food, both at oral and post-oral levels, is conditioned by the post-ingestive state of satiety and its duration (Capretta, 1962, 1964; Le Magnen, 1957a, 1957b, 1957c).

REFERENCES

Aggleton, J.P. and Passingham, R.E. (1982). An assessment of the reinforcing properties of foods after amygdaloid lesions in rhesus monkeys. *Journal of Comparative and Physiological Psychology*, **96**, 71–77.

Aggleton, J.P., Petrides, M. and Iverson, S.D. (1981). Differential effects of amygdaloid lesions on conditioned taste aversion learning by rats. *Physiology and Behavior*, **27**, 397–400.

Akil, H., Mayer, D.J. and Liebeskind, J.C. (1976). Antagonism of stimulation-produced analgesia by naloxone, as narcotic antagonist. *Science*, **191**, 961–963.

Aleksanyan, Z.A., Buresova, O. and Bures, J. (1976). Modification of unit responses to gustatory stimuli by conditioned taste aversion in rats. *Physiology and Behavior*, **17**, 173–179.

Aravich, P.F. and Sclafani, A. (1980). Dietary preference in rats fed bitter tasting quinine and sucrose octa acetate adulterated diets. *Physiology and Behavior*, **25**, 157–160.

Archer, T. and Sjoden, P.O. (1979). Positive correlation between pre- and post-conditioning saccharin intake in taste-aversion learning. *Animal Learning and Behavior*, **7**, 144–148.

Archer, T., Sjoden, P.O., Nilsson, L.G. and Carter, N. (1979). Role of exteroceptive background context in taste-aversion conditioning and extinction. *Animal Learning and Behavior*, **7**, 17–22.

Bellisle, F. (1979). Human feeding behaviour. *Neuroscience and Biobehavioural Review*, **3**, 163–169.

Bellisle, F. and Le Magnen, J. (1981). The structure of meals in humans: eating and drinking patterns in lean and obese subjects. *Physiology and Behavior*, **27**, 649–658.

Bellisle, F., Lucas, F., Amrani, R. and Le Magnen, J. (1984). Deprivation palatability and the microstructure of meals in human subjects. *Appetite*, **5**, 85–94.

Berg, H.W., Pangborn, R.M., Roessler, E.B. and Webb, A.D. (1963). Influence of hunger and olfactory acuity. *Nature*, **197**, 108.

Berger, B.D., Wise, C.D. and Stein, L. (1973). Area postrema damage and bait-shyness. *Journal of Comparative and Physiological Psychology*, **82**, 475–479.

Bernstein, I.L. and Goehler, L.E. (1983). Chronic lithium chloride infusions; conditioned suppression of food intake and preference. *Behavioral Neuroscience*, **97**, 290–298.

Bodnar, R.J., Brutus, M., Glusman, M. and Kelly, D.D. (1978). Analgesia induced by 2-deoxy-D-glucose, an antimetabolic glucose analogue. *Federal Proceedings*, **37**, 470.

Bodnar, R.J., Kelly, D.D., Spiaggia, A. and Glusman, M. (1978). Biphasic alterations of nociceptive thresholds induced by food deprivation. *Physiological Psychology*, **6**, 391–395.

Booth D.A. (1972). Conditioned satiety in rats. *Journal of Comparative and Physiological Psychology*, **81**, 457–471.

Booth, D.A. and Davis, J.D. (1973). Gastrointestinal factors in the acquisition of oral sensory control of satiation. *Physiology and Behavior*, **11**, 23–30.

Booth, D.A. and Simson, P.C. (1974). Taste aversion induced by an histidine-free amino acid load. *Physiological Psychology*, **2**(3A), 349–351.

Borison, H.L. and Wang, S.C. (1953). Physiology and pharmacology of vomiting. *Pharmacological Review*, **5**, 193–230.

Boudreau,J.C., Hoang, N.K.,Oravec, J. and Do, L.T.(1983). Rat neurophysiological taste responses to salt solutions. *Chemical Senses*, **8**, 131–150.

Braveman, N.S. and Jarvis, P.S. (1978). Independence of neophobia and taste aversion learning. *Animal Learning and Behavior*, **6**, 406–412.

Burghardt, G.M. (1970). Chemical perception in reptiles. In J.W. Johnston, Jr., D.G. Moulton and A. Turks (Eds), *Communications by Chemical Signals*, Appleton-Century-Crofts, New York, pp. 241–308.

Burton, M.J., Mora, F. and Rolls, E.T. (1975). Visual and taste neurones in the lateral hypothalamus and substantia innominata: modulation of responsiveness by hunger. *Journal of Physiology (London)*, **252**, 50P.

Burton, M.J., Rolls, E.T. and Mora, F. (1976). Effects of hunger on the responses of neurones in the hypothalamus to the sight and taste of food. *Experimental Neurology*, **53**, 508–519.

Cabanac, M. (1979). Sensory pleasure. *Quarterly Journal of Biology*, **54**, 29P.

Capretta. P.J. (1962). Saccharin consumption under varied conditions of hunger drive. *Journal of Comparative and Physiological Psychology*, **55**, 656–660.

Capretta, P.J. (1964). Saccharin consumption and the reinforcement issue. *Journal of Comparative and Physiological Psychology*, **57**, 448–450.

Chang, F.C. and Scott, T.R. (1984). Conditioned taste aversions modify neural responses in the rat nucleus tractus solitaris. *Journal of Neuroscience*, **4**, 1850–1862.

Chaput, M. and Holley, A. (1976). Olfactory bulb responsiveness to food odour during stomach destension in the rat. *Chemical Senses and Flavour*, **2**, 189–202.

Cohen, E., Lieblich, I. and Ganchrow, J.R. (1982). Saccharin preferences in prepubertal male and female rats: relationship to self-stimulation. *Behavioral and Neural Biology*, **36**, 88–93.

Deutsch, J.A. and Gonzalez, M.F. (1980). Gastric nutrient content signals satiety. *Behavioral and Neural Biology*, **30**, 113–116.

Deutsch, J.A., Gonzalez, M.F. and Young, M.G. (1980). Two factors control meal size. *Brain Research Bulletin*, **5**, (suppl 4), 55–58.

Deutsch, J.A. and Hardy, W.T. (1977). Cholecystokinin produces bait shyness in rats. *Nature*, **266**, 196.

Desor, J.A., Maller, O. and Turner, R. (1973). Taste in acceptance of sugars by human infants. *Journal of Comparative and Physiological Psychology*, **84**, 496–501.

Duclaux, R., Feisthauer, J. and Cabanac, M. (1973). Effets du repas sur l'agrement d'odeurs alimentaires et non alimentaires chez l'homme. *Physiology and Behavior*, **10**, 1029–1034.

Dugas du Villard, X., Her, C. and MacLeod, P. (1981). Qualitative discrimination of sweet stimuli: behavioural study on rats. *Chemical Senses*, **6**, 143–148.

Dum, J., Gramsch, C.H. and Herz, A. (1983). Activation of hypothalamic endorphin pools by reward induced by highly palatable food. *Pharmacology, Biochemistry and Behaviour*, **18**, 443–447.

Ettenberg, A. (1980). Conditioned taste preference and response rate as measures of brain-stimulation reward: a comparison. *Physiology and Behavior*, **24**, 755–758.

Ettenberg, A., Sgro, S. and White, N. (1982). Algebraic summation of the affective properties of a rewarding and an aversive stimulus in the rat. *Physiology and Behavior*, **28**, 873–878.

Faurion, A. (1982). Etude des mecanismes de la chimioreception du goût sucré. Universite de Paris.

FitzGerald, R.E. and Burton, M.J. (1981). Effects of small basolateral amygdala lesions on ingestion in the rat. *Physiology and Behavior*, **27**, 431–438.

FitzGerald, R.E. and Burton, M.J. (1983). Neophobia and conditioned taste aversion deficits in the rat produced by undercutting temporal cortex. *Physiology and Behavior*, **30**, 203–206.

Fonberg, E. (1969). The role of the hypothalamus and amygdala in food intake, alimentary motivation and emotional reactions. *Acta Biologica Experimentalis*, **29**, 335–358.

Frenk, H. and Rogers, G.H. (1979). The suppressant effects of naxolone on food and water intake in the rat. *Behavioral and Neural Biology*, **26**, 23–40.

Furchtgott, E. and Friedman, M.P. (1960). The effects of hunger on taste and odor RLs. *Journal of Comparative and Physiological Psychology*, **53**, 576–587.

Ganchrow, J.R., Lieblich, I. and Cohen, E. (1981). Consummatory responses to taste stimuli in rats selected for high and low rates of self-stimulation. *Physiology and Behavior*, **27**, 971–976.

Glenn, J.F. and Erickson, R.P. (1976) Gastric modulation of gustatory afferent activity. *Physiology and Behavior*, **16**, 561–568.

Goetzl, F.R. and Stone, F. (1947). Diurnal variations in acuity of olfaction and food intake. *Gastroenterology*, **9**, 444–453.

Green, K.F. and Garcia, J. (1971). Recuperation from illness: flavor enhancement for rats. *Science*, **173**, 749–751.

Guttman, N. (1953). Operant conditioning, extinction and periodic reinforcement in relation to concentration of sucrose used as a reinforcing agent. *Journal of Experimental Psychology*, **46**, 213–424.

Harris, L.J., Clay, J., Hargreaves, F.J. and Ward, A. (1933). Appetite and choice of diet: the ability of the vitamin B deficient rat to discriminate between diets containing and lacking the vitamin. *Proceedings of the Royal Society of London (Series B)*, **113**, 162–190.

Hasegawa, Y. (1981). Recuperation from lithium-induced illness: flavor enhancement for rats. *Behavioral and Neural Biology*, **33**, 252–256.

Kemble, E.D. and Nagel, J.A. (1973). Failure to form a learned taste aversion in rats with amygdaloid lesions. *Bulletin of the Psychonomic Society*, **2**, 155–156.

Kogure, S., Onada, N. and Takagi, S.F. (1980). Responses to lateral hypothalamic neurons to odours before and during stomach distension in unanaesthetized rabbits. *28th International Congress of Physiological Sciences*, Budapest.

Kolakowska, L., Larue-Achagiotis,. C. and Le Magnen, J. (1984). Effets comparés de la lésion du noyau basolatéral et du noyau lateral de l'amygdale sur la néophobie et l'aversion gustative conditionee chez le rat. *Physiology and Behavior*, **32**, 647–651.

Kratz, C.M., Levitsky, D.A. and Lustick, S. (1978). Differential effects of quinine and sucrose octo-acetate on food intake in the rat. *Physiology and Behavior*, **20**, 665–668.

Larue, C. (1978). Oral cues involved in the rat's selective intake of fats. *Chemical Senses and Flavor*, **3**, 1–6.

Le Magnen, J. (1956). Hyperphagie provoquée chez le rat blanc par alteration du mecanisme de satiete peripherique. *Comptes Rendus de la Societe de Biologie*, **150**, 32.

Le Magnen, J. (1957a). Etude d'un facteur post-ingestif de l'establishment des appetits chez le rat blanc. *Archives Sciences Physiologiques (Paris)*, **11**, 263–271.

Le Magnen, J. (1957b). Les effets respictifs de durée de jeûne avante et apres le repas sur l'etablissement de l'appetit. *Archives Sciences Physiologiques (Paris)*, **11**, 263–271.

Le Magnen, J. (1957c). Effet de la durée du jeûne post-prandial sur l'establissement des appetits chez le rat blanc. *Comptes Rendus de la Société Biologie (Paris)*. **151**, 229–231.

Le Magnen, J. (1959). Effets des administrations post-prandiales de glucose sur l'etablissement des appetits. *Comptes Rendus de la Société Biologie*, **153**, 212–215.

Le Magnen, J. (1960). Effets d'une pluralite de stimuli alimentaires sur le determinisme quantitatif de l'ingestion chez le rat blanc. *Archives Sciences Physiologique*, **14**, 411–419.

Le Magnen, J. (1971). Advances in studies on the physiological control and regulation of food intake. In E. Stellar and J.M. Sprague (Eds), *Progress in Physiological Psychology*, vol. 4, 204–261.

Le Magnen, J. (1983). Body energy balance and food intake: a neuro-endocrine regulatory mechanism. *Physiological Review*, **63**, 314–386.

Le Magnen, J. (1985). Hunger, *Problems in the Behavioural Sciences*, Cambridge University Press, Cambridge.

Le Magnen, J., Marfaing-Jallat, P., Miceli, D. and Devos, M. (1980). Pain modulating and reward systems: a single brain mechanism? *Pharmacology, Biochemistry and Behavior*, **12**, 729–733.

Lieblich, I., Cohen, E., Ganchrow, J.R., Blass, E.M. and Bergmann, F. (1983). Morphine tolerance in genetically selected rats induced by chronically elevated saccharin intake. *Science*, **221**, 871–872.

Louis-Sylvestre, J. (1983). Phase cephalique de la secretion d'insuline et varieté des aliments au cours du repas chez le rat. *Reprod. Nutr. Develop.*, **23**, 351–356.

McCutcheon, B. and Brown, L. (1983). Response to NaCl taste in mixture with sucrose by sodium deficient rats. *Physiology and Behavior*, **30**, 405–408.

Mackintosh, N.J. (1974). *The Psychology of Animal Learning*, Academic Press, London.

Madden, J., Akil, H., Patrick, R.L. and Barchas, J.D. (1977). Stress-induced parallel changes in central opioid levels and pain responsiveness in the rat. *Nature*, **265**, 358–360.

Marfaing-Jallat, P. and Le Magnen, J. (1982). Induction of high voluntary ethanol intake in dependent rats. *Pharmacology, Biochemistry and Behavior*, **17**, 609–612.

Marfaing-Jallat, P. and Le Magnen, J. (1984). Further study of induced behavioural dependence on ethanol in rats. *Alcohol*, 259–273.

Mora, F., Rolls, E.T. and Burton, M.J. (1976). Modulation during learning of the responses of neurones in the lateral hypothalamus to the sight of food. *Experimental Neurology*, **53**, 508–519.

Morley, J.E., Levine, A.S., Gosnell, B.A., Kneip, J. and Grace, M. (1983). The kappa opiate receptor, ingestive behaviours and the obese mouse (ob/ob). *Physiology and Behavior*, **31**, 593–602.

Morley, J.E., Levine, A.S., Yim, G.K. and Lowy, M.T. (1983). Opioid modulation of appetite. *Neuroscience and Biobehavioural Review*, **7**, 281–305.

Nachman, M. and Ashe, J.H. (1974). Effects of basolateral amygdala lesions on neophobia, learned taste aversions and sodium appetite in rats. *Journal of Comparative and Physiological Psychology*, **87**, 622–643.

Norgren, R. (1976). Taste pathways to hypothalamus and amygdala. *Journal of Comparative Neurology*, **166**, 17–30.

Oomura, Y. (1976). Significance of glucose, insulin and free fatty acids on the hypothalamic feeding and satiety neurons. In D. Novin, W. Wyrwicka and G.A. Bray (Eds), *Hunger: Basic Mechanisms and Clinical Implications*, Raven Press, New York, pp. 145–148.

Pager, J. (1974). A selective modulation of the olfactory bulb electrical activity in relation to the learning of palatability in hungry and satiated rats. *Physiology and Behavior*, **12**, 189–196.

Pager, J. and Royet, J.P. (1976). Some effects of conditioned aversion on food intake and olfactory bulb electrical responses in the rat. *Journal of Comparative Physiological Psychology*, **90**, 67–77.

Pager, J., Giachetti, I., Holley, A. and Le Magnen, J. (1972). A selective control of olfactory bulb electrical activity in relation to food deprivation and satiety in rats. *Physiology and Behavior*, **9**, 573–579.

Parker, L., Failor, A. and Weidman, C. (1973). Conditioned preference in the rat with an unnatural need state: a morphine withdrawal. *Journal of Comparative and Physiological Psychology*, **82**, 294–300.

Pfaffman, C. (1936). Differential responses of the newborn cat to gustatory stimuli. *Journal of Genetic Psychology*, **49**, 61–67.

Pfaffman, C. and Bare, J.K. (1950). Gustatory nerve discharges in normal and adrenalectomized rats. *Journal of Comparative and Physiological Psychology*, **43**, 320–324.

Pfaffman, C. and Hagstrom, E.C. (1955). Factors influencing taste sensitivity to sugars. *American Journal of Physiology*, **183**, 651.

Ricardo, J.A. and Koh, E.T. (1978). Anatomical evidence of direct projections from the nucleus of the solitary tract to the hypothalamus amygdala and other forebrain structures in the rat. *Brain Research*, **153**, 1–26.

Richter, E.P. (1941). Biology of drives. *Psychosomatic Medicine*, **3**, 105.

Richter, C. (1957). Hunger and appetite. *Journal of Clinical Nutrition*, **5**, 141.

Ritter, S., McGlove, Y.Y. and Kelley, K.W. (1980). Absence of lithium-induced taste aversion after area postrema (AP) lesion. *Brain Research*, **201**, 501–506.

Rogers, P.J. and Blundell, J.E. (1980). Investigation of food selection and meal parameters during the development of dietary-induced obesity. *Appetite*, **1**, 85 (abstract).

Rolls, B.J., Rowe, E.A. and Rolls, E.T. (1982). How sensory properties of food affect human feeding behaviour. *Physiology and Behavior*, **29**, 409–418.

Rolls, B.J., Van Duijvenvoorde, P.M. and Rowe, E.A. (1983). Variety in the diet enhances intake in a meal and contributes to the development of obesity in the rat. *Physiology and Behavior*, **31**, 21–29.

Rolls, B.J., Rowe, E.A., Rolls, E.T., Kingston, B., Megson, A. and Gunary, R. (1981). Variety in a meal enhances food intake in man. *Physiology and Behavior*, **26**, 215–222.

Rolls, E.T., Burton, M.J. and Mora, F. (1976). Hypothalamic neuronal responses associated with the sight of food. *Brain Research*, **111**, 53–66.

Rolls, E.T. and Rolls, B.J. (1973). Altered food preferences after lesions in the basolateral region of the amygdala in the rat. *Journal of Comparative and Physiological Psychology*, **83**, 284–259.

Roth, S.R., Schwartz, M. and Teitelbaum, P. (1973). Failure of recovered lateral hypothalamic rats to learn specific food aversions. *Journal of Comparative and*

Physiological Psychology, **83**, 184–197.

Rozin, P. and Kalat, J.W. (1971). Specific hungers and poison avoidance as adaptative specialization of learning. *Psychological Review*, **78**, 459–486.

Saper, C.B., Loewy, A.D., Swanson, L.W. and Cowan, W.M. (1976). Direct hypothalamo-autonomic connections. *Brain Research*, **117**, 305–312.

Schwartz, M. and Teitelbaum, P. (1974). Dissociation between learning and remembering in rats with lesions in the lateral hypothalamus. *Journal of Comparative and Physiological Psychology*, **87**, 384–398.

Sclafani, A. and Springer, D. (1976). Dietary obesity in adult rats: similarities to hypothalamic and human obesity syndromes. *Physiology and Behavior*, **17**, 461–471.

Simson, P.C. and Booth, D.A. (1973). Effects of CS-US interval on the conditioning of odour preferences by amino-acid loads. *Physiology and Behavior*, **11**, 801–808.

Steiner, J. (1973). The gusto-facial response: observations on normal and anencephalic newborn infants. In J.F. Bosma (Ed.), *Oral Sensation and Perception: Development in the Fetus and Infant*, US Department of Health, Education and Welfare, Bethesda, Maryland, pp. 254–278.

Treit, D., Spetch, M.L. and Deutsch, J.A. (1983). Variety in the flavor of food enhances eating in the rat: a controlled demonstration. *Physiology and Behavior*, **30**, 207–211.

Wike, E.L. and Casey, A. (1954). The secondary reward value of food for satiated animals. *Journal of Comparative and Physiological Psychology*, **47**, 441–443.

Wise, R.A. (1982). Neuroleptics and operant behavior: the anhedonia hypothesis. *The Behavioral and Brain Sciences*, **5**, 39–52.

Zahorik, V., Maier, S. and Pies, R.W. (1974). Preferences for tastes paired with recovery from thiamine deficiency in rats. *Journal of Comparative and Physiological Psychology*, **80**, 1083–1091.

Eating Habits
Edited by R.A. Boakes, D.A. Popplewell and M.J. Burton
© 1987 John Wiley & Sons Ltd

CHAPTER 7

Signals Determining Meal Size

J. Anthony Deutsch
Department of Psychology, University of California, San Diego, La Jolla, California 92093, USA

This chapter focuses on the problem of what mechanisms terminate eating. When factors which initiate eating such as food deprivation do not vary, the amount that a rat eats during a meal is typically rather constant. What produces such a constancy of amount eaten? What signals tell the rat when to stop eating?

One supposition might be that during a period of food deprivation the animal's tissues run short of a certain amount of nutrient, so that when it eats the rat simply restores the amount lost. The problem with this view is that each is rather short, say, 10 to 20 minutes, but it may take hours for the eaten food to be digested and absorbed and so find its way back to the depleted tissues. Thus, the animal must have some way to predict whether it has eaten enough to make up for the missing nutrient when it decides to stop eating and so terminate a meal.

How does the rat make this prediction? Some headway has been made in identifying the relevant predictive signals, but as yet there is very little idea of how they are calibrated to match stimulation of the mouth with the nutritive outcome.

Consider the control of meal size. When an animal is permitted to eat and the food eaten is allowed to drain out either through an oesophageal fistula in dogs or gastric fistula in rats, eating becomes very excessive. This experiment has been repeated many times since the work of Hull, Livingstone, Rouse and Barker (1951). Davis and Campbell (1973) and Snowdon (1970) showed that, when food is withdrawn from the stomach after a meal is finished, fairly accurate compensatory ingestion occurs. Investigations in our laboratory

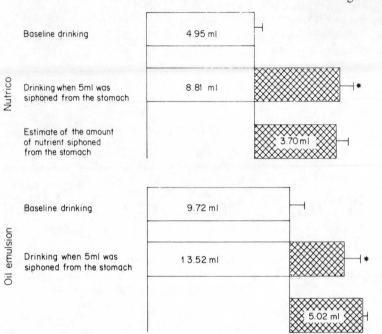

Figure 1.   Compensatory drinking after nutrient has been siphoned from the stomach for Nutrico and oil–emulsion. (The asterisks indicate $p < 0.01$ in this and following figures)

started at this point by measuring the accuracy of compensation for measured amounts lost from the stomach by the rat as it was eating a familiar diet. A tube was implanted in the stomach of the rat. (A detailed description of this surgical technique is contained in Young and Deutsch, 1981). A set amount of nutrient was siphoned from the stomach during a meal. The results of two such experiments are illustrated in Figure 1. In the top diagram the rats were drinking Nutrico, a complete liquid diet. (Deutsch and Gonzalez, 1980). In the bottom diagram they were drinking an emulsion, made up of 50% corn oil and 50% water (Deutsch and Gonzalez, 1981). As can be seen, the amount drunk in excess over baseline matches quite well the amount of nutrient siphoned from the stomach. Such compensation is immediate in two different senses. First, it occurs within the meal; the rat keeps drinking for longer. Second, the rat compensates accurately even the first time siphoning occurs. Care must be taken that the rat is thoroughly accustomed to the situation and that the diet is familiar.

What do these experiments reveal? First, they show that the animal does not simply swallow a set amount of food in response to a particular taste. Instead, it seems to eat until a certain amount of food is present in the upper gastrointestinal tract. The second thing to be learned from the experiments is that whatever it is that measures the amount of food required to produce satiety it is not signals from the mouth. Of course, the mouth in conjunction with other sensory systems is important in identifying what to eat, or what is being eaten, but the signal that induces the termination of eating by a mechanism not yet specified does not come from the mouth. If the mouth made any contribution to the signals arriving at the brain to terminate feeding, then removing food from the stomach should not cause the rat to compensate completely for the amount lost. The signals from the mouth would already have been received in the normal manner and would be unaffected by the removal of the food from the stomach. However, as discussed later, the mouth is important in selecting what end point of ingestion is relevant.

WHERE DO THE SIGNALS THAT SWITCH OFF EATING COME FROM?

When nutrient is removed from the stomach, the rat responds by compensatory eating within the same meal. This would make it seem that the stomach is the site of origin of the signals that stop eating. However, if food is disappearing from the stomach, food flow to the duodenum may also be reduced. In other words, the site at which the signals that stop eating are generated may be below the stomach. To test this possibility an inflatable cuff was implanted around the pylorus. (The pylorus marks the boundary between the stomach and the duodenum.) If satiety signals are generated below the stomach, then shutting off the flow of food to the duodenum should prevent such signals from being generated. Overeating should result. But when the pylorus is closed by inflation of the cuff, the amount eaten is essentially unchanged, as shown in Figure 2 (Deutsch and Gonzalez, 1981). This has been shown repeatedly in our laboratory (e.g. Deutsch and Gonzalez, 1980, 1981) and also by Kraly and Smith (1978).

These experiments show that sites above the pylorus produce satiety signals large enough to terminate a meal within the normal limits. These findings were confirmed and extended by investigating the rats' ability to compensate for food removed from the digestive tract when the cuff was inflated (Deutsch and Gonzalez, 1980). Again, the compensation for the amount withdrawn was as good when the pylorus was closed as when it was open, as can be seen from Figure 3.

In this particular experiment seven rats with implanted gastric tubes and pyloric cuffs were habituated to drinking Nutrico while 15 h hungry. In the test session, they were run under two conditions. In both conditions they were allowed to drink for 10 min without the pyloras occluded and for 30 min after that with the pylorus occluded. In the first condition (baseline), no nutrient was withdrawn from the stomach. In the second, a mean of 4.14 ml was withdrawn from the stomach as soon as the pylorus was occluded. There was about one-third of a ml difference in intake betwen the two conditions in the first 10 min (4.29 ml, sem ± 1.39 in the first condition and 4.64 ml, sem ± 1.07 before siphon condition.). Figure 3 shows that there is excellent compensation even with the duodenum

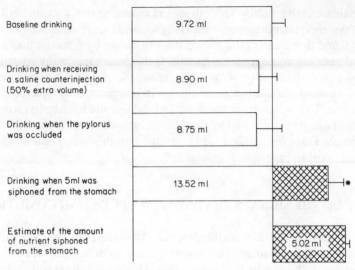

Figure 2. Nutrient intake when extra volume was placed in the stomach when siphoning of nutrient from the stomach occurred, and when the pylorus was occluded

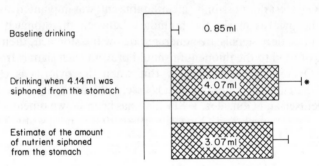

Figure 3. Compensatory drinking of Nutrico after pylorus was occluded with implanted cuff

unaffected by the withdrawal of nutrient. (The figure does not show intake in the first 10 min. It only shows intake after the pylorus in occluded.) We conclude that at least the major signal of satiety comes from the stomach and that duodenal signals are not necessary to produce satiety.

STOMACH DISTENTION

It seems that the stomach signals some consequences of food ingestion. What property of the food generates this signal? One obvious change that occurs during eating is that the stomach distends. To find out whether a certain level of distention produces the satiety signal the following experiment was performed.

Sixteen rats implanted with pyloric cuffs and stomach tubes drank milk from U-tubes. In half the tests an equal volume of saline was automatically injected into the stomach at the same rate at which the animals drank. If distention signals shut off eating, then the rats should have terminated their meal very much earlier than usual because excess volume was placed in the stomach. This was, in fact, the result; but only for some animals. Other animals drank the same amount whether extra volume was pumped into the stomach or not (Deutsch, Gonzalez and Young, 1980).

There was a correlation between the amount normally drunk and the decrease that took place in drinking when extra volume was injected into the stomach ($r = 0.744$, $p < 0.001$). The same experiment run with cuff inflated gave similar results ($r = 0.744$, $p < 0.002$). In other words, the rats that reduced their intake by mouth to keep stomach volume the same tended to be large drinkers, while the rats that did not reduce their intake when double the volume ended up in their stomach were on the whole small drinkers. Thus stomach distention does play a part in stopping further eating, but only at the upper limit of stomach capacity. It seems from our data that rats are in general unwilling to end up with more than 20–25ml in the stomach. At lower volumes distention does not operate to terminate intake, but something else does. In passing, it should be noted that very similar results are obtained whether the duodenum is excluded or not.

As it stands, the experiment could mean that there are two kind of rats and that these control the amount they eat by different mechanisms. Further, the membership of each group correlates with the amount eaten during a meal. An alternative interpretation is that all rats have a mechanism that terminates eating when the integrity of the stomach is threatened by excessive volume, and that they also have another mechanism that senses nutrient content independent of volume before the volume mechanism comes into play. To distinguish between these two alternatives, rats were fed on calorically dense nutrients. Thus they could all drink to satiety by drinking a low volume.

In one experiment (Deutsch and Gonzalez, 1980) the rats ($n=11$) drank Nutrico, a complete high calorie diet, for 30 mins. As shown in Figure 4, they drank a mean of 4.95 (sem $\pm$ 0.32) when they were drinking normally. When saline was pumped into the stomach at 50% of the volume of the rats' own intake the rats drank a mean of 5.09 ml (sem $\pm$ 0.68). In another experiment rats ($n=6$) drank a 50:50 Mazola corn oil-water emulsion for 30 min. In the normal condition the animals drank a mean of 9.72 ml (sem $\pm$ 0.89). When saline at half the rate at which they were drinking was pumped into the stomach they drank a mean of 8.90 ml (sem $\pm$ 1.35). These results support the idea that all rats sense nutrient content regardless of volume or dilution and use this to terminate intake, provided that certain absolute levels of volume are not exceeded.

The existence of two separable factors controlling intake is confirmed using transection of the two nerves that contain afferent fibres from the stomach. Section of the vagus abolishes regulation by distention, though regulation by

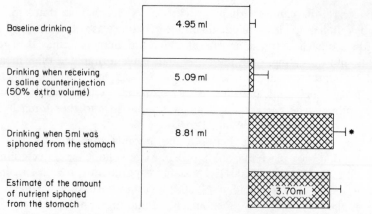

Figure 4. Drinking of Nutrico when gastric siphoning occurs and when extra volume is pumped into the stomach as rat drinks. (Data from Deutsch and Conzalez, 1980)

amount of nutrient is left intact (Gonzalez and Deutsch, 1981). On the other hand, section of the splanchnic nerve abolishes regulation by amount of nutrient (Deutsch and Ahn, 1986).

SIGNALS FOR NUTRIENT CONTENT

What aspect of the nutrient does the stomach sense? Some preliminary progress has been made in answering this question. It seems obvious that if taking nutrient out of the stomach as the rat ate increased the amount drunk by mouth, then placing nutrient in the stomach as the rat drinks should decrease intake. To confirm this prediction oil emulsion was pumped into the stomach as the rat was drinking it and surprisingly showed that such nutrient was not more effective than saline in equal volume (Gonzalez and Deutsch, in press). Then it became obvious what was wrong. Nutrient, such as fat, cannot directly be sensed. It must be broken down and, in bypassing the mouth, Ebner's glands on the lower part of the tongue are also bypassed. These glands secrete the lipase that is thought to produce gastric lipolysis (Plucinski, Hamosh and Hamosh, 1979).

To test this idea donor rats were used, who first drank the oil before it was siphoned from the stomach and then infused into the stomachs of the experimental rats. Separating the predigested oil into the oily and aqueous fractions, it can be seen from Figure 5 that it is the oily fraction that carries most of the satiating ingredients.

Furthermore, it does not seem from the results of a conditioned taste aversion experiment that predigested oil causes nausea. Rats (n=10) drank two flavours of 50:50 corn oil–water emulsion. For half the subjects one flavour of emulsion was paired with a simultaneous gastric injection of 5 ml of the same oil–water

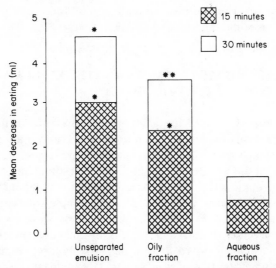

Figure 5. Decrease in meal size (in ml) of oil emulsion when 5 ml of predigested oil emulsion was injected during meal, or when the oily fraction or the aqueous fraction was injected

emulsion, but predigested. For the other half of the subjects the other flavour was paired with such an injection. The second flavour in each case had no concomitant injection with it. On the third day the rats were given a choice between the two flavours of emulsion. The whole procedure was repeated three times. There was no significant trend to decrease choice of the flavour paired with gastric injection. Nor was the absolute amount of the paired flavour drunk on any of the days significantly smaller.

In passing it should be noted that intragastric infusion of undigested oil in this experiment appears not to be aversive. We have shown that under other conditions such aversion occurs (Deutsch, Molina and Puerto, 1976). The explanation of the aversion produced by such gastric injections (Deutsch, 1978) was that digestive breakdown products of oil on entering the duodenum normally prevent further gastric eflux. But the introduction of oil directly in the stomach would greatly reduce or even eliminate such digestion, thus leading to the dumping of oil into the duodenum. In the experiment where oil is gastrically introduced when oil is also being normally ingested, breakdown products of oil digestion would be present probably in adequate quantity to prevent dumping. The aversive consequences of gastric injection of undigested oil should therefore not occur.

What has been learned about the stomach and satiety from the foregoing experiments? When the animal eats it continues until some preset level of signal has arrived in the brain. This signal is generated by the stomach. There are two main kinds of signal. The first is generated only by high volumes of intake and signals distention via the vagus. The second signals nutrient content via the splanchnic nerve regardless of volume or dilution; presumably what is actually signalled is some digestive breakdown product.

NOVEL VERSUS FAMILIAR FLAVOURS AND THE EFFECTIVENESS OF GASTRIC SIGNALS

How can the stomach measure the amount of a substance in the stomach independent of dilution of volume, even though denied information about the volume of the stomach when the vagus is cut? A chemical sensor, like a taste bud, can only signal the dilution of the substance that stimulates it and not its volume. Such information without an indication of volume cannot tell the brain the total amount of nutrient. However there is a simple solution, as I have suggested elsewhere (Deutsch, 1978). The surface of the stomach stretches as stomach volume increases. If nutrient receptors are embedded in the surface of the stomach, it may be supposed that an increasingly large number will be exposed as the volume in the stomach increases. This could be caused by having membranes slide over each other, or by the placing of receptors in pits or folds. If the volume in the stomach increases through dilution and more receptors are exposed, each individual receptor will be stimulated less than because of such dilution. Total output from such receptors would signal total amount of nutrient irrespective of volume or dilution. Alternatively, the receptors could be exposed all the time, but increase in chemical sensitivity when stretched.

If such a system for measuring nutrient content exists, then the evidence that has accumulated so far by restricting nutrient to the stomach shows only that the stomach does produced satiety signals. If such a system were in fact operating, some signals could also be generated by the duodenum as well, given the evidence available. This is because the system described is one where the parts are interchangeable. If there were similar receptors in the duodenum which normally contribute to the summed activity of the whole upper gastrointestinal tract, then preventing access of nutrient to such receptors in the duodenum could be compensated for by placing more nutrient in the stomach itself. However, the contribution of any such possible postgastric sites must, if the hypothesized system is operating, be limited to the proportion of nutrient arriving there during a meal, because there is no overeating when possible postgastric sites are excluded. (In fact, if anything, the opposite tendency is observed.) This means that any possible postgastric sites must be equally weighted in terms of the amount of nutrient they signal or, in other words, report the amount of nutrient present at these sites in such a way that the same signal would be generated if the same amount of nutrient were impinging on gastric sites.

It should be noted that it would not be the total amount of nutrient that would be measured but the total amount of some digestive breakdown product of nutrient. Such a breakdown product might already be present in large quantities in some foods. If the satiety signal derived from a given amount of breakdown product was 'hard wired' and had a fixed value than some foods would produce satiety signals out of all proportion to their actual nutrient value. Such foods would then be underconsumed, while other foods would be overconsumed. This would result in a somewhat ineffecient regulatory system.

Such a source of inefficiency does not in fact exist. It can be shown that animals learn to calibrate a satiety signal from the stomach in accordance with the taste signal from the mouth. This was implied in the earlier statement that the mouth is important in selecting what end-point of ingestion is relevant. The amount of satiety signal from the stomach required to switch off eating may be different depending on the food being tasted.

Some recent experiments have shed some light on this. When a familiar food is removed from the stomach for the first time the amount of compensatory eating that results within the same meal is very accurate as described earlier. On the other hand, if a familiar food is diluted or fortified and then given to the rat to eat, it takes the rat at least one session to compensate in terms of intake (Booth, 1972; Booth and Davis, 1973). It is strange that these two situations should be different. In both situations the relationship between the amount eaten and the nutrient yield is altered, but there is one probable difference. If food is diluted calorically by taking a portion out of the stomach, the taste in the mouth is not altered. The reason that the rat compensates within a meal when food is siphoned from the stomach may be that the flavour of the food is familiar. But when the nutrient that the rat is drinking is suddenly diluted, it is somewhat altered in taste, and then gastric messages may no longer control intake to satiety. To test whether such an idea is right in accounting for the paradox that has just been outlined, rats (n=24) were implanted with stomach tubes and accustomed to drinking an unflavoured oil–water emulsion (Deutsch, 1983). Then their compensation for siphoning 6 ml from the stomach on the first day was measured under two conditions. In the first, they drank the unflavoured oil emulsion as usual. In the second, they drank the same emulsion but flavoured with banana extract for the first time. (Half the group drinking the banana flavour emulsion was run without any siphoning to see if the flavour alone would alter the amount drunk.) We found that addition of the flavour to the emulsion did not altar the amount drunk. The mean when the normal unflavoured emulsion was drunk without siphoning was 13.7 ml (sem ± 1.56) and the mean when the flavoured emulsion was drunk for the first time was 13.3 ml (sem ± 1.1). Siphoning from the stomach did not produce any compensation when the new flavour was added to the emulsion, the mean amount drunk being 14.2 ml (sem ± 1.56). However, good compensation for siphoning occurred when the rats drank the familiar unflavoured emulsion, the mean drunk being 17.8 ml (sem ± 0.85). It looks as if the animal uses satiety signals from the stomach to regulate intake only when drinking a familiar flavour. When the flavour is new, stomach signals are disregarded and mouth signals determine intake instead. However, after a few days experience the animals, as they continue to be siphoned, compensate well with the new flavour, presumably because it has now become familiar. After 7 days, for instance, the siphoned animals with the new flavour drink a mean of 17.9 ml (sem ± 2.45).

If it is correct that the animal fails to compensate for caloric change in the diet because the change in taste is too large, then there should be a compensation for dilution if such a change is kept below some threshold. That this is effective is shown by the following experiment (Deutsch, 1983) in which after training on a 5:5 oil–water emulsion for some subjects, the corn oil emulsion was diluted using five parts of oil to nine parts of water. If the rats compensated for this dilution, given their average intake, they would drink a mean of 6 ml more. (This maintained comparability with the previous siphoning experiment where 6 ml was withdrawn.) Initially all the rats were trained to drink the normal 5:5 oil–water emulsion. Then half the animals were given an emulsion with a banana flavour, while a non-flavoured emulsion was given to the others. For half the rats for which the emulsion was suddenly flavoured, it was watered down at the same time. All the rats given the flavoured emulsion, whether watered down or not, drank the same amount, about 14 or 15 ml. In other words, there was no compensation for dilution when the novel flavour was added. Further, there was also no decrease or increase in the amount drunk as a result of addition of the novel flavour. The group receiving the unflavoured emulsion was treated similarly. One half of this group was given the watered down emulsion and compensated appropriately by drinking almost 21 ml, while the other half stayed on the 5:5 mixture and drank the usual amount of about 14 ml. In this case, when no new flavour was introduced, compensation for dilution was immediate and complete. This was in spite of the fact that a rat, in order to compensate, had to distend its stomach well beyond the habitual amount. This again makes it clear that distention at low volumes (below 12 to 15 ml) is not the regulatory cue and that an animal can measure nutrient content quickly independent of dilution or volume. As might be expected, the rats drinking the flavoured diluted solution do learn to compensate after a few days.

As stated earlier, intragastric injection of about 5 ml of predigested oil emulsion produces a compensatory reduction. The amount of oil emulsion drunk by mouth decreases by about 4.5 ml. Another experiment was designed to show whether a similar compensation would occur the first time the rat tasted a novel flavour. If the presence of a novel flavour leads to a disregarding of gastric cues when siphoning occurs, they should also be ignored here. Predigested intragastrically injected oil is also ignored and no downward compensation takes place. However, the rat does react to LiCl under such conditions. It is interesting to note that the rats respond to cues of sickness although the flavour is novel, but do not respond to gastric satiety signals. This finding could be used to construct a test of whether a procedure produces satiety or malaise, but this is a lead we have not followed up.

It seems then as if the animal must be familiar with the taste of the nutrient before regulation can occur on the basis of stomach satiety signals. The relationship of such stomach signals following of novel tasting of food to some long-term metabolic satisfaction must be learned before these stomach signals are used. It looks as if the animal builds up a whole catalogue of different flavours, each of which sets its own separate level to which stomach signals must rise to produced satiety.

Another case where oropharyngeal, and not gastric, signals regulate intake is reported by Mook, Bryner, Rainey and Wall (1980). They found that alteration of the gastric consequences of saccharin intake does not alter the amount drunk by mouth. Further, it was observed that glucose intake is also regulated oropharyngeally when allowed to escape through the oesophagus as the rat drinks. We may therefore hypothesize that, when gastric signals are present, they regulate intake in the case of familiar food. When such gastric signals are not generated, as in the case of saccharin and glucose that does not reach the stomach, oropharyngeal metering takes over. It is to be noted that the rat may be different from the dog in this regard. Dogs with an oesophageal fistula eat excessive amounts (Hull, Livingstone, Rouse and Barker, 1951) when there is no stimulation of gastric receptors. In the rat it seems that such excessive eating occurs only when there is some stimulation of gastric receptors. When glucose drains out through an oesophageal fistula in the rat, oropharyngeal signals take over the task of regulation and meal size becomes normal. Similarly, when the splanchnic nerve is sectioned, gastric nutrient signals no longer reach the central nervous system and oropharyngeal signals regulate meal size (Deutsch and Ahn, 1986).

PROBLEMS ARISING FROM PLACING SUBSTANCES IN THE STOMACH

The method of introducing material directly into the stomach described above is different from that generally used. There have been experiments that have attempted to measure the effectiveness of various substances placed in the stomach to produce satiety. (An excellent summary for the very large number of such studies is given by Houpt, 1982.) The general method used heretofore takes the substance and places it in the stomach at various times before a meal, when the animal is not ingesting any food. The validity of the method is based on the assumption that the placing of a substance in the stomach while the animal is not eating is equivalent in all important respects to the arrival of that food in the stomach during normal eating. When this assumption is examined experimentally it is found to be invalid on a variety of grounds.

1.   Placing of food in the stomach does not evoke the normal cephalic phase of digestion nor is the food mixed with ptyalin or lingual lipase. It has been shown (Molina, Thiel, Deutsch and Puerto, 1977; Plucinski, Hamosh and Hamosh, 1979) that in consequence the digestive breakdown of food in the stomach is much less efficient.

2.   Abnormalities of intragastric pressure arise. When the rat swallows, the stomach relaxes to accommodate the extra load, so that as volume increases,

pressure stays level (Young and Deutsch, 1980). However when food is placed directly in the stomach, pressure rises linearly with volume. There is no receptive relaxation of the stomach (Cannon and Lieb, 1911) and so undigested food is propelled down the pressure gradient prematurely into the duodenum. Such a state of affairs is aversive (Deutsch, Puerto and Wang, 1977).

3. It is assumed that satiety signals have their normal effect when the signals are novel or when a food is tasted which has not previously been paired with the stomach signals present. These assumptions are no longer tenable. Stomach signals produce satiety through a process of learning (Deutsch, 1983) and are initially disregarded. The introduction of a novel substance in the stomach while the rat eats a familiar food is disregarded, even though that substance can become a satiety signal through a process of learning, as will be shown below. It therefore seems unlikely that a substance introduced into the stomach when the rat is not tasting any food, and when such a substance is novel as well, would have anything like its normal satiety effect. It might, on the other hand, induce thirst or nausea. The method described in the next section was devised keeping the above difficulties in mind. The substance to be placed in the stomach is introduced while the rat itself drinks nutrient. This leads to no abnormal pressures as we have shown (Young and Deutsch, 1980).

THE SPECIFICTY OF GASTRIC SATIETY SIGNALS

To recapitulate, it has been shown that it is signals from the stomach which terminate a meal. There are two types of signal. The first are generated by the volume in the stomach and operate only when a large intragastric volume is exceeded. Of more interest are the second type, which are generated by intragastric nutrient content and which do not depend, within limits, on volume or dilution. Such gastric nutrient signals assume a regulatory role only after a number of exposures to a novel food, showing that learning is necessary for such signals to become effective. However, a change in the flavour of a food presented to oral receptors (such as addition of a banana or almond flavour to a corn oil–water emulsion) is sufficient to switch control to oropharyngeal metering and to render previously effective gastric signals ineffectual in the control of intake of that food. Thus, gastric signals must be separately calibrated for different foods through a process of learning, and no such calibration is available for the gastric signals generated by novel foods. Further, the substances that generate satiety signals are produced by the digestive breakdown products of nutrients such as oil, rather than by the oil itself.

If signals emanating from the stomach function as satiety signals through a process of learning, then it should be possible to associate novel foods with arbitrary gastric signals in order to study the system used in the control of food intake. This is shown by the results of the following experiments.

Rats were implanted with intragastric catheters and, upon recovery, introduced for the first time to a 50:50 corn oil–water emulsion. As they drank this emulsion, some dissolved substance was pumped into the stomach at a fixed percentage of the rate of drinking. Control groups had saline pumped into the stomach at the same rate. After intake had become asymptotic, 4 days were taken as baseline, and the experimental manipulation occurred on the fifth. On that day the gastric infusions of the control and experimental groups were switched: the experimental group received saline, and the control group the dissolved substance for the first time. The substances used and the experiment results are presented in Table 1.

To perform these experiments initially we chose amino acids and maltose, because these are digestive breakdown products of proteins and amylose, respectively, and might thus reasonably be expected to act on chemoreceptors concerned with food intake regulation. However, we report here only the experiments involving amino acids. These substances were paired with corn oil emulsion, because such a pairing would not occur naturally as a result of the normal ingestion of corn oil emulsion. Rats completely unfamiliar with oil or oil emulsion were prepared with gastric cannulae. They were then introduced to the corn oil emulsion. Every time they drank it a small amount of amino acid was pumped into their stomach through the cannula. The gastric infusion was always in the same small proportion of the amount ingested by mouth. For instance, an 8% solution of amino acid was intragastrically infused at 10% of the rate that the animal drank the corn oil emulsion. A control group was intragastrically infused with saline at the same 10% rate. As was to be expected, the caloric consequences of the amino acid infusion were minimal and the control and experimental groups drank almost identical amounts of corn oil.

Whether the substance infused into the stomach had in fact come to be utilized as a satiety signal was tested as follows. After intake had become stable the group of rats receiving the intragastric infusion of amono acids was switched to a saline infusion in the same volume. On the first day the calorically negligible amino acids were omitted a significant increase in intake took place (Deutsch and Tabuena, 1986). Such an increase would be expected if these substances had become conditioned signals of satiety. What was difficult to predict was what would happen when an amino acid was suddenly infused into the stomachs of the control rats that had been infused with saline as they drank the corn oil emulsion. There were various reasons for uncertainty.

1.   The novel intragastric stimulus would be unexpected, as it was not connected by learning to the taste being drunk. It might, therefore, produce complete cessation of drinking, or it might be completely ignored. Or it might switch control from intragastric signals to oropharyngeal signals, much as a novel flavour presented to the mouth. There was no *a priori* way to rule out any of these possibilities.

2.   Another reason for uncertainty is based on the concept of channel. It is possible that all the various chemical stimuli in the stomach act on a single

Table 1.   Results of introducing various substances into the stomach or omitting them. % rate of drinking infused stomach = the rate that the solution is infused into the stomach as the rat drinks, as a percentage of its own drinking rate. Mean % change when introduced = the percentage change in volume of oral intake when a solution is infused for the first time (substituted for saline). Mean % change when omitted = the percentage change in oral intake volume, when saline is substitued for solution of a substance. Probabilities were evaluated by the use of a correlated t-test (two-tailed)

Substance	Concen-tration	% rate of drinking infused stomach	mean % change when introduced	mean % change when omitted	SEM	n	p
L-Lysine	4%						
+L-Threonine	4%	20		+58.1	11.21	9	0.002
+L-Tryptophan	1%						
L-Lysine	4%	20		+26.69	8.13	6	0.05
+L-Threonine	4%		+0.35		10.9	6	n.s.
L-Lysine	3%	20		+37.35	6.01	6	0.002
			−13.7		5.36	6	n.s.
L-Tryptophan	0.8%			+25.5	4.4	7	0.002
			+13.09		6.8	7	n.s.
Oleic acid	100%	5		+35	15.38	10	0.05
	100%	10	−52		9.93	11	0.002
		20	−58.28		8.6	11	0.002
Predigested Oil Emulsion	100	100 (5 ml infused)	−4.8 ml		0.93	11	0.002
		(5 ml withdrawn)		+4.1 ml	1.29	6	0.05

The following points about the results should be made:

1.   The sudden omission of all substances that had been infused directly into the stomach during training to drink new food produces large increases in intake.

2.   Large decreases in intake occur when some substances are suddenly introduced into the stomach. Substances causing such decreases are those that were present in the stomach during training in lesser quantity due to the digestive breakdown of corn oil, the orally consumed nutrient. These substances are oleic acid (Plucinski, Hamosh and Hamosh, 1979) and predigested oil emulsion.

3.   The sudden introduction of substances (such as amino acids) that were not present in the stomach during training produces no decrease in intake.

4.   The fact that some substances do not cause a decrease in intake upon being introduced shows that release from malaise or nausea is not a plausible explanation of an increase in intake when they are omitted.

5.   Where sudden introduction produces large decreases in intake (oleic acid, predigested oil) we have run two-bottle taste aversion tests. After three pairings and three tests we were unable to detect any trend to avoid the neutral taste paired with the above substances in the quantities and rates of infusion used in the main experiment.

6.   Gastric reflux to the mouth has been considered as an explanation. But when oral flavour changes, the rat ignores gastric factors and persists in drinking the baseline amount.

7.   To produce the effects observed here, the gastrically introduced substances are acting as

receptor, or that the outputs from all the various classes of receptor converge so that information from them becomes pooled. Thus, chemical information from the stomach could be transmitted to the central nervous system via a single channel. Satiety would then be signalled by variations in the magnitude of a signal arriving in the CNS. The omission of a part of the stimulus contributing to such a single signal should produce an increase in intake and the introduction of a new stimulus to which the system was sensitive should reduce intake. On the single channel hypothesis the new chemical signal could not be perceived as such, but only as an overall increase in intensity. We had no way of knowing whether the satiety signals ascended a single channel or many channels.

However, the results of introducing a novel chemical stimulus were clear. It had been established that the novel stimulus used could be sensed by the system because of the increase in intake when the same stimulus had suddenly been withheld. But when such a stimulus was suddenly introduced, there was no change in intake. From this we can conclude that there is more than one channel that conveys satiety messages to the CNS. It seems as if the satiety system can discriminate amino acid (or maltose) from free fatty acids and glycerol. If no discrimination were possible (if there were a single channel), then the addition of substances that can be sensed by the satiety system could only be registered as an increase of a quantitive kind and thus lead to a decrease in intake. Such a decrease in intake is seen when we know that the substances introduced into the stomach produce only a quantitative increase. For when we infused predigested oil emulsion into the stomach of rats that are used to drinking oil emulsion, oral intake decreased by the amount infused into the stomach, as seen above.

While there must be more than one channel conveying satiety information, we do not yet know how the novel information functions. One possibility is that the satiety system simply ignores a novel stimulus. Another possibility is that control is switched from gastric signals to oropharyngeal signals, as in the case where a novel flavour is first introduced via the mouth. As described earlier (see also Deutsch 1983), the siphoning of nutrient from the stomach no longer leads to compensatory drinking when a novel flavour is first added to a food.

Intake increases when a chemical substance, whose intragastric infusion is customarily correlated with intake, is suddenly omitted. This fact reveals that such a substance is capable of stimulating some receptor whose activity signals satiety. It does not reveal whether such a substance can be discriminated from other substances by that receptor; or if it is discriminated by the receptor, whether the activity of that receptor is pooled with that of other receptors before the satiety signal ascends to the CNS. In other words, we do not know

---

signals, and are not reversing hunger metabolically. For instance, the sudden intragastric introduction of L-tryptophan that amounts to about 0.16% of the calories of the meal, causes no change in intake. However, the omission of the same amount of L-tryptophan causes an increase of about 25% of intake. A metabolic explanation is rendered unlikely both because of the asymmetry of the effect and the size of the effect.

whether the information arriving in the nervous system concerning the contents of the stomach arrives through a single pathway capable only of quantitative variation. In fact, the experiment omitting a substance from the stomach suggests that this single channel hypothesis is correct and shows that the information regarding the quality of the signal is discarded at some point in the processing of satiety information, though this discarding may take place only after such information has arrived in the CNS.

That this discarding of information concerning the quality of the signal takes place only after such information has arrived in the CNS is shown by the results of experiments in which substances are newly infused into the stomach. When the substances infused are the same as those already utilized as signals, intake is immediately reduced by the correct amount. For instance, as is shown in Table 1, when predigested oil emulsion is first intragastrically infused into rats that are used to drinking oil emulsion, oral intake goes down by the amount intragastrically infused. Infusion of the same volume of saline has no effect. Thus, a sudden increase of the signal already utilized leads to a decrease in oral intake. On the other hand, when the substances infused are different from those already utilized the response of the satiety mechanism changes. We know that the novel substances infused can be sensed by the mechanism, because omission of these substances, previously given in the same volume and concentration, led to a large increase in intake in another group of rats. But when the novel substances are infused into the stomach, no decrease in oral intake takes place. This indicates that such novel substances are recognized as different from the substances resulting from the breakdown of oil emulsion and thus there must be another channel ascending to the CNS besides that which is stimulated by the breakdown of the oil emulsion as a part of the satiety mechanism.

THE LOGIC OF MEAL SIZE REGULATION

The experimental results summarized above are the properties of a mechanism or system. Based on these results it is possible to hypothesize how the mechanism of meal size regulation operates. Critical to the mode of operation of such a mechanism is its input. As described above, if the input is familiar, that is, if it consists of a set of afferent messages that have all arrived simultaneously many times before, regulation is based on gastric signals. If, on the other hand, the input consists of a set of afferent messages only some of which have arrived simultaneously many times before, regulation is switched to control by oropharyngeal signals. In terms of a mechanism this suggests that simultaneously arriving afferent signals are connected at the same time to an 'and' gate and also to an 'or' gate. The 'and' gate functions only when all the previously simultaneous afferent signals arrive together. However, the 'or' gate functions if only some, but not all, of the previously simultaneous signals arrive together again. However, the output of the system controlled by the 'or'

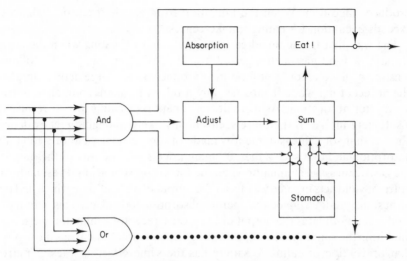

Figure 6.   Diagram of hypothetical system, controlling meal size. → = excites → =
inhibits –o = enables. AND = unit that turns on only when all its inputs are active, OR
= unit that turns on when all or some of its inputs are active. ADJUST = unit that
changes gain of signal from AND unit to SUM (summator,) SUM = summator of gastric
afferent signals, EAT = unit that activates ingestive behaviour. Arrows leading into the
AND and OR units are from cephalic chemoreceptors. Arrows leading to the connections between the STOMACH and SUM units are from various AND units

gate is inhibited by the output of the system controlled by 'and' gates. Control
by gastric signals is switched on when an 'and' gate is active. Control by
oropharyngeal signals occurs when no 'and' gate is active. There is a large
number of 'and' gates, one of which is thrown into activity when a familiar food
is present. When a property of a familiar food is changed on some dimension so
that it becomes unfamiliar, some of the previously associated signals will be
missing and so no 'and' gate will be activated. But one or many 'or' gates will be
activated. In such a case the most highly activated 'or' gate will inhibit the less
activated 'or' gates.

The activated 'and' gate selects its own particular set of gastric signals and its
own particular level to which these will be adjusted in the following way. When
specific food is being eaten it does two things. First, when it arrives in the
stomach it gives rise to activity in a number of afferent channels signalling from
gastric chemoreceptors via the splanchnic nerve. Second, such a food also
activates a specific 'and' gate through stimulating a variety of olfactory,
gustatory, and other cephalic receptors. The concomitant activity of a specific
'and' gate and gastric afferent channels during learning leads, as a result of such
learning, to the opening of such gastric channels when the particular 'and' gate
is on, so that messages from such channels can proceed to a further stage. At
this further stage the messages from the gastric receptors are all summed. After
this the summed messages act to inhibit the neural systems whose excitation

produces ingestion. When the inhibition from gastric receptors balances or exceeds excitation for eating, intake ceases.

The way that the summed gastric signals shut off eating when the correct amount of food has been ingested also involves learning, for the following reason. A given amount of food may produce a very large activity in gastric chemoreceptors, while it satisfies only a relatively small amount of nutrient need after absorption. As a result, termination of eating would result after insufficient intake. It therefore seems highly likely, though direct evidence is absent, that some measurement is made of the nutrient yield of a food after absorption and that such a measurement affects the intensity of the output of the gastric message summator when the food is present again. Presumably the nutrient yield acts in some way to set the output of an 'and' gate which had been on at some predetermined time before absorption took place. This output of an 'and' gate modulates the output of the gastric receptor summator, perhaps by inhibiting the summator to some degree. Such a simple system has the property that prevention of eating to satiety has the same effect as a lesser nutrient density. A parallel system exists to control intake when afferent messages are present, only some of which have arrived simultaneously before. The output of such a system is inhibited by the output of the gastric message summator. However, evidence at present is insufficient for a more detailed hypothesis concerning the system subserving oropharyngeal metering.

SUMMARY

Meal size is determined by one of two regulatory mechanisms, each acting exclusively. The first mechanism utilizes gastric, the second oropharyngeal signals. The first (gastric) mechanism operates when the diet is familiar. The second (oropharyngeal) mechanism supplants the first when the food ingested is somewhat novel or gastric nutrient signals are absent (saccharin, splanchnic section). Both these mechanisms can be overriden by a third. When gastric volume becomes excessive, then signals from gastric distention terminate eating via a separate vagal pathway. The first gastric mechanism signals the amount of nutrient independent of volume or dilution via the splanchnic nerve. Nutrient content is detected by different chemoreceptors stimulated by by-products of the digestive breakdown of the nutrient. The nutrient signals have to be calibrated through a process of learning and can be arbitrarily associated with different foods.

REFERENCES

Booth, D.A. (1972). Conditioned satiety in the rat. *Journal of Comparative and Physiological Psychology*, **81**, 457–471.
Booth, D.A. and Davis, J.D. (1973). Gastrointestinal factors in the acquisition of oral sensory control of satiation. *Physiology and Behavior*, **11**, 23–29.

Cannon, W.B. and Lieb, C.W. (1911). The receptive relaxation of the stomach. *American Journal Physiology*, **29**, 267–273.

Davis, J.D. and Campbell, C.S. (1973). Peripheral control of meal size in the rat: Effect of sham feeding on meal size and drinking rate. *Journal of Comparative Physiological Psychology*, **83**, 379–387.

Deutsch, J.A. (1978). The stomach in food satiation and the regulation of appetite. *Progress in Neurobiology*, **10**, 135–153.

Deutsch, J.A. (1983). Dietary control and the stomach. *Progress in Neurobiology*, **20**, 313–332.

Deutsch, J.A. and Ahn, S.J. (1986). The splanchnic nerve carries satiety signals. *Behavioral Neural Biology*, **45**, 43–47.

Deutsch, J.A. and Gonzalez, M.F. (1980). Gastric nutrient content signals satiety. *Behavioral Neural Biology*, **30**, 113–116.

Deutsch, J.A. and Gonzalez, M.F. (1981). Gastric fat content and satiety. *Physiology and Behavior*, **26**, 673–676.

Deutsch, J.A. and Tabuena, O.O. (1986). Learning of gastrointestinal satiety signals. *Behavioral Neural Biology*, **45**, 282–299.

Deutsch, J.A. Gonzalez, M.F. and Young, W.G. (1980). Two factors control meal size. *Brain Research Bulletin*, **5**, suppl. 4, 55–57.

Deutsch, J.A., Molina, F. and Puerto, A. (1976). Conditioned taste aversion caused by palatable nutrients. *Behavioral Biology*, **16**, 161–174.

Deutsch, J.A., Peutro, A. and Wang, Ming-Li (1977). The pyloric sphincter and differential food preference. *Behavioral Biology*, **19**, 543–547.

Gonzalez, M.F. and Deutsch, J.A. (1981). Vagotomy abolishes cues of satiety produced by gastric distention. *Science*, **212**, 1283–1284.

Gonzalez, M.F. and Deutsch, J.A. (1985). Intragastric injections of partially digested triglyceride suppress feeding in the rat. *Physiology and Behaviour*, **35**, 861–865.

Houpt, K.A. (1982). Gastrointestinal factors in hunger and satiety. *Neuroscience and Biobehavioral Reviews*, **6**, 145–164.

Hull, C.L., Livingston, J.R., Rouse, R.D. and Barker, A.N. (1951). True, Sham and oesophageal feeding as reinforcements. *Journal of Comparative Physiology Psychology*, **44**, 236–245.

Kraly, F.G. and Smith, G.P. (1978). Combined pregastric and gastric stimulation by food is sufficient for normal meal size. *Physiology and Behavior*, **21**, 405–408.

Mook, D.G., Bryner, C.A., Rainey, L.D. and Wall, C.L. (1980). Release of feeding by the sweet taste in rats: Oropharyngeal satiety. *Appetite*, **1**, 299–315.

Molina, F., Thiel, T., Deutsch, J.A. and Puerto, A. (1977). Comparison between some digestive processes after eating and gastric loading in rats. *Pharmacology Biochemistry Behavior*, **7**, 347–350.

Pluckinski, T.M., Hamosh, M. and Hamosh, P. (1979). Fat digestion in rat: Role of lingual lipase. *American Journal of Physiology*, **237**(6), E541–E547.

Snowdon, C.T. (1970). Gastrointestinal sensory and motor control of food intake. *Journal of Comparative and Physiological Psychology*, **71**, 68–76.

Young, W.G. and Deutsch, J.A. (1980). Intragastric pressure and receptive relaxation in the rat. *Physiology and Behavior*, **25**, 974–975.

Young, W.G. and Deutsch, J.A. (1981). The construction, surgical implantation and use of gastric catheters and pyloric cuff. *Journal of Neuroscience Methods*, **3**, 377–384.

CHAPTER 8

Cognitive Experimental Psychology of Appetite

D.A. Booth
Department of Psychology,
University of Birmingham, Birmingham, B15 2TT

Eating and drinking are among the most common of our cognitively rich activities (Szalai, 1972). Substantial parts of any human culture concern cuisine and the social meanings of eating and drinking occasions (Simoons, 1976). Even in affluent countries, food production and marketing constitute the biggest single industry (Pyke, 1968). Food and drink are not merely essential to life and health: in affluence, individually sensible eating and drinking habits (concerning fats or alcohol, for example) are widely believed to be second only to ceasing to smoke in their importance for avoiding degenerative diseases (Turner, 1981). Most women and increasing numbers of men try at some time to eat less in order to be healthily or fashionably slim (Jeffery, Folsom, Luepker, Jacobs, Gillum, Taylor and Blackburn, 1984; Lewis and Booth, 1986). All in all, a very considerable proportion of our thoughts, impressions, and feelings revolve around the ingestion of foods and drinks.

Yet, for all its importance, appetite (the organization within a person's eating and drinking) remains remarkably poorly understood. One particular job for experimental psychology is to characterize the thinking processes that go into an individual's behaviour. Yet, like other aspects of motivation, human appetite research has been a very specialized interest among psychologists, largely arising in the social and clinical psychology of obesity, with occasional forays from investigators primarily interested in physiological influences more easily studied in animals. Some experimental psychologists have recently commented on the relative neglect of 'hot cognition', i.e. emotion and

175

motivation (e.g., Clarke and Fiske, 1982). Perhaps some of the growth points and challenges reviewed in this book will begin to attract wider attention in psychology.

Outside academic psychology, the food industry and its market researchers have collected a great deal of data. Yet even the psychologists involved have analysed very little of such research to elucidate what is going on in the mind of the individual purchaser or eater (Moskowitz, 1983). Notwithstanding claims to the contrary (King, 1981), the standard analysis of survey data as opinion frequencies may provide social and market data but is a basis for no more than indirect speculation about what any individual may think or do: maybe there is nobody who holds all of the commonest opinions; the average attitude may not have been rated by many respondents at all. Smaller quantities of social data are collected to assess the nutritional status of nations or certain categories of people. More accurate measurements of food samples are obtained at the individual level as dietary records, but even these data are not used to test hypotheses about the organization of eating behaviour.

A psychologist must ask whether such research would not be more useful in marketing or nutrition if it were designed to describe how the individual actually thinks and behaves. Market or long-term health consequences normally predicted from the social data could still then also be calculated from the psychological results in samples of people representing the population of interest. The individual psychology, however, would show us how and why some people have the nutrient intakes, the food purchasing patterns and the eating habits that they do. Just such information on individual motivation is what the nutritionist or the marketer needs most in order to decide on action.

Yet the food business has a vast fund of practical experience and clear, even if often challengable, interpretations of it. It has the expertise in food technology and the 'feel' for the market that are essential for realistic psychological research on eating. For nutritional research, medical physiology is crucial in addition, but no less is food science, and social psychology. So, as in other applications of their discipline, psychologists have to come to terms with much equally relevant expertise if their involvement in such research is to tell us much about real-life eating and drinking and its mechanisms.

APPETITE AS A DISPOSITION

This chapter will be misunderstood if it is read with inappropriate terminological and conceptual assumptions. The underlying approach to psychological phenomena adopted here relies on avoiding certain philosophical preconceptions about mental processes, language, consciousness, and behaviour that still pervade appetite research and many other areas. So some explanation is needed of the concept of appetite used here, although neither verbal nor operational definitions help very much in science.

Usually, 'having an appetite', 'feeling hungry', and 'wanting something to eat' (typically something to drink with it too) all mean exactly the same in ordinary parlance — currently possesing the disposition to eat food (and perhaps to drink) (Ryle, 1949; Booth, 1976). This motivational state is observable in the individual's behaviour of searching for and selecting, preparing and ingesting materials regarded as edible or potable.

The interpretation of such behavioural evidence has to be so complex, in the case of human beings at least, that there is no doubt that thought is involved in wanting to ingest. Appetite and its cognitive complexity are also evidenced in those aspects of what people say that observably succeed in expressing that ingestive disposition. So, like much of ordinary mental language, 'appetite' or, alternatively, 'hunger' and 'thirst' are eminently viable as scientific labels for the psychological processes involved in eating and drinking (Booth, Lovett, and McSherry, 1972; Silverstone, 1976; Bolles, 1980).

Nevertheless, words like 'appetite', 'hunger', 'thirst', and 'satiety' get diverted from their scientifically useful ordinary meaning in the service of a particular view of the mind or even of a particular theory of the mechanisms involved. There are two levels of dispute over the use of such psychological words, although these are thoroughly intertwined in the history of appetite research.

Objective Measurement of Mental States

One dispute involves body-mind dualism. The Introspectionist psychologists, many of their Behaviourist antagonists, and medical physiologists to this day, have assumed that mental phenomena (if they exist) must be states of consciousness that the brain somehow produces under the influence of sensory inputs. Thus appetite, hunger, thirst, satiety, palatability or whatever are supposed to be distinctively human experiences — varieties of sensation or affect — stimulated by food volatiles up the nose, emptiness or fullness of the stomach, glucoreceptors in the brainstem or hypothalamus, and the like (Figure 1).

This view betrays a systematic misunderstanding of commonsense language concerning the phenomena of behaviour and consciousness, dramatically exposed by the later Wittgenstein (1953). He demonstrated how people's expressions of their subjective experiences in words must have been learned from public interactions and that it is incoherent to regard such talk about sensations or how things seem as descriptions based on inspection of an inner private world. Successful thought (e.g. following a rule correctly) is evident in a person's linguistic or other performance. That is, the objective mental processes are in the organization of what a person says (or does in other ways). What is going on in a person's mind cannot simply be read off the grammar of face assertions. The cognitive processes can be identified only by controlled investigation of the objective organization of conduct. That is, thoughts may or may not be adequately described by the words uttered under their influence or

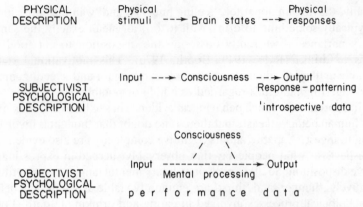

Figure 1.   Three types of description of a person's relationship to the environment: the physics and physiology of the interactions, the description in terms of the subjective experiences referred to in the language for expressing personal viewpoints, and the description of the information-processing achieved by the person by interacting with the environment

indeed fully or accurately represented by the contents of consciousness (Ericsson and Simon, 1980). Undoubtedly the speaker is aware of a great deal but the language of social interchange and attribution is misunderstood when taken to be an authoritative self-report, rather than an expression of a personal viewpoint and cultural role (Coulter, 1979). Complaints about sensations of a grumbling or full 'stomach', expressions of interest in eating or how pleasing a particular food is — even declaration of intent to eat a certain amount — are all speech acts with a common function of 'asking' for food. Therefore these verbal expressions do not necessarily refer to different phenomena. It follows that introducing the notion of quantity, by rating intensities of fulness, pleasantness, desire, etc., cannot be assumed to make the words measure different things (Teghtsoonian Becker & Edelmann, 1981; Blundell and Hill, 1985). Indeed, all these different ratings are often highly intercorrelated (Table 1), i.e. reflect one main underlying variable. Concretely expressed motivation — the pleasantnesses of eating staple foods — is the most valid of these ratings, e.g. as a measure of the satiating effect of absorbed carbohydrate energy (Table 3 in Booth, Mather and Fuller, 1982). The discriminative performance that dualists read off such vocabulary must be shown by independent psychophysical control (Booth, 1981b).

One or more levels of description of human beings and their environment are provided by the physiochemical and physiological sciences. Another description of people is provided by mentalistic or socially informed language. Unhaunted by Descartes' 'ghost' (Ryle, 1949), we can describe the operation of the same biological 'machine' as a person's culturally meaningful interpretations and intentions with regard to the situation that she or he is in. The correctness of these informational characterizations, and of their detailed development as general hypotheses about cognitive processes, can be tested against people's performances in specifiable 'tasks' (Figure 1). The products of

Table 1. Intercorrelations among appetite ratings to bodily sensations, the pleasantness of foods or the amount of food that the rater would like to eat at the time.

Rating	Average correlations to 'how hungry are you'?*	Average loadings on main hunger factor†	Average before-after meal difference loadings on first factor‡
How hungry	–	0.92	–
Hunger sensation	0.91	0.83	0.60
Satiety sensation	–0.73	–0.61	–0.95
Desire to eat	0.86	0.82	–
Pleasantness of a staple food	–	0.90	0.77
Energy of wished menu	0.50	0.63	0.47

* Unpublished data from Experiment 1, Booth, Mather and Fuller, 1982.
† Experiment 2, Mather and Booth (unpublished), factor accounting for 75% of variance.
‡ Experiment 1, S. Rawle and D.A. Booth (unpublished), factor accounting for 80% of variance.

'introspection' are tests only when treated as observable evidence of abilities and dispositions.

Cognitive psychology has been protected by its hypothesis-testing experimental tradition from the worst confusions of introspectionism, or indeed of behaviouristic overreactions on the same dualist assumptions. Even so, in areas such as psychophysics and social psychometrics, what Torgerson (1958) called the 'subjectivist' approach has held sway in psychology itself, as well as in other fields studying psychological phenomena, such as (for appetite) the sensory evaluation of foods, or the assessment of appetite-suppressant diets or drugs or of symptoms in eating disorder and gastrointestinal distress.

That is, numerically interpretable talk about food or eating has been taken to be a measurement of subjective experience, rather than potential objective evidence of perceptual discrimination of identification or of motivational orientation. Naturally then, such verbal 'subjective measures' are regarded as unique to our species. What they are assumed to measure is assigned its own name (for some, appetite not hunger; for others hunger not appetite!), to distinguish it from some objective desire to eat. On the contrary, until a procedure is demonstrated to do so, we should not assume that it avoids 'stimulus error', i.e. distinguishes the contents of consciousness from cognitive achievement, or let alone measures the intensity of sensation or affect. We should be content to take what people say in the language of consciousness as more evidence of what they are objectively wanting to do, doing or perceiving.

Drive and Incentive

It is a simple step from regarding a mental state as the private side of the brain's physical input or output to using the mentalistic word as a label for the physical cause or effect of the cognitive process, not for the process itself. Thus, 'hunger' and 'thirst' are often redefined as influences on eating from need states in the internal environment and 'appetite' as influences on eating from the external environment (e.g. foods, time on the clock, or other people). In some medical textbooks, the same distinction is made in terms of 'drive' versus 'craving'. The problem with this usage is that it redefines the motivational state of being disposed to eat (or drink) into two categories of putative physical causes of that disposition. The conflation of a psychological phenomenon with its causes does nothing to advance even the physiological explanation of that behaviour, and will hold back research if the behaviour is badly investigated as a result.

One connection of this theoretical move with the philosophical dispute is the linguistic fact that the phrase 'appetite sensation' does not exist in ordinary English, unlike 'hunger sensation' and 'thirst sensation'. Such usage may well arise merely because we have occasion to distinguish between the bodily sensations associated with the particular dispositions to eat food or to drink water, within what in other circumstances is often an undifferentiated general disposition to take a meal or snack with fluid. Contrary to widespread conceptions (e.g. Rolls and Rolls, 1982), the hunger, thirst or satiety itself is a disposition and cannot be a sensation: for, the sensation describable as epigastric pang, dryness of the mouth or abdominal fullness can identified as a sensation of hunger/thirst/satiety only by its relevance to oral acceptance or refusal of food or water. Furthermore, some people typically want to eat and drink without obviously instigating bodily sensations (Monello and Mayer, 1967), a claim that only makes sense if hunger is wanting to eat, not having a sensation. Also, satiety cannot be a visceral sensation because oral stimulation alone (Booth, 1976, 1977a; Rolls and Rolls, 1977) and the sight of an empty plate (Pudel, 1976) produce satiety, i.e. inhibit the disposition to ingest. The high correlation of sensation ratings with motivation ratings of various sorts (Table 1) may in part be the disposition to refuse or accept food 'affectively contaminating' the rated intensity of sensations of fullness or emptiness, as can happen to intensity ratings of a food's characteristic flavour (Moskowitz, 1983). That is another reason why sensation ratings cannot be assumed to be perceptions of gastric fullness or flavouring concentration, until they are demonstrated to be so by quantitative and differential control of the rating by the presumed physical stimulus — i.e. by an unconfounded psychophysical experiment.

THE STRUCTURE OF APPETITE

Having identified appetite as the disposition to eat and drink, what sorts of cognitive, behavioural, perceptual, and emotional structure do we assume these objective mental processes to have? Research approaches are strongly influenced by formal theoretical presuppositions and their associated methodology. The rest of this chapter is organized to bring out such assumptions.

First we shall consider the classical two-process analysis of influences on appetite. The limitations of such a bipartite structuring will lead us to consider whether eating at base is a large collection of reflex reactions, with conceptual attributions built up from these behaviour processes. The third paradigm is an unavoidable dimensionalizing of mind which describes all the processes within appetite as values on a set of orthogonal dimensions that are integrated into the disposition to eat and drink. Finally, is each of these three approaches an over-simplification of what is actually a tangled knitwork of processes? If so, how can we practicably design research to improve such a complex systematic theory of appetite?

THE TWO-PROCESS MODEL OF APPETITE

One of the oldest and, at first sight, simplest ideas about appetite is that it is a battleground between 'internal' and 'external' controls. Two physical environments, separated by the skin, are relevant to a person's eating; the *milieu internale* of Claude Bernard and the habitat that concerns the ecologists.

The biomedical reduction of human appetite to service of nutritional needs very soon collapses on consideration of everyday facts about eating and drinking. Even in species that have to forage for their food, physiological needs have very few proven direct connections with food choices (Rozin, 1976; Booth, 1985).

Indeed, purely external, 'cognitive' control of appetite has been proposed, with somatic states totally irrelevant to eating and drinking under conditions of affluence. S.C. Wooley (1971) and O.W. Wooley (1971) could find no immediate or longer-term effect of the energy content of familiar foods on intake or appetite ratings. Rather, the foods appear to have had the effects people expected of them. Stunkard and Fox (1971) found little relation between epigastric hunger pangs and minimally invasive measurements of gastric motility, although Coddington and Bruch (1970) reported some relation between fulness ratings and volume tubed to the stomach. However, such experiments need to be done again now with new physiological techniques and with cognitive experimental designs that allow the autosuggestive elaboration on perceptible somatic processes (Booth, 1980). When unfamiliar foods are used to administer disguised carbohydrate energy and non-habitual food or rating situations are used to test its somatic effect on appetite, then internal influences are clearly seen (Booth, Campbell and Chase, 1979; Booth, 1981a; Booth, Mather and Fuller, 1982).

Thus, human appetite definitely is subject to both categories of influence. The question is whether external and internal influences are independent and, if so, whether they simply add. The classical theory assumes that both answers are 'yes'. A general agitation of somatic drive or even specifically signalled hunger and thirst are guided by palatability and other situational incentives, and then palatability is countered by somatic effects of ingested food and drink.

The distinction between externally and internally originating processes within appetite should not be allowed to lapse back into the confused notion of sensations generated by physical stimulation of exteroceptors and interoceptors. A particular attribution of appetite to something in the situation or in the body may have little to do with its actual source(s). The cognitive model must allow for the possibility that these sources of perceptions or attributions are integrated preconsciously into the desire to eat and the analytical awareness of appetite is dominated by personal theory. There may be 'straight-through' responding to situations (Booth, 1979), or even an appetite 'module' (Fodor, 1983), and then a cultural superstructure of conventional 'accounts' justifying our eating and drinking (Peters, 1954; Harré, Clarke and De Carlo, 1984).

It should also be kept clear that the internal/external distinction being considered is between physical locations — within the body or otuside the body. Despite attempts by environmentalists (e.g. Skinner, 1977), as well as physiologists, to equate the subjective world with what is under the skin, the classical distinction between sources of appetite is not between the person (or the mind) and other agencies, the environment or luck, nor between the centre and the periphery of a person's attention. Neither is a person whose appetite is under strong external influence necessarily a stimulus seeker or an extrovert — nor any less (or more) hungry. These conceptual distinctions between control by internal and external environments and other senses of 'internality' and 'externality' have been been readily sustained psychometrically (Nisbett and Temoshuk, 1976).

Palatability and Post-Ingestional Satiation

If palatability and somatic hunger were not the same appetite arising from different sources, it should be possible to distinguish their behavioural effects. Perhaps the best chance of drawing such a distinction would be by temporal microanalysis of eating. Bellisle, Lucas, Amrani and Le Magnen (1984) characterized aspects of eating movements that are sensitive to variations in palatability among test foods. Kissileff, Thornton and Becker (1982) found that a quadratic equation was the best fit to the negatively accelerated cumulative intake curve often observed when someone eats a single homogeneous test diet available in unlimited amount (Jordan, Wieland, Zebley, Stellar and Stunkard, 1966). Kissileff and colleagues suggested that the linear (initial eating rate) term reflects excitatory processes, including palatability, while the negative quadratic term reflects cumulative satiation processes, including visceral filling. However, neither of these lines of work provides evidence of differences in eating behaviour between palatability and absence of post-ingestional satiety. Similarly, ratings of appetite/satiety do not distinguish food-specific satiety from post-ingestional satiety in ingestive pattern, only in selectivity among the materials towards which the (inhibition of) eating is directed.

A major interest in distinguishing between the influences on appetite from foods and from the body is comparison of individuals for traits of sensitivity to such external and internal influences. Meyer and Pudel (1972) suggested that people with 'latent' obesity do not slow normally during a test meal. Cabanac and Duclaux (1972) claimed that failure of drinking concentrated glucose to suppress rated appetite for sweet water was characteristic of reduced obese people. However, Kissileff, Thornton and Becker (1982) point out that their linear and quadratic terms are correlated, that is, the technique does not disconfound excitation and inhibition: an individual's lack of deceleration may not be an internal satiety defect but may arise from high deprivation or palatability.

No such analysis of output by itself (whether behaviour or ratings) is likely to elucidate mediating processes unambiguously (compare Figure 1). Neither of the above lines of experiment has factored out internal from external inputs to satiation/appetite. The excitation of appetite attributed to food ('palatability') remains uncharacterized perceptually, let alone quantified psychophysically. The quadratic maximum that Kissileff, Thornton and Becker (1982) suggest is somatically determined is never reached during their test meal, and they have to consider the operation of other factors in meal termination, such as boredom with the food, learned avoidance of oversatiation, and concerns to limit intake deliberately. To progress beyond mere speculation, we must design experiments with parametric control of both external and internal factors independently.

The internal effects of chronic or even acute deprivation are almost impossible to disconfound from external cues, such as the time since the last meal (Wooley, 1976). The rapid change in internal state involved in normal satiation is more easily managed, if the physiologically repleting food component can be distinguished and its effects not overwhelmed by habit.

For this reason, physiologically oriented human appetite research 15 to 20 years ago moved from gut- or tissue-aroused appetite to post-ingestional satiation (e.g. Jordan, Wieland, Zebley, Stellar and Stunkard, 1966; Booth, Campbell and Chase, 1970; Cabanac, Minaire and Adair, 1968; Wooley, Wooley and Dunham, 1972). However, the food technology to separate internal and external effects of ordinary foods is limited. Therefore very few effective measurements of relative external and internal sensitivities have been compared between supposedly unusually responsive people and controls.

Ratings that have been assumed to be sensitive to processes of palatability and satiation (e.g. sensations of sweetness or fullness) have not been shown to measure individuals' perceptions (e.g. of sugar concentration or gut contents), let alone how the psychophysics affects eating. General appetite would *prima facie* be assessed by ratings of the pleasantness of a range of normal foods and drinks — so long as people are expressing their wish to ingest the food, not the intensities of the sensual pleasures that food sometimes gives but that may not be behaviourally predictive (Cabanac, 1971). A reduction of rated pleasantness as a result of ingestion is therefore putative satiation, so long as there is no change in food perception (hence 'negative alliesthesia' is an unfortunate term for pleasantness satiation). Nevertheless, attribution of the pleasantness to a percept such as food flavour or abdominal sensation still does not identify the actual sources of such appetite and its satiation. Some specificity of the satiating effect of eating a food to the sensory characteristics of that food has been demonstrated in both pleasantness ratings and food intake (Booth, 1977a; Rolls and Rolls, 1977; Rolls, Rolls, Rowe and Sweeney, 1981). No nutrient-specificity of appetite or its satiation has been shown in people, except between food and water, where perceptual mechanisms for identifying the nutrient in the ingested material are obviously available (Rolls, Rolls and Rowe, 1983). The post-ingestional action of starch suppresses rated pleasantness of eating all staple foods more clearly than it changes rated strengths of hunger or satiety sensations or pleasantness of low-calorie foods or of drinks normally taken throughout a meal (Booth, Mather and Fuller, 1982). This result also supports the notion that a unitary eating motivation is integrated from internal and external sources.

The unitary output also means that excitatory and inhibitory factors cannot be identified directly. Does sugar stimulate eating by its high palatability or its resistance to satiation? The question needs reformulating to give us a basis for adequate experimental design or we end up in circularity.

Externality

Some external influences are more readily manipulated experimentally than internal influences, by physical arrangement of the environment of the eater. Also, given sufficient ingenuity, more or less controlled selections can be made among real-life situations involving different degrees of external influence over eating. One of the most remarkable and still influential programmes of research into appetite used such techniques to pursue the possibility that a personal trait of over-responsiveness to external influences is a cause of obesity (Schachter, 1971a, 1971b). The appetite mechanisms in the 'Externality' theory are not as cognitively elaborate as those in Schachter and Singer's (1962) controversial theory that the emotions are social attributions of diffuse bodily arousal. Rather, eating motivation is assumed to be elicited by internal and/or external cues, such as an empty stomach and/or the sight of food or of a clock showing the time for a meal. So people who react strongly to the external cues are liable to eat when they otherwise would not, because those cues often do not coincide with relevant internal cuing. Extra eating could contribute to weight gain. Such 'externality' theory fits common experience of succumbing to the temptation to eat snacks and, indeed, the tendency of those with weight problems to blame the strength of such temptations. However, such attributions could be quite delusory. Theorists should treat intuition with empirical caution.

The 'externality' research programme almost destroyed itself by the (still widespread) strategic error of pursuing a theory of the causation of obesity by reliance on comparisons between obese (or even moderately overweight) people and those in the recommended weight range. Bodyweight (relative to height) is very convenient for its objectivity. Nevertheless, degree of over-weight is an absurd criterion to set for a psychological theory of fattening appetite. Extent of overweight at a given point in time is the cumulative result of a history of all the influences on eating, including efforts to lose perceived over-weight, as well as of individual differences in physical activity and meta-bolism. A psychological trait such as 'external' responsiveness should not be expected to correlate substantially with over-weight, and, in fact, it does not.

If other major factors did not blur the picture, 'externality' might correlate with tendency to gain weight. Rodin, Slochower and Fleming (1977) indeed showed, for girls at a summer camp, that weight gain related to 'externality' (while degree of over-weight did not). Rodin (1985) reports greater fat-depositing physiological responses in highly responsive subjects. We have found that high responsiveness goes with poor learning from post-ingestional effects of unfamiliar snack-foods (Booth, 1978; Booth, Fuller and Lewis, 1983). So, despite the doubts expressed by many, including Rodin herself (1981), an individual characteristic like 'externality' is still worthy of intensive investigation as a likely contributor to weight problems.

However, there are problems with the externality construct. One flaw is a risk of circularity in deciding whether mouth stimuli count as external or internal factors (Rodin, 1976). Conceptually more serious is an assumption that turns out to underly the choice of the term 'externality'. The personal characteristic in question was operationally defined by Schachter and Rodin (1974) as an unusually great emotional/motivational response to a physically intense stimulus (Figure 2). The crucial stimulus parameter was identified as salience, not external location. It does not seem very plausible to assume that external stimuli are always more salient than internal stimuli. The overrespon-siveness to salience is elicitable by non-food stimuli, and can be shown not only in food intake but also in strength of emotional reaction, distraction of attention, etc. Therefore, 'emotional (over)responsiveness' would be a better term than 'externality'. This disentanglement of the construct from the mere location of the stimuli also takes some of the bite out of Krantz's (1979) argument that the 'externality' effects in fact reflect sensitivity to social demands on eating.

Schachter and Rodin (1974) recognized that their construct of high arous-ability by strong or salient stimuli is related to easy sensitization or the ready elicitation of (general) 'drive', in Hull's (1943) sense. Yet a persisting state of drive is induced by deprivation of food, among other manipulations. Thus, the stable high responsiveness to strong (external) stimuli is the same behaviour as is sensitive to (potential) stimuli that are presumably largely internal — the need state induced by lack of food. The 'externality' assumption in the over-responsiveness construct relies on the two-factor model in its strong additive form.

However, more attention has been paid to another possible implication of the similarity between Schachterian 'externality' and high arousability or

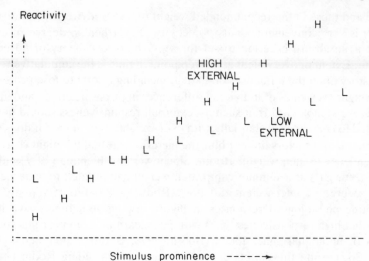

Figure 2.   Functions of response vigour on stimulus salience for high and low 'External' people, following Schachter and Rodin (1974)

chronic drive. Maybe emotional over-responsiveness is secondary to efforts to reduce weight by eating less. Hibscher and Herman (1977), following Nisbett (1972), suggested that externality (and a liability to breach one's diet with a binge) was created by living below one's 'set point' of obesity.

However, this suggestion is self-contradictory. The person who has lost most weight will thereby be the most need-aroused. Yet the person has been the most successful at resisting temptations to eat and so restraining energy intake. The person with the worst weight-control problem is the least physically deprived. This inattention to the physiological as well as cognitive dynamics of weight control shows in the psychometric weaknesses (Drewnowski, Riskey and Desor, 1982; Lewis, 1981; Lewis and Booth, 1985; Ruderman, 1983) of the Dietary Restraint Questionnaire (Herman, 1978; see Figure 3).

Also, it is odd for social psychologists again to invoke a physiological mechanism for a cognitively rich emotional problem. Furthermore, the notion of an inherited proper amount of fat in the body is highly dubious (Booth, Toates and Platt, 1976; Booth, 1980): there is no known mechanism for fat cells to register their deviation from a fixed proper size; in any case, fat mass can 'regulate' itself by uncalibrated negative feedback (Booth and Mather, 1978). When the stress of prolonged self-deprivation does involve bodily signals, time with an empty stomach and lack of repletion of the liver are likely to be far stronger internal signals than reduced size of fat cells.

There are ample sources of purely psychosocial stress for dieters. They must be 'aroused' by the frustration of refraining from eating on occasions at which they can remember eating in the past and when many others can indulge. So the theory that dietary restraint causes difficulties in reducing weight ends up equivocating between somatic need and cognitive distress (Herman, 1978).

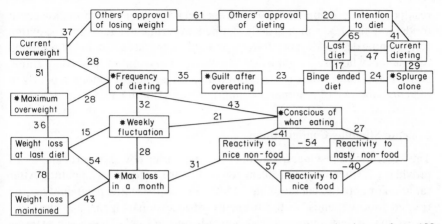

Figure 3.   Significantly intercorrelated responses to questionnaire items, from 100 English Midlands women who professed to be dieters (Lewis and Booth, 1986). The content of each question is indicated by the phrase in the box; asterisks indicate items from Herman's (1978) dietary restraint questionnaire. The number between each pair of related items is the value of the correlation coefficient X 100

This shows in the complex structure of responses to the questionnaire that purported to encapsulate the mechanisms of dietary restraint in a single score (Figure 3).

Experimental analysis of hypothesized cognitive processes in emotional responsiveness has proved productive when pursued. The stronger the emotionality with which a person generally reacts to a salient stimulus, the less likely is that person to be efficient at processing any information also provided by that stimulus. In other words, the reaction to physical intensity would be more liable to distract from meaning. That deduction is consistent with use of better processing of stimuli ('stimulus binding') as a criterion of emotional overresponsiveness (Rodin, 1973), because this was in very simply structured and briefly executed tasks such as reaction time. A task that better relates over-responsiveness to intake control is the extraction of information from food and/or the body about the consequences of eating, in the presence of salient but less informative food tastes or somatic hunger pangs. The emotionally highly responsive do indeed prove to be bad at learning the satiating potential of a new snack food, while extent of overweight and dietary restraint score do not relate to poor information acquisition (Booth, 1980; Booth, Fuller and Lewis, 1983).

Herman, Polivy, Pliner, Threlkeld and Munic (1978) found complex relationships between dietary restraint score and distractability. They correctly called for more research on the high-arousal construct of 'externality'. Despite the rich possibilities for experimental 'hot cognition', very little such research has so far ensued. This may be because the complexities are not resolved by taking a simple score like over-weight or dieting. Even a modest improvement of specificity in the assessment of the weight-control problems can be productive. We have found that scoring relative success or not at losing weight as a result of 'dieting' distinguishes good from bad acquisition of information about foods and the body in a strictly defined experimental test. In a satiation conditioning design (Booth, 1977a; Booth, Mather and Fuller, 1982), we found that dieters who lose weight learn well about conjections of food composition and somatic state, whereas dieters who do not lose weight condition poorly to the combinations of external and internal cues (Booth and Toase, 1983).

Appetite Stimulus Configurations

The experiments just mentioned on learned satiating power of particular foods provide a further major problem for two-factor theories of appetite. After satiation or appetite conditioning (Booth, 1977a, 1985), the palatability of the trained food depends on the trained post-ingestional signal, and the post-ingestional satiety/appetite effect depends on the food. That is, an external influence and an internal influence are integrated into a configuration in control of eating: appetite is based on *Gestalten* (where a *Gestalt* is understood objectively as an unanalysed entry of stimuli into performance). Thus, the palatability of a flavour is not always a constant to which the appetising effect of an empty stomach is added or from which the satiating effect of gastrointestinal filling is subtracted. As a result of learning that different after-effects follow the eating of arbitrarily assigned flavours in different stages of a meal, the relative preference between two foods can reverse from the start to the finish of a meal (Booth, Mather and Fuller, 1982). This kind of learning creates discrete combinations of external and internal cues. It is quite independent of the culturally established reversal of preference from 'savory' to 'sweet' recipes when going from entrée to dessert (Booth, 1977a).

Such configurational diet-body percepts were demonstrated with ordinary foods at mealtimes. So, appetite *Gastalten* are likely to be common in everyday life. The impression of internal sources of satiety subtracting from palatability arises from artificial tests on single-food meals.

CONDITIONING OR COGNITION?

Such acquired control of eating by discrete combinations of dietary and somatic cues has been described as classical conditioning of preference or aversion to compound stimuli (Booth, 1977a, 1980, 1985). Many psychologists seem to regard human conditioning as necessarily non-cognitive. For example, human awareness of the CS-US contingency has been interpreted as proof that real classical conditioning cannot be occurring (Brewer, 1974). However, even theories of learning in animals have developed a cognitive style over the last decade (Dickinson, 1980). Acquisition of a conditioned response has been characterized as the animal's perception of a causal contingency (Mackintosh, 1979). The learned appetite-satiation reaction to an external-internal configuration (i.e., the learned internal-state dependency of the palatability of a particular food) is similar to the mood-dependent recall observed by Bower, Monteiro and Gilligan (1978) and Teasdale (1983). More complex cognitive processes have since proved to be involved in sadness and no doubt there is also more to appetite than particular percepts eliciting unitary motivation. Nevertheless, a process such as coactivation of a node in an associative memory net is needed in cognitive theory to account for even the simple state-dependency effects. Indeed, it is not obvious how to distinguish such an account experimentally from configural conditioning or conditional discriminative learning (Bower, Monteiro and Gilligan, 1978).

More broadly, complex cognitive performance can be simulated by computations that rely on 'productions', which are condition-act routines that look remarkably like S-R habits (Anderson, 1983). Once allow that Chomsky had it as wrong in one direction as Skinner in the other and even language can be seen to start as an increasingly well-adapted set of production-like conditioned responses (Harrison, 1972; Booth, 1977b). So appetite cognition and language may be founded on an increasingly versatile collection of classically conditioned ingestive reflexes (Booth, 1980).

We are born equipped with highly organized ingestive motor patterns, extending from reflex sequences of sipping, sucking, and swallowing to a smile-like grimace and the intimate sociality of feeding at the breast. There is also an egestive pattern, the incipient or partial elicitation of which may contribute to those reductions of intake and choice that justify the invocation of aversion as opposed to mere lack of preference, both in satiation (Booth, 1985) and in toxin avoidance (Berridge and Grill, 1984). Nevertheless, apart from some effects of sweet taste and of an empty gut, human appetite has to be acquired (Birch, this volume). Socialization of appetite could be based largely on habituation and associative processes differentiating the control of ingestive (and egestive) patterns. Hunger, thirst, and satiety sensations, palatabilities, eating occasions, and the appetite *Gestalten* would be well represented in the language and habits of the culture. In addition, any frequent or strong aspect of appetite is likely to come to its possessor's awareness directly (compare Bem, 1972). Thus, a verbalized attributional structure of eating habits (compare the latent variables in Figures 1 and 7) could be built up from observations of the complex collection of highly differentiated, acquired reaction patterns that are common in the culture.

So there are not mutually exclusive alternatives: the answer is conditioning *and* cognition.

Perhaps because it fits well to cognitive processes in eating and drinking, the stimulus-conditioning analysis is proving to be a productive model for human appetite (Birch and Deysher, 1985; Booth, 1976, 1977a,c, 1980, 1985; Hawkins, 1977; Rodin and Marcus, 1982; Smuckler and Tantam, 1984; Stunkard, 1975; Zellner, Rozin, Aron and Kulish, 1983). It is also convenient methodologically to have the discipline of rather precise questions to investigate about the behavioural and verbal effects of changes in contingencies among nutritional events and between them and other events. Furthermore, a cognitive-behavioural approach ensures the tie of perception and thought to action that is expected of the psychology of motivation.

DIMENSIONAL ANALYSES OF APPETITE

Two Factors or Many?

A serious danger for the conditioning approach may be unmanageable fragmentation. Yet the two-factor approach is unrealistic. Could appetite be usefully regarded as the additive result of many more than two relatively discrete, graded influences? This is no more than to assume the General Linear Model which of course pervades nearly all empirical investigation and has proved very powerful in exploring data structures and testing hypotheses.

At first sight, if appetite *Gestalten* are as important as suggested above, additive multifactor models would be as unrealistic as additive two-factor models. However, moderate deviations from a *Gestalt* might be perceived dimensionally and such dimensions of dissimilarity (or generalization decrement, in behaviour process terminology) might be identical for many distinct *Gestalten*. That is, a multidimensional approach to appetite may be viable, so long as the investigations keep variables in a familiar or natural range, rather than expecting it to be useful to extend variables to their physical limits (whether in pursuit of an illusory theoretical universality or merely to obtain striking experimental differences). The notorious barrenness of multivariate data-grubbing can be avoided in other ways too, for example, qualititative analysis; indeed, ethnography or a conceptual study is an essential preliminary when plausible dimensions have not already been identified.

Even limiting its scope, however, the implausibility of the strong dimensional assumptions of classical multivariate science must be recognized. In the end, much of appetite may prove not to be analysable as linear combinations of functions along discrete dimensions.

Even if functional variables can be identified, their influence has to be measured, i.e. scaled in some empirical rather than merely statistical sense. As summarized below, an 'appetite psychophysics' has begun for certain perceptually simple food constituents, using the region of peak preference. Equally strong experimental control of stimuli and ratings or behaviour is needed for visceral cues. The dimensional approach seems ill-suited to most interpersonal and cultural influences on eating and drinking, but any objective social psychophysics (Wegener, 1982) of appetite could be a powerful theory-building tool.

Even if dimensions of appetite can be identified psychophysically in some important instances, we then need additive combinations or linearizable relations among orthogonal dimensions. That is most likely for the relatively narrow 'dynamic ranges' of influences on appetite that are found in everyday life. Improved ecological validity is achieved also if experimentally convenient but artificial extremes are avoided, whether sensory, physiological or social.

Linear combination of dimensions of influence is of course a long tradition in motivation, from Hull's (1943) multiplication of drive and habit and Spence's (1956) mixed model to the now almost equally moribund two- or three-dimensional multiplicative models of human achievement motivation (Atkinson and Birch, 1970).

Even if the original two factors of deprivation-repletion (drive) and innate preference-aversion (incentive) do operate independently, they are not likely to be linear (Booth, 1977a, 1979). Such departures from interval scaling can yield linear interaction, however, in the sense of the addition of suitably transformed measurements or of variances. Yet innate preference-aversion is a very special case. Also, the influence of food- or water-deprivation on human appetite may not be a wide-range dimension: nobody has determined how few discriminable levels of visceral hunger there are.

Nevertheless, first let us try to identify and scale some important dimensions.

Psychophysical Identification of Dimensions of Appetite

Some of the influences of food constituents on appetite are the easiest to 'dimensionalize' effectively. Sensory evaluation has used multivariate analyses — most recently, response surface methodology (e.g. Drewnowski, 1984) — to identify statistical dimensions of description and preference in uncontrolled sets of foods or drinks, rated out of their context of use (Moskowitz, 1983). However, measurement of the psychological strength of a sensory influence on appetite requires more than statistics: it requires experimental designs founded on a psychophysics of normal individual preference. The relevant principles of cognitive experimental psychology have recently been applied to this problem (Booth, Thompson and Shahedian, 1983; Booth, Conner, Marie, Griffiths, Haddon and Land, 1986), as follows.

Psychophysicists have traditionally used perceptual vocabulary for the responses they collect from assessors, e.g., how loud or sweet the stimulus seems. Hedonic ratings (how pleasant it is), preferences or other motivational vocabulary have been considered to follow a 'different psychological law' (Moskowitz, Kluter, Westerling and Jacobs, 1974) or to introduce unmanageable noise into otherwise 'objective' sensory tests.

Nonetheless, the relationship between an individual's preference for different strengths of stimulus is often just as systematic as the traditional intensity function. The difference is that preference is single-peaked (Coombs, 1964), while perception is monotonic: there is a preferred level of loudness or sweetness in a real-life hearing or tasting situation.

On this principle, Frijters and Rasmussen-Conrad (1982) successfully interconverted individuals' separate intensity and hedonic ratings of sucrose solutions. There is no need to collect separate ratings, however. For example, sweetness or saltiness of a food can very reliably be rated relative to the assessor's own ideal for sugar or salt in the food (Booth, Fuller and Lewis,

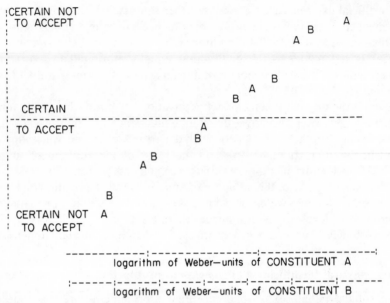

Figure 4.   Typical data pattern from an individual, plotted as psychophysical functions of preference ratings on amounts of a food or drink constituent expressed in units yielding constant Weber ratio (Booth et al., 1983; Booth, Conner, Marie, Grifiths, Haddon and Land 1986). Data points A: raw values of preference ratings when concentration of constituent A is varied with minimum bias around the ideal point (the mid-category). B: preference rating values when only B's concentration is varied. Such continuous linear functions arise when variations in a constituent are presented in an otherwise well-liked formulation. If however the context is not liked, the inverted V of the 'folded' preference function is rounded to a U, i.e., a discontinuity appears between colinear extremes in the functions illustrated.

1983; Booth, Conner, Marie, Griffiths, Haddon and Land, 1986). The same rating can be made also relative to the two intolerable extremes of excess and insufficiency of the perceived characteristic.

Indeed, a precise psychophysical function can be obtained from ratings purely of the motivation towards the object, without mention of the characteristic being varied by the experimenter. The high-level (excess) descending limb of the preference ratings can then be plotted, above the peak-preferred level, as a continuation of the monotonic relationship seen in the ascending (deficiency) limb (Figure 4). Two (or even three) constituents can be varied around the assessor's ideal points for each, either in separate preference-rating experiments (Figure 4) or in the same session (Booth et al., 1986).

To be reasonably sure of obtaining a peak preference or ideal point, the samples have to be a familiar food or drink in which the salt or sugar (say) is a normal constituent. However, as usually obtained, the single-peaked preference function and even the monotonic intensity function relative to ideal are mathematically indeterminate. So an individual's preference cannot be accurately interpolated from the curve and it is almost impossible to quantify the importance of the substance in the palatability of that food to that person. However, the functions become linear (i.e. the peak is a symmetrical triangle) for variations in an otherwise ideal formulation (Figure 4) on two conditions. First, the test procedure must be designed individually to eliminate known cognitive biases (Poulton, 1979). Secondly, the physical unit used in the psychophysical function must represent an aspect of the substance which has a constant Weber ratio over the range tested (Thurstone, 1927; Booth, Thompson and Shahedian, 1983). Concentration units meet this condition in the case of sugar and salt in the soft drinks, soup and bread we have begun to look at.

The resulting psychophysical function of degree of preference on level of a food constituent measures the influence of the sensory characteristics of that substance on the assessor's appetite for such a sample. In particular, it provides an estimate of the individual's most preferred level of food or drink constituent (Figure 4). It also provides information on the motivational effect of lower or higher levels of the constituent, at least relative to preference reductions produced by variations in other constituents (Figure 4).

This 'preference psychophysics' has been developed initially for constituents that are, relatively speaking, perceptually simple and easily managed physically. The tastants sodium chloride and sucrose are particularly convenient. They are also strong contributors to both sensory and attitudinal determinants of appetite. Furthermore, their consumption is relevant to health. With foods containing substantial amounts of salt or sugar, little or no deliberation is needed to be aware of the perceptual basis of preference and so 'analytical' or descriptive of sweetness or saltiness relative to the most preferred level give functions of similar precision to these from 'straight-though' ratings of overall preference that make no reference to taste sensations (Booth et al., 1986). However, preference functions could well turn out to be more precise than intensity functions when the perceptual effect is hard to put into words.

Individuals' peak preferences estimated by this method are self-consistent over many weeks and they are valid relative to real-life choices, so far as we have been able to determine to date (Booth et al., 1985). Our results so far confirm the impression from cruder methods (such as preference frequency polls) that most people prefer formulations close to those marketed. The immediate reason for this is, of course, manufacturers' efforts to meet majority preference. However, in the longer term, many such preferences are likely to have been induced by the formulations traditionally available on the market. So the precise preference estimation method should be used to determine the robustness and generality of the recent evidence that preferred salt level goes up and down after several months on a diet containing less salt (Bertino, Beauchamp and Engleman, 1982).

Good individualized measurements of sugar preference in various foods have enabled us to test the concept of a 'sweet tooth' (Booth et al., 1986).

People do indeed vary reliably in the level of sugar they prefer on average across contrasting foods (with exceptions for tea and coffee). However, the simple concept of a food-independent trait was also refuted: some people seem to react differently from others to sugar in the presence of sour or bitter tastes.

The method also permits an individual psychological measurement approach to subtler issues such as the elasticities of tolerances for non-ideal levels of food characterstics and the extent to which different characteristics trade off against each other (see the 'cognitive algebra', below). The smallest amount of constituent that the assessor professes would make a difference to their appetite for the test foodstuff (an 'hedonic JND' or preference Weber ratio) can be calculated from the response variance and the slope of the psychophysical function. The hedonic JND cannot be smaller than the perceptual limit, i.e. the actual JND (McBride and Booth, 1986). A substantial proportion of assessors seem to tackle the preference rating task at this limit of discriminative ability; however, some express less discriminating preference, for example for salt level in bread (Griffiths, Clifton and Booth, 1985). These variations in psychophysical preference 'slope' have been validated on everyday choice behaviour (Booth et al., 1986). However, the cognitive mediation of sensory influences into both rating slopes and eating behaviour needs much elucidation before we will have generalizable principles for validating preference ratings on choice behaviour (Blamires, 1980).

Extension to Non-Psychophysical Designs

When the psychophysics of such sensory motivation has been established, it can then be used to interpret results obtained under less controlled but more widely relevant conditions. For example, people are often faced with choices between variants of the same foodstuff. The preference responses to a set of variants, whether expressed unanalytically or perceptually described, can be screened for serious biases and then whatever is known of the physical origins of the perceptual descriptors can be used for at least semiquantitative estimation of the individual's likes and dislikes (Figure 5). When the ratings are demonstrably undistorted, they provide a sounder basis also for the merely statistical operations of multidimensional scaling too.

The descriptors are not limited to sensory characteristics, nor need the food samples be free of brand names or other extrinsic attributes, including the culinary or even interpersonal context of normal use. Any rated attribution could be scaled onto preference, i.e. appetite. Indeed, a sensory, social or somatic factor could be controlled within the otherwise uncontrolled set of actual or described test situations and the unscaled attributions calibrated on the psychophysically scaled attributes.

This extension of the psychophysical design would also improve the assessment of choices between different types of foodstuff: a major aspect of

```
                    Inedibly                    Just                    Inedibly
                    too little                  right                   too much
                    ----------------------------*----------------------------

CHOCOLATEY          C  B  MN    LS  R  *   D
                    8  7  36    25  4  >>> 1

POWDERY             C  R              SL  D  M        B  N
                    8  4          << 52  1  3         7  6

SWEET                         D C LB  *    MN  R S
                              1 8 27  >    36  4 5

MILKY               C             B L* R D N    S        M
                    8             7 2< 4 1 6    5        3

AFTERTASTE                    SC B  DMN LR
                              58 7  136 24
                                   <*
```

Figure 5. An example of an individual's preference-relevant characterizations of chocolates in a self-chosen vocabulary. Each characteristic's intensity is rated relative to ideal intensity and inedibly low and high intensities. In this assessor, the chocolatey and powdery ratings were highly correlated, but the others were relatively independent. Each letter represents a different brand of milk chocolate, rated 'blind'. The number on each letter represents the brand's rank in ratings of overall liking by that individual. The arrows represent the direction in which the apparent ideal point should be corrected to allow for the evident range bias on the ratings of that characteristic (Booth, Conner, Marie, Griffiths, Haddon and Land, 1986)

preference that is missed by assessing reactions to variations in the constitution of a single test foodstuff.

Statistical Importance of Different Influences on Appetite

Questions about the strengths of foods' influences on appetite can be broadened to issues like the one we started with: are internal variables at all important in human appetite? However, these issues have not usually been tackled by objective measurement, i.e. mapping the several input dimensions onto the same appetite output variable. Even when some parametric control has been introduced, a subjective (sensation numbering) approach and merely statistical data reduction have been applied.

Schutz and Wahl (1981) surveyed the verbal terms 'appearance', 'texture', and 'flavour' for 94 foods. Situational effects on food purchase have been assessed (e.g. Belk, 1974; Miller and Ginter, 1979). Such comparisons emphasize or even totally rely on the variances covered by the different influences (p values of effects), not on measurements of the psychological sizes of the influences. Even prediction is often impracticable, because the setting conditions of the variances are not measured and so the results cannot be extrapolated to other conditions. The relative strengths of two sorts of influence (food characteristics and somatic processes) on the same intake-measuring parameters were reported by Booth, Mather and Fuller (1982), but the setting conditions on the triggering of expected satiation by food characterstics were not measured.

Psychological measurement not only requires effective design of experiments or controlled observations. It also requires analysis first at the individual level. Raw data cannot be grouped, making the unwarranted assumption that the numbers obtained from one individual mean the same as the numbers obtained from another on the same response. Furthermore, the relationships among different data outputs from an individual may bear little or no resemblance to the relationships between the data correlated across a set of individuals. When strengths of influences within each individual's mind have been measured, then we can determine whether there is a common conceptual structure — even perhaps similarities of parameter values. Overall or segmented aggregation procedures can then be justified, avoiding the fallacious presumption that the group average represents something that goes on in any real person's mind, let alone the majority or all.

Multidimensional Cognitive Algebra

If several such 'dimensions' of appetite can be truly measured, we should consider trying to combine them additively in a 'cognitive algebra' of appetite (Anderson, 1981). Klitzner and Anderson (1972) showed that rated liking for described sandwiches could be factored into a multiple of verbal attributions of moderate hunger and palatability, whereas price added in. The simplicity of the algebra ($\times$ or $+$) depends on linear functions of ratings on stimulus differences. Our evidence (above) is that responses well distributed over moderate ranges measure influences on appetite quite linearly. Anderson's designs use medium-range variants of familiar stimuli (verbally presented). He argues (with most plausibility for the case of a mixed additive-multiplicative interaction) that he demonstrates linearity 'functionally' in his ANOVA cell plots.

A further alternative to our 'empirical' (psychophysical) measurement and Anderson's 'functional' measurement of two or three dimensions of appetite is axiomatic measurement (Coombs, 1964). For example, at least ordinal measurement properties of two or more responses (behavioural or verbal) can be established by the technique of conjoint measurement. This has been done for foods with ratings of flavour and price (McCullough and Best, 1979). Even disparate attributes can add easily enough to be traded off against each other (e.g. Johnson, 1974).

A Single Causal Nexus of Appetite Determinants?

All three theoretical approaches (two-factor, conditioned reactions, multidimensional) have been considered so far on the assumption that a unitary ingestive motivation results from influences converging at a single summation point (Figure 6). The visceral, dietary, social, and other influences on appetite at any one instant, interpreted through memory, are integrated into the momentary disposition to eat or to drink something of what is available (or to

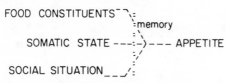

Figure 6.   Categories of influence converging in appetite

refuse to ingest). On this assumption, the moment-to-moment persistence or change of these combinations of facilitatory and inhibitory influences on the individual's ingestive behaviour accounts for search for and avoidance of food, the timing of eating and drinking, the selection of food and drink, and the amounts consumed.

It has been more usual in psychology to draw a sharp distinction between 'cool' discriminative instrumental behaviour and affect-filled elicited behaviour. However, the distinction is in practice very difficult to operationalize conclusively for appetite (Booth, 1980). No doubt a very close look at eating and drinking appetite will bring out distinctions. Different conditioned reaction patterns may contribute in different ways. Different sets of the many influences may converge at several different points in a hierarchy or some other type of network of processes. The network may prove to have several fundamentally different outputs. None of the three approaches considered so far need to be confined to a single causal nexus. At present, though, only one need be postulated.

Furthermore, some of the more complex models are not as different from the unitary output model as might appear at first sight.

A hierarchy of conscious processes might work separately 'above' a single preconscious nexus (Figure 1), but nevertheless always through it. Eating is often an unreflective and involuntary reaction to a complex situation, even though the individual is also eating intentionally, i.e. there are elements of instrumental discriminative control as well. Social-emotional influences (verbally explicit or indexed less directly) could enter the single causal nexus alongside the power of rational considerations.

Marketers call such customer behaviour towards fast-moving goods like foods 'non-involved'. That does not mean unmotivated. It means without agonies of (in)decision, i.e. without the sort of problem-solving deliberation represented by the complex serial processing typical of cognitive theorizing of the last 20 years. Cognition is still relevant, but it may well be parallel processing, such as the cognitive algebra of integrating information straight through into a unitary disposition towards food and drink. We should expand the model to include less directly measurable cognitive processes such as preconscious affect (Zajonc, 1980) or contents of consciousness like sensations (Figure 7) only when the data require such latent variables.

A distinction must then be drawn between the logical structure of a task and the causal structure of its performance. A series of multiple regressions may be statistically more powerful than a single one (Fishbein and Azjen, 1976).

```
C - - - [S ] - - - - D              C - - - [S ] - - - - D
1       1  \       1                1      \  1          1
            \                              \
             ) - - A                        ) - - - - - A
            /                              /
           /                              /
C - - - [S ] - - - - D              C - - - [S ] - - - - D
 2       2           2               2      2            2
```

Figure 7.   Food sensations as latent variables in causal models of the effects of food constituents on food preference. Left: appetite as a response based on integration of conscious and described percepts (compare Triesman and Gelade, 1980). Right: appetite as a direct response to unanalysed or preattentive integration of sensory input. The different sorts of information processing may occur in different circumstances (Farell, 1984). C: a constituent, S: a sensation, D: descriptor of a sensory characteristic, A: overall appetite or acceptance response, [] : an unobserved variable

Nevertheless, the beliefs and values in each attitude, and the attitudes and situational perceptions in an intention, can all operate within a person's momentary action, whether or not they were also operative in any prior deliberation.

COGNITIVE NETWORKS IN APPETITE

The fourth approach to the psychology of eating and drinking is to assume that we already need such a theoretical system of interacting cognitive processes. However, cognition should not be confused with other parts of the whole system surrounding appetite.

Non-Cognitive Networks

The biographical backgrounds of eaters are not the same as the information-processing in their minds. Consumer behaviour textbooks tend to conflate the temporal progress of an individual customer through the market with the theoretical arrows and boxes of the experimental psychologists of perception and memory. Awareness of information concerning a food product is followed by comparisons and then decision and purchasing behaviour, finally reaching use. Temporal sequence of behaving has been mapped into implausibly extended serial cognitive processing.

Other sorts of causal network that differ from cognition, but undoutedly lie behind appetite, are the nutritional physiology and the sociological processes bearing on eating and drinking. Appetite (like indeed any psychological phenomenon) is an aspect of a multi-level system. Indeed, more than that, the determinants and consequences of ingestive behaviour are now recognized to constitute one of the strongest examples of a truly psychobiosocial system, in which cognitive processes in the individual person's behaviour intertwine equally with her or his visceral processes and with the culture and economy in which s/he lives (Booth, 1976, 1981c; Rodin, 1977; Rodin and Marcus, 1982; Wooley, 1976; Wooley, Wooley and Dyrenforth, 1979). These precursors and consequences of appetite operate over finite time, adapt each other and the cognitive processing (learning), and include much re-entrant causation (i.e. an influence leading back onto itself).

Such processes cannot be accommodated by one main causal nexus. Yet, when they have been allowed for, would a single integration point account for most of the appetite in the mind of the eater, i.e. the cognitive psychology as such?

Dieting

An informal institution has grown up around the consequences of the fact that undereating is an indispensable part of the cure for obesity, even though there need not have been any overeating contributing to the slimmer's (or his weighing scales') original 'downfall'. The dieting culture provides a rich mine for fundamental and potentially useful cognitive-behavioural research.

Herman and Polivy's (1975) concept of 'dietary restraint' has played a major role in drawing attention to the need for more realistic approaches to the psychology of appetite in weight control. However, the unitary construct of Dietary Restraint scored by questionnaire (Herman, 1978; Herman and Polivy, 1982) can no longer be sustained (Drewnowski, Riskey and Desor, 1982; Ruderman, 1983; Stunkard and Messick, 1984), despite its original success in distinguishing between compensatory and overeating responses in normal-weight and mildly overweight students in the original 'breakdown of restraint' experiments (e.g. Hibscher and Herman, 1977). One of the simplest possible sketches of major causal influences within and around appetite in dieting is given in Figure 3. This diagram includes the only reliable correlations observed amongst some of the items in Herman's (1978) dietary restraint questionnaire in 100 women dieters (Lewis and Booth, 1986). It also shows how several poorly inter-related items correlated well with responses to a variety of other questions about dieting reasons, emotional responsiveness, and body weight.

Of course, it is not possible to test a whole system of this sort by means of a fully controlled experiment. The traditional topic of productive experiments is a single key causal step. With a more complex design, a particular re-entrant causal circuit or one multifactor integration process can be characterized. Other methods are needed to provide adequate tests overall of the hypothesized causal 'knitting'.

Quantitative and Qualitative Investigation

Experimental psychologists, psychometricians, and qualitative researchers all should recognize that well-formulated and decently operationalized theoretical networks can now be compared quantitatively, given enough data.

Appetite has suffered (like most of social cognitive experimental psychology) from a separation between the experimental tradition — with controlled independent variables, one measured dependent variable (or very few quite distinct measurements), and correspondingly tight but narrow hypotheses about causal processes — and the multivariate tradition, with a much weaker grasp on causation or even no theoretical interests at all, but a wider-ranging relevance and more concern with variation amongst individuals. Nevertheless, in recent years, appetite research has featured combined experimental-psychometric studies, such as on dieting (see above). The area should join other fields of applied cognitive social psychology as a testing ground for the growing rapprochement of correlational and univariate statistics, and the extension of experimental and quasi-experimental investigation to the new multivariate tests of systematic theories that invoke hypothetical processes, i.e. causal modelling with latent variables (Bentler, 1980; Bagozzi, 1980). Such testing of covariance structures can distinguish rival hypothetical variables (latent processes), when the theories are sufficiently well-developed from piecemeal experiments, observations or speculations, and when a high enough proportion of all the variables has been observed (manifest processes).

These and more traditional multivariate analyses require many cases. Also, the usual calculations assume that all individuals studied have the same structure. The causal links in the network have to perform linearly and combine additively at the nodes. However, if the sizes of influences of causes on effects within a network can be specified after such modelling, then aspects of overall performance (and indeed subsystem performance) can be calculated for an individual, who is represented by particular values of the parameters of the cause-effect equations. Also, generalizations can be abstracted from such quantitative simulations, for comparison with observed group means and variances, and then extrapolation to new conditions.

This movement between nomothetic (general theory) and idiographic (individual difference) traditions is occurring piecemeal, e.g. in preference psychophysics (above). It has been attempted holistically for the behavioural-physiological interactions within the appetite system (Booth, 1976, 1978b), including the conditioning processes likely to be fundamental to some cognitive and social influences in eating (also above). The psychology of dieting can now provide a whole cognitive system for causal modelling.

When fully effective, the causal modelling approach on data from structured questions and answers relates people's own accounts of what they are and do to objective aspects of the situations they are in and of the tasks they perform in such circumstances. Psychophysical measurements, multi-correlational explorations, experimental-psychometric programmes are all needed before a causal model can be constructed and tested. Psychologists would be well advised also to precede the piecemeal parameterization and the formulation of an overall model by some careful qualitative investigation, i.e. disciplined ethnography. This cultural mapping should not be distorted by the focus on a particular food product and the speedy conclusions that are needed in qualitative market research. Also, merely statistical analysis of repertory grid data or the like is insufficient as a basis for elucidating the structure of the internalized norms (Harre, Clarke and De Carlo, 1985). Very little detailed work on dietary ethnography and the cognitive anthropology of food has yet been done. The structures likely to be revealed are well illustrated by Murcott's work on the proper Sunday lunch (1982) and on what spouses expect of each other in cooking (1986).

Personal Theory of Energy

Ordinary people's accounts of food energy and body weight illustrate the elaborate 'lay' cognition in everyday eating. With admirable etymological rectitude, 'energy' is everyday parlance for a person's vigour in either mental or physical activity. However, the precise scientific use of the word has also entered people's theories of themselves: specifically of the foods they eat, of the effects of foods on the weight and fatness of the body, and even of their body's use of energy in exercise, tissue maintenance and the generation of body warmth. Just like the cognitive psychology of mathematics, grammar or object recognition, we can investigate the thinking processes in this lay thermodynamic theory and we can objectively characterize their success in reflecting actual energy and try to explain errors and biases. Such personal energy theory is of considerable practical importance: for reduction of unhealthy or unfashionable overweight, in the rationalization of risky compulsions to starve, vomit or abuse laxatives, and when prevention of heart disease depends to some extent on appreciating that fats contain more than twice as much energy as any other foodstuff in dry form. Some structured investigations of aspects of this thinking were reviewed by Booth, Lewis and Fuller (1981) and are sketched here with some additions.

It has been pointed out repeatedly that the only genuine 'regulation' of body weight, food intake or energy expenditure yet demonstrated is human rule-following behaviour relative to some target of food calories, miles jogged or weight read off the bathroom scales and body shape seen in the mirror, felt against the waistband or expressed in another's comment (Booth, 1980).

Booth, Lewis and Fuller (1981) reported that the cognitive 'set point' provided by the publicized tables of desirable weight for height was reproduced with considerable bias towards overweight for short people — 10–20 lb (4½–9 kg) in excess for men's weights judged by men, and about half as much for women about women — whatever the judge's own overweight or height.

Self-perception in sufferers from anorexia nervosa has been much studied. The clinical impression of gross misperception of shape may arise from the anorexic's attempt to make sense of a compulsion to starve that may well have been acquired because of stress-reducing or even rewarding effects of resisting eating on a chronically empty stomach. When pressed to be realistic, these patients have been reported to characterize themselves more nearly as emaciated as they are (Szmuckler, 1986). Unfamiliar and artificial methods of eliciting estimates of body dimensions have been difficult to use, with normal weight and obese people often giving the overestimates professed by the anorexic. Fuller (1978; Booth, Lewis and Fuller, 1981) used the ecologically more valid perceptual task of estimating by sight the waist and hip dimensions of different sizes of unlabelled clothing. She found underestimates of up to 3 inches (7½ cm) in some untreated young women who had met the diagnostic criteria for anorexia nervosa, while normal-weight controls showed no bias. However, most of the bias was attributable to absolute judgement of the clothing dimensions, not the judge's statement of her own dimensions. That is, again the evidence points to no genuine misperception of self but attribution of a wish to wear smaller clothes and such like.

The energy contents of foods may be reflected in behaviour more effectively than they are in untrained estimation of the kilocalories per gramme. Calorie judgements, even with exemplars to scale on, are often parametrically less well related to actual energy content than ratings of how filling or how fattening the food is (Booth, 1980; Booth, 1983). That is also to say that filling and fattening ratings correlate well — and why is that? Do people have an energy theory of satiation, similar to recent physiological psychology (Booth, 1972, 1978b)? Or do normal people, as well as those with eating disorders, in effect suppose that the experience of feeling full leaves a residue of fat deposited in the abdomen? In any case, veridical judgments in such terms seem much more likely to be useful in food choices for people who want to control energy intake than are calculations based on energy labelling (where available). It should be noted that these energy perceptions are in turn influenced by the implications of advertising slogans ('helps you work, rest and play') and even of officially approved qualitative nutritional labels ('low fat'). Table 2 shows that two samples of yogurt differing only in label on the pack are thought to differ in 'calories' and in fattening power (specifically — not in mood effects), even though there was in fact no difference in energy contents of the packs.

Table 2.   Differences between ratings on sight of equicaloric portions of the same brand and flavour of yoghurt, labelled 'low fat' or 'whole milk', without eating of samples ($n = 40$).

Rating	'Low fat'	'Whole milk'	Difference p value*
How many calories	3.9	6.8	<0.01
How fattening	3.4	4.8	<0.001
How energizing	2.9	3.0	n.s.
How calming	1.7	1.8	n.s.

* By within-subject t-tests (n.s. > 0.1). Calories, fattening and filling ratings were highly intercorrelated, and they and the energizing and calming ratings were nearly orthogonal across the subjects.

Other Nutrient Perceptions

Such work on quantitative lay conceptions is needed for other nutrients in food and for the related intake-output balances across one's body surface — protein (i.e. essential amino acids and nitrogen balance), salt, cholesterol, vitamin D, and so on. There has recently been an unfortunate tendency to extend from animals to people the practice of calculating the proportions of different nutrients in the observed dietary selection and then assuming that the eating behaviour is under the control of those nutrients. Yet even a non-verbal animal selects its diet on the basis of sensory cues and eating habits which may be causally unrelated to nutrient proportions (Booth, 1981, 1985; Miller and Teates, 1984). Human linguistic communication concerning eating provides false and misunderstood as well as truly remembered information about nutritional composition. It influences choices amongst foods in many ways entirely irrelevant to the intake of nutrients as such. So until the cognitive and perceptual bases of someone's dietary selection have been identified or controlled, their intakes should not be treated as nutrient-specific selection.

FUNDAMENTS AND PRACTICE

Healthy eating habits cannot be effectively promoted by informing and persuading people and providing attractive nutritious choices, unless we understand adequately their nutritional psychology and its biocultural context. Nutrition education and food advertising need to make salient the relevant, and indeed the best-fitting (e.g. good tasting and disease-risk avoiding), percepts and concepts. However, emotions and involuntary reactions influence behaviour as well as informed intentions. Also, in the long-term, beliefs and attitudes based on the secondhand experience or the conceptualised theory that is relayed as largely verbal information must be sustained by direct experiences such as social-affective and nutritional conditioning or observational learning. The only way in which appropriate eating can be induced is by the integration of information and environment through reasoning and emotions, in a manner that does in fact yield in usual contexts the habitual choices that are desirable. Appetite research truly is a 'hot topic' for cognitive psychology.

REFERENCES

Anderson, J.R. (1983). *The Architecture of Cognition*, Harvard University Press, Cambridge, Massachussetts.

Anderson, N.H. (1981). *Foundations of Information Integration Theory*, Academic Press, New York.

Atkinson, J.W. and Birch, D. (1970). *The Dynamics of Action*, Wiley, New York.

Bagozzi, K.P. (1980). *Causal Models in Marketing*, Wiley, New York.

Belk, R.W. (1974). An exploratory assessment of situation effects in buyer behavior. *Journal of Marketing Research*, **11**, 156–163.

Bellisle, F., Lucas, F., Amrani, R. and Le Magnen, J. (1984). Deprivation, palatability and the micro-structure of meals in human subjects. *Appetite*, **5**, 85–94.

Bem, D.J. (1972). Self-perception theory. In L. Berkowitz (Ed.), *Advances in Experimental Social Psychology*, Vol. 6, Academic Press, New York.

Bentler, P.M. (1980). Multivariate analysis with latent variables: causal modelling *Annual Review of Psychology*, **31**, 419–456.

Berridge, K.C. and Grill, H.J. (1984). Isohedonic tastes support a two-dimensional hypothesis of palatability. *Appetite*, **5**, 221–231.

Bertino, M., Beauchamp, G.K. and Engelman, K. (1982). Long-term reduction in dietary sodium alters the taste of salt. *American Journal of Clinical Nutrition*, **36**, 1134–1144.

Birch, L.L. and Deysher, M. (1985). Conditioned and unconditioned caloric compensation: evidence for self-regulation of food intake in young children. *Learning and Motivation* in press.

Blamires, C. (1980). Pricing research techniques: a review and a new approach. *Journal of the Market Research Society*, **23**, 103–126.

Blundell, J.E. and Hill, A.J. (1985). Analysis of hunger: inter-relationships with palatability, nutrient composition and eating. In J. Hirsch and T.B. Van Itallie (Eds.), *Recent Advances in Obesity Research*, vol. IV, John Libbey, London, pp. 118–129.

Bolles, R.C. (1980). Historical note on the term 'appetite'. *Appetite* 1, 3–6.

Booth, D.A. (1972). Satiety and behavioral caloric compensation following intragastric glucose loads in the rat. *Journal of Comparative and Physiological Psychology*, **78**, 412–432.

Booth, D.A. (1976). Approaches to feeding control. In T. Silverstone (Ed.), *Appetite and Food Intake*, to feeding control. T. Silverstone (Ed.), Abakon/Dahlem, Berlin, pp. 417–478.

Booth, D.A. (1977a). Appetite and satiety as metabolic expectancies. In Y. Katsuki, M. Sato, S.F. Takagi and Y. Oomura (Eds.), *Food Intake and Chemical Senses*, University of Tokyo Press, Tokyo, pp. 317–330.

Booth, D.A. (1977b). Language acquisition as the addition of verbal routines. In R.N. Campbell and P.T. Smith (Eds). *Recent Advances in the Psychology of Language. Formal and Experimental Approaches*, Plenum Press, New York, pp. 219–241.

Booth, D.A. (1977c). Satiety and appetite are conditioned reactions. *Psychosomatic Medicine*, **39**, 76–81.

Booth, D.A. (1978a). Acquired behavior controlling energy intake and output. *Psychiatric Clinics of North America*, **1**, 545–579.

Booth, D.A. (1978b). Prediction of feeding behaviour from energy flows in the rat. In D.A. Booth (Ed), *Hunger Models*, Academic Press, London, pp. 227–278.

Booth, D.A. (1979). Preference as a motive. In J.H.A. Kroze (Ed.) *Preference Behaviour and Chemoreception*, IRL Press, London, pp. 317–334.

Booth, D.A. (1980). Acquired behavior controlling energy intake and output. In A.J. Stunkard (Ed.) *Obesity*, Saunders, Philadelphia, pp. 101–143.

Booth, D.A. (1981a). The physiology of appetite. *British Medical Bulletin*, **37**, 135–140.

Booth, D.A. (1981b). How should questions about satiation be asked? *Appetite*, **2**, 237–244.

Booth, D.A. (1981c). Momentary acceptance of particular foods and processes that change it. In J. Solms and R.L. Hall (Eds), *Criteria of Food Acceptance: How Man Chooses what he Eats*, Forster, Zurich, pp. 49–68.

Booth, D.A. (1985). Food-conditioned eating preferences and aversions with interoceptive elements: conditioned appetites and satieties. *Annals of the New York Academy of Sciences*, 22–37.

Booth, D.A. and Mather, P. (1978). Prototype model of human feeding, growth and obesity. In D.A. Booth, (Ed.), *Hunger Models*, Academic Press, London, pp. 279–322.

Booth, D.A. and Toase, A.–M. (1983). Conditioning of hunger/satiety signals as well as flavour cues in dieters. *Appetite*, **4**, 235–236.

Booth, D.A., Campbell, A.T. and Chase, A. (1970). Temporal bounds of post-ingestive glucose induced satiety in man. *Nature*, **228**, 1104–1105.

Booth, D.A., Conner, M.T., Marie, S., Grifiths, R.P., Haddon, A.V. and Land, D.G. (1986). Objective tests of preference amongst foods and drinks. In C. Leitzmann and J.M. Diehl (Eds), *Measurement and Determinants of Food Habits and Food Preferences, Euro-Nut Report 5*, Agricultural University, Wageningen.

Booth, D.A., Fuller, J. and Lewis, V.J. (1983). 'External' (salience) responsiveness causes intake control problems (whether or not obesity results). *Proceedings of the Fourth International Congress of Obesity, New York City*, C.B. Slack, Thorofare, New Jersey.

Booth, D.A., Lee, M. and McAleavey, C. (1976). Acquired sensory control of satiation in man. *British Journal of Psychology*, **67**, 137–147.

Booth, D.A., Lewis, V.J. and Fuller, J. (1981). Human control of body weight: cognitive or physiological? Some energy-related perceptions and misperceptions. In L.A. Cioffi, W.P.T. James and T.B. Van Itallie (Eds), *Body Weight Regulatory System: Normal and Disturbed Aspects*, L.A. Cioffi, W.P.T. James and T.B. Van Itallie), Raven, New York, pp. 305–314.

Booth, D.A. Lovett, D. and McSherry, G.M. (1972). Postingestive modulation of the sweetness preference gradient. *Journal of Comparative and Physiological Psychology*, **78**, 485–512.

Booth, D.A., Mather, P. and Fuller, J. (1982). Starch content of ordinary foods associatively conditions human appetite and satiation, indexed by intake and eating pleasantness of starch-paired flavours. *Appetite*, **3**, 163–184.

Booth, D.A., Thompson, A.L. and Shahedian, B. (1983). A robust, brief measure of an individual's most preferred level of salt in an ordinary foodstuff. *Appetite*, **4**, 301–312.

Booth, D.A, Toates, F.M. and Platt, S.V. (1976). Control system for hunger and its implications in animals and man. In D. Novin, W. Wyrwicka and G.A. Bray (Eds), *Hunger*, Raven Press, New York, pp. 127–142.

Bower, G.H., Monteiro, K.P. and Gilligan, S.G. (1978). Emotional mood as a context for learning and recall. *Journal of Verbal Learning and Verbal Behaviour*, **17**, 573–585.

Brewer, W.F. (1974). There is no convincing evidence for operant or classical conditioning in adult humans. In W.B. Weimer and D.S. Palermo (Eds.), *Cognition and the Symbolic Processes*, Wiley, New York, pp. 1–42, 57–62.

Cabanac, M. (1971). Physiological role of pleasure. *Science*, **173**, 1103–1107.

Cabanac, M. and Duclaux, R. (1972). Obesity, absence of satiety aversion to sucrose. *Science*, **168**, 496–497.

Cabanac, M., Minaire, Y. and Adair, E.R. (1986). Influence of internal factors on the pleasantness of a gustative sweet sensation. *Communications in Behavioral Biology*, **A1**, 77–82.

Clarke, M.S. and Fiske, S.t. (Eds.) (1982). *Affect and Cognition*, Erlbaum, Hillsdale, New Jersey.

Coddington, R.C. and Bruch, H. (1970). Gastric perceptivity in normal, obese and schizophrenic subjects. *Psychosomatics*, **11**, 571–579.

Coombs, C.H. (1964). *A Theory of Data*, New York, Wiley.

Coulter, J. (1979). *The Social Construction of Mind*, Macmillan, London.

Dickinson, A. (1980). *Contemporary Animal Learning Theory*, Cambridge University Press, London.

Drewnowski, A. (1984). New techniques: multidimensional analyses of taste responsiveness. *International Journal of Obesity*, **8**, 599–607.

Drewnowski, A., Riskey, D. and Desor, J.A. (1982). Feeling fat yet unconcerned: self-reported overweight and the restraint scale. *Appetite*, **3**, 273–279.

Ericsson, K.A. and Simon, H.A. (1980). Verbal reports as data. *Psychological Review*, **87**, 215–251.

Farell, B. (1984). Attention in the processing of complex visual displays: detecting features and their combinations. *Journal of Experimental Psychology: Human Perception and Performance*, **10**, 40–64.

Fishbein, M. and Ajzen, I. (1975). *Belief, Attitude, Intention and Behavior*, Addison-Wesley, Reading, Massachusetts.

Fodor, J.A. (1983). *The Modularity of Mind*, MIT Press, Cambridge, Masachussetts.

Frijters, J.E.R. and Rasmussen-Conrad, E.L. (1982). Sensory discrimination, intensity perception and affective judgement of sucrose-sweetness in the overweight. *Journal of General Psychology*, **107**, 233–248.

Fuller, J. (1980). Human appetite and body size control: the roles of individual differences and food dependencies in human appetite and body size control processes. PhD Thesis, University of Birmingham.

Geliebter, A.A. (1979). Effects of equicaloric loads of protein, fat and carbohydrate on food intake in the rat and Man. *Physiology and Behavior*, **22**, 267–273.

Griffiths, R.P., Clifton, V.J. and Booth, D.A. (1985). Measurement of an individual's optimally preferred level of a food flavour. In J. Adda (Ed.) *Progress in Flavour Research 1984*, Elsevier, Amsterdam.

Harré, R., Clarke, D. and De Carlo, N. (1984). *Motives and Mechanisms*. Methuen, London.

Harrison, B. (1972). *Meaning and Structure: an Essay in the Philosophy of Language*, Harper and Row, New York.

Hawkins, R.C. (1977). Learning to initiate and terminate meals: theoretical, clinical and developmental aspects. In L.M. Barker, M.R. Best and M. Domjan (Eds). *Learning Mechanisms in Food Selection*, Baylor University Press, Texas, pp. 201–224.

Herman, C.P. (1978). Restrained eating. *Psychiatric Clinics of North America*, **1**, 593–607.

Herman, C.P. and Polivy, J. (1975). Anxiety, restraint and eating behavior. *Journal of Abnormal Psychology*, **84**, 666–672.

Herman, C.P. and Polivy, J. (1982). Weight change and dietary concern in the overweight: are they really independent? *Appetite*, **3**, 280–281.

Herman, C.P., Polivy, J., Fliner, P., Threlkend, J. and Munic, D. (1978). Distractibility in dieters and nondieters: and alternative view of 'externality'. *Journal of Personality and Social Psychology*, **36**, 536–548.

Hibscher, J.A. and Herman, C.P. (1977). Obesity, dieting and the expression of 'obese' characteristics. *Journal of Comparative and Physiological Psychology*, **91**, 374–380.

Hull, C.L. (1943). *Principles of Behavior*, Appleton-Century-Crofts, New York.

Jeffery, R.W., Folsom, A.R., Leupker, R.V., Jacobs, D.R., Gillum, R.F., Taylor, H.L. and Blackburn, H. (1984). Prevalence of overweight and weight loss behavior in the metropolitan adult population: the Minnesota Heart Survey experience. *American Journal of Public Health*, **74**, 349–352

Johnson, R.M. (1974). Trade-off analysis of consumer values. *Journal of Marketing Research*, **11**, 121–127.

Jordan, H.A., Wieland, W.F. Zebley, S.P., Stellar, E. and Stunkard, A.J. (1966). Direct measurement of food intake in man: a method for objective study of eating behavior. *Psychosomatic Medicine*, **28**, 836–842.

King, S. (1981). *Eating Behaviour and Attitudes to Food, Nutrition and Health*. J. Walter Thompson, London.

Kissileff, H.R., Thornton, J. and Becker, E. (1982). A quadratic equation adequately describes the cumulative intake curve in man. *Appetite*, 3, 255–272.

Klitzner, M.D. and Anderson, N.H. (1972). Motivation × Expectancy × Value: a functional measurement approach. *Motivation and Emotion*, 1, 347–365.

Krantz, D.S. (1978). The social context of obesity research: another perspective on its place in the field of social psychology. *Personality and Social Psychology Bulletin*, 4, 177–184.

Lewis, V.J. (1981). Attitudes to dietary change: evaluation of body weight and foods. M.Sc. Thesis, University of Birmingham.

Lewis, V.J. and Booth, D.A. (1986). Causal influences within an individuals dieting thoughts, feelings and behavior. In C. Leitzmann and J.M. Diehl (Eds), *Measurement and Determinants of Food Habits and Food Preferences*, University Department of Human Nutrition, Wageningen.

Mackintosh, N.J. (1977). Conditioning as perception of causal relations. In R.E. Butts and J. Hintikka (Eds), *Foundational Problems in the Special Sciences*, D. Reidal, Dordrecht.

McBride, R.L. and Booth, D.A. (1986). The method of constant *hedonic* differences using classical psychophysics to measure preference (submitted).

McCullough, J. and Best, R. (1979). Conjoint measurement: temporal stability and structural reliability. *Journal of Marketing Research*, 16, 26–31.

Meyer, J.E. and Pudel, V.E. (1972). Experimental studies on food intake on obese and normal weight subjects. *Psychosomatic Medicine*, 16, 305–308.

Miller, K.E. and Ginter, J.L. (1979). An investigation of situational variation in brand choice behavior and magnitude. *Journal of Marketing Research*, 16, 11–123.

Miller, M.G. and Teates, J.F. (1984). Oral somatosensory factors in dietary self-selection after food deprivation and supplementation. *Behavioral Neuroscience*, 98, 424–434.

Monello, L.F. and Mayer, J. (1967). Hunger and satiety sensations in men, women, boys and girls. *American Journal of Clinical Nutrition*, 20, 253–261.

Moskowitz, H.R. (1983). *Product Testing and Sensory Evaluation of Foods. Marketing and R & D Approaches*, Food & Nutrition Press, Westport, Connecticut.

Moskowitz, H.R., Kluter, R.A., Westerling, J. and Jacobs, H.L. (1974). Sugar sweetness and pleasantness: evidence for different psychological laws. *Science*, 184, 583–585.

Murcott, A. (1982). On the social significance of the 'cooked dinner' in South Wales. *Social Science Information*, 21, 677–694.

Murcott, A. (1986). The study of food habits: objectives, methods and consequences. In C. Leitzmann and J.M. Diehl (Eds), *Measurement and Determinants of Food Habits and Food Preferences*, University Department of Human Nutrition, Wageningen.

Nisbett, R.E. (1972). Hunger, obesity and the ventromedial hypothalamus. *Psychological Review*, 79, 433–453.

Nisbett, R.E. and Temoshuk, L. (1976). Is there an 'external' cognitive style? *Journal of Personality and Social Psychology*, 33, 36–47.

Peters, R.S. (1954). *The Concept of Motivation*, Routledge & Kegan Paul, London.

Poulton, E.C. (1979). Models for biases in judging sensory magnitude. *Psychological Bulletin*, 86, 777–803.

Pudel, V.E. (1976). Experimental feeding in man. In T. Silverstone, (Ed.), *Appetite and Food Intake*, Abakon/Dahlem, Berlin, pp. 245–264.

Pyke, M. (1968). *Food and Society*, John Murray, London.

Rodin, J. (1973). Effects of distraction on the performance of obese and normal subjects. *Journal of Comparative and Physiological Psychology*, 83, 68–78.

Rodin, J. (1976). The role of perception of internal and external signals on the regulation of feeding in overweight and nonobese individuals. In T. Silverstone (Ed.), *Appetite and Food Intake*, Abakon/Dahlem, Berlin, pp. 265–283.

Rodin, J. (1977). Research on eating behavior and obesity: where does it fit in personality and social psychology? *Personality and Social Psychology Bulletin*, **3**, 333–355.

Rodin, J. (1981). The current status of the internal-external obesity hypothesis: what went wrong? *American Psychologist*, **36**, 361–372.

Rodin, J. (1985). Insulin levels, hunger, and food intake: an example of feedback loops in body weight regulation. *Health Psychology*, **4**, 1–25.

Rodin, J. and Marcus, J. (1982). Psychological factors in human feeding. *Pharmacology and Therapeutics*, **16**, 447–468.

Rodin, J. and Slochower, J. (1976). Externality in the obese: effects of environmental responsiveness on weight. *Journal of Personality and Social Psychology*, **33**, 338–344.

Rodin, J., Slochower, J. and Fleming, B. (1977). The effects of degree of obesity, age of onset, and energy deficit on external responsiveness. *Journal of Comparative and Physiological Psychology*, **91**, 586–597.

Rolls, B.J. and Rolls, E.T. (1982). *Thirst*, Cambridge University Press, London.

Rolls, B.J., Rolls, E.T. and Rowe, E.A. (1983). Sensory-specific and motivation-specific satiety for the sight and taste of food and water in Man. *Physiology and Behavior*, **30**, 185–192.

Rolls, B.J., Rolls, E.T., Rowe, E.A. and Sweeney, K. (1981). Sensory specific satiety in man. *Physiology and Behavior*, **27**, 137–142.

Rolls, E.T. and Rolls, B.J. (1977). Activity of neurones in sensory, hypothalamic, and motor areas during feeding in the monkey. In Y. Katsuki, M. Sato, S.F. Takagi and Y. Oomura (Eds), *Chemical Senses and Food Intake*, University of Tokyo Press, Tokyo, pp. 525–549.

Rozin, P. (1976). Psychobiological and cultural determinants of food choices. In T. Silverstone (Ed.), *Appetite and Food Intake*, Abakon/Dahlem, Berlin, pp. 285–312.

Ruderman, A.J. (1983). The restraint scale: a psychometric investigation. *Behavioural Research and Therapy*, **21**, 253–258.

Ruderman, A.J. (1985). Restraint, obesity and bulimina. *Behavioural Research and Therapy*, **23**, 151–156.

Ryle, G. (1949). *The Concept of Mind*, John Murray, London.

Schachter, S. (1968). Obesity and eating. *Science*, **61**, 751–756.

Schachter, S., (1971a). Some extraordinary facts about obese humans and rats. *American Psychologist*, **26**, 129–144.

Schachter, S. (1971b). *Emotion, Obesity and Crime*, Academic Press, New York.

Schachter, S. and Rodin, J. (1974). *Obese Humans and Rats*, Erlbaum/Wiley, New York.

Schachter, S. and Singer, J.E. (1962). Cognitive, social and physiological determinants of emotional state. *Psychological Review*, **69**, 379–399.

Schutz, H.G. and Wahl, D.L. (1981). Consumer perception of the relative importance of appearance, flavour and texture. In *Criteria of Food Acceptance: How Man Chooses What He Eats*, Forster, Zurich, pp. 97–105.

Silverstone, T. (1976). Introduction. In T. Silverstone (Ed.), *Appetite and Food Intake* Abakon/Dahlem, West Berlin, pp. 11–14.

Simoons, F.J. (1976). Food habits as influenced by human culture: approaches in anthropology and geography. In T. Silverstone (Ed), *Appetite and Food Intake* Abakon/Dahlem, Berlin, pp. 313–329.

Skinner, B.F. (1977). Why I am not a cognitive psychologist. *Behaviourism*, **5**, 1–10.

Spence, K.W. (1956). *Behavior Theory and Conditioning*, Yale University Press, New Haven, Connecticut.

Stunkard, A.J. (1975). Satiety is a conditioned reflex. *Psychosomatic Medicine*, **37**, 383–387.

Stunkard, A.J. and Fox, S. (1971). The relationship of gastric motility and hunger. *Psychosomatic Medicine*, **33**, 123–134.

Stunkard, A.J. and Messick, S. (1985). Three-factor eating questionnaire to measure dietary restraint, disinhibition and hunger. *Journal of Psychosomatic Research*, **29**, 71–83.

Szmukler, G. and Tantam, D. (1984). Anorexia nervosa: starvation dependence. *British Journal of Medical Psychology*, **57**, 303–310.

Szalai, A. (1972). *The Use of Time*, The Hague.

Teasdale, J.D. (1983). Affect and accessibility. *Philosophical Transactions of the Royal Society*, *B*, **302**, 403–412.

Teghtsoonian, M., Becker, E. and Edelman, B. (1981). A psychophysical analysis of perceived satiety: its relation to consumatory behavior and degree of overweight. *Appetite*, **2**, 217–229.

Torgerson, W.S. (1958). *Theory and Methods of Scaling*, Wiley, New York.

Treisman, A.M. and Gelade, G. (1980). A feature-integration theory of attention. *Cognitive Psychology*, **12**, 97–136.

Turner, M.R. (1981). *Preventive Nutrition and Society*, Academic Press, London.

Wegener, B. (Ed.) (1982). *Social Attitudes and Psychophysical Measurement*, Erlbaum, Hillsdale, New Jersey.

Wittgenstein, L. (1953). *Philosophical Investigations*, Blackwell, Oxford.

Wooley, O.W. (1971). Long-term food regulation in the obese and non-obese. *Psychosomatic Medicine*, **33**, 436–440.

Wooley, S.C. (1971). Physiologic versus cognitive factors in short term food regulation in the obese and nonobese. *Psychosomatic Medicine*, **34**, 62–68.

Wooley, S.C. (1976). Psychological aspects of feeding — Group Report 3. In T. Silverstone (Ed.), *Appetite and Food Intake*, Abakon/Dahlem, Berlin, pp. 331–354.

Wooley, S.C., Wooley, O.W. and Dunham, R.B. (1972). Calories and sweet taste: effects on sugar preference in the obese and nonobese. *Physiology and Behavior*, **9**, 765–768.

Wooley, S.C., Wooley, O.W. and Dyrenforth, S. (1979). Theoretical, practical, and social issues in behavioral treatment of obesity. *Journal of Applied Behavior Analysis*, **12**, 3–25.

Zajonc, R. (1980). Feeling and thinking. *American Psychologist*, **35**, 151–175.

Zellner, D.A., Rozin, P., Aron, M. and Kulish, C. (1983). Conditioned enhancement of human liking for flavor by pairing with sweetness. *Learning and Motivation*, **14**, 338–350.

Name Index

Principal page references are in italics

211

Subject Index

221